1945: YEAR ZERO

Other Books by John Lukacs

THE GREAT POWERS AND EASTERN EUROPE

TOCQUEVILLE: THE EUROPEAN REVOLUTION/CORRESPONDENCE
WITH GOBINEAU (*Editor*)

A HISTORY OF THE COLD WAR

DECLINE AND RISE OF EUROPE

HISTORICAL CONSCIOUSNESS

THE PASSING OF THE MODERN AGE

THE LAST EUROPEAN WAR: SEPTEMBER 1939/DECEMBER 1941

1945: YEAR ZERO

JOHN LUKACS

DOUBLEDAY & COMPANY, INC.

GARDEN CITY, NEW YORK

1978

ISBN: 0-385-11502-4
Library of Congress Catalog Card Number 76-56314
Copyright © 1978 by John Lukacs
All Rights Reserved
Printed in the United States of America
First Edition

THIS BOOK IS DEDICATED

TO

DWIGHT MACDONALD

CONTENTS

PART I

I.   Nineteen Forty-five   3

II.   Hitler's Testament   15

III.   Churchill: The Chill of Old Age   49

IV.   Roosevelt Near Death   81

V.   Josef Vissarionovich Djugashvili "Stalin"   109

VI.   Truman and His Circle   133

VII.   A Sketch of the National Mind: American Public Opinion (and Popular Sentiment) in 1945   171

VIII.   Year Zero   215

PART II

Recalling Zero   249

Notes   315

Index   317

1945: YEAR ZERO

PART I

I. NINETEEN FORTY-FIVE

1945 The new year's figure is always strange when it comes around, but soon one gets used to it. Still, 1945 was different from other years. Some of us may remember: there was something surrealistic in this conjunction of figures, 1945. That gray, modern number 19 marking the twentieth century, and the 45, pulling in different directions: the German-marching 4 succeeded by the jaunty, bowlegged American 5: a colt number, an American figure, a cowboy cipher, a far Western year.

Was it the beginning of a new age? Surely it was the end of a terrible experiment.

The terrible experiment that failed was the German attempt to sway the destinies of the world through their ruling Europe; and the Japanese attempt to carve out a large empire for themselves along the far Eastern curvatures of the globe was, in more than one way, only consequent to it.

And now, in January 1945, the once implacable German armies were crowding back into their Reich. On the twelfth night of the new year, New Year's Eve in the old Russian calendar, on the mournful plains of Poland after long months the Russian guns broke their strange and deadening silence. The Russian soldiers poured across the Vistula in the morning. The Germans were fleeing to the west, hundreds of thousands of women and children and old people. For the first time in many hundreds of years they were fleeing in misery from the marches of their Reich that their ancestors had settled and ruled. The medievalized German towns of the east, emptied of their stiff citizenry, were to be tramped down into rubble by the conquering Russians.

Over the Mediterranean, across what Churchill used to call the soft underbelly of Europe, silvery under a frosting sun, the two aging men in whom the hopes of so many people resided were winging to the east. They were to meet Stalin, in a curious cinematic setting, in dead-white palaces of the Tsars refurbished by the Soviets, in the Crimea, near where the Light Brigade had charged ninety years before. During cold and sunny mornings Churchill, Stalin, Roosevelt slept. In the afternoons and evenings they were driven to each other's palaces to assemble and speak and eat and drink: Stalin, stubby and suspicious; Churchill, orotund and voluble; Roosevelt, waning and wearing his smile. He and Stalin agreed to divide up the Far East, in exchange for Stalin's promise to send an army against Japan at a given time. They also agreed to pretend that they had not divided up Europe, even though by the time of Yalta that was an accomplished fact.

The day after Churchill, Roosevelt, Stalin departed the Crimea, an entire German city burned to the ground. The English and American bombers came and went; they cast a fire storm in which 135,000 Germans died in the city of Dresden. She had been largely bereft of soldiers, though she lay along the path of the advancing Russians.

Smoke and fire billowed forward over much of Germany, day and night. Hitler ordered a counterattack—not along the borders of the Reich, but on the muddy plains of western Hungary, his last remaining ally, even as the fortress of Buda had already fallen. For a moment the Russians were astounded; they reeled back; but they rallied soon, there were not enough Germans to defeat them this late, in this place. As March moved into its sunny half, the Germans stumbled out of what was left of Hungary. Soon the Russians were to break into Vienna, the city of young Hitler's dreams and nightmares, blackened by fire and half destroyed.

The German people were now told that they must fight till death, because the Russian advance meant the advance of a curtain of iron, behind which marched the reign of darkness, with its relentless rule of rape and robbery and Siberia. There was much truth to that, though it was not the entire truth. In those eastern European lands across which the Russians were pouring westward there reappeared scenes from a long-forgotten and primitive past, of peasant drunkenness, coarse meals, horse-drawn carts, a muddy and green Eastern village world, freshly rusting, not yet mechanical and ironbound to conform to the standards imposed by Stalin's Soviet Union, though that was to be forced on it soon.

Over the Rhine and over the Apennines the American and British warplanes came and went, came and went; and at long last, for the first time in the war, the Germans were helpless underneath their ceaseless death-bearing traffic. A day came in March when the Rhine was no longer a barrier: the Americans drove across an undemolished bridge, and the British began to stream across the bends of the Rhine further to the north.

Before the advancing Americans rows of German windows overnight went white. The German people were hanging out their sheets, in fear and in hope. They had washed their sheets, hoping that they had washed them free of the stains of their recent nightmares and of their protracted daydreams, hoping that they, too, would be taken for white by the Americans driving in from the German roads.

April came, cruel and customary, with its relentless sights. When the German slave camps were abandoned by their guards, the Americans found these stockades inhabited by skeletons moving among the corpses; and no matter how often these Americans had heard story after story about the murderous crimes of the Germans, they were startled and sickened by what they saw.

Suddenly Roosevelt died. Before the end of the month a group of Italian Communists shot Mussolini. In a spasm of public and theatrical hatred his body and that of his faithful mistress were hung upside down from a steel beam, before which scene thousands of people milled and cursed the dead flesh of their former national idol.

Hitler, hanging on the edge of despair, put things in order. In his bunker quarters, beneath a lid of concrete, still intact under the ruins of his capital city, he had his aides witness his formal marriage with his bland mistress. He wrote his testaments; he appointed his successors; he ordered his body to be burned to ashes. Then he shot himself. Did he know that by doing this he would instantly relieve not only his people but his principal enemies from a further mental agony? We do not know; God alone knows.

Even before he died Russians and Americans had met along the flooded banks of the river Elbe amidst the wreckage of spring and of war. Among the soldiers of the 58th Russian Guards Division there were some whose home was Vladivostok, who came to the middle of Europe from the shores of the western Pacific; among the soldiers of the U.S. 69th Division there were some whose home was San Francisco; they, too, had been sent to conquer halfway around the world. They met in the middle of Germany, and in the middle of European history: for Torgau on the Elbe is about midway between Wittenberg, where Luther's fire of great revolutions had started, and Leipzig, where Napoleon's course of great victories had ended. On that day of the meeting at Torgau the United Nations convened for the first time, in San Francisco: but of these two meetings the first was immeasurably more important than the second.

The Germans hoped that they would be overrun by the Americans, not the Russians: they had far less to fear from the former: they were surrendering to them in droves. The Americans, because of this, could have reached Berlin and Prague and perhaps even Vienna before the Russians arrived, but they chose not to do so; and in early May the gunfire died, the war in Europe was over.

In May 1945 the cities and towns of Central Europe stank with their corpses. One day this writer, thin as a rail and famished, was going up to the hills above his native city with a beautiful woman, to lie on a green meadow spangled with wildflowers. Like the landscape, she, too, was recovering: she had been violated by Russians but a few weeks before. Wending his way through the ruined streets, he bought a handful of apricots from a peasant woman for a handful of paper money. He had to wend his way between the enormous heaps of collapsed houses under some of which lay hundreds of bodies freshly dead. Their smell swam in his nostrils, as did the scent of the apricots and the flowers.

The sun slowly came up over Western Europe. Sea gulls flew inland. White-jacketed waiters appeared on certain terraces in Paris. The memories of war began to fade. In gray justicial palaces gray-faced men were being tried by gray-faced men for the things they had said during the war.

Under the impassive sun of the Pacific the great war went on. The Japanese tried to turn suicide into self-sacrifice, driving their planes into the steel decks of American warships. They clung to the uttermost rocks of islands in the western Pacific. Death was imaginable for them; defeat was not. Yet the carcasses of their ships lay rusting and bubbling under the seas around Japan, and their cities burned like matchsticks. Those among their leaders who, together with their Emperor, knew that the war was now lost, tried to signal peace to America, through Russia if need be: but their signals were not yet apt, Americans were not yet ready to listen.

Under a different brazed and burnished sky, in the American West—yes, this was a far Western year—men put together a new kind of fire, like the Indians once in the unrecorded and unhistoried past, in the desert. They constructed a bomb out of the electric particles of matter. Most of these scientists, too, had made a long journey. They had grown up in gray *Mietkasernen*, dark Wilhelmine apartment houses in the gloomy streets of Central European capitals; and now they were in the western American desert, in baggy suits, pinned with badges marking Very Important Persons, chattering and excited under the complicated eyes of their American military masters, alternately wringing and clapping their hands as the hour of the sorcerer's apprentices drew near.

They saw the future, and it worked. The first atomic bomb burst over the desert at dawn. Three weeks later atomic bombs were dropped over Japan. One hundred and twenty thousand Japanese burned to death. The government of Japan signaled its surrender; and so the war ended.

The American people were awestruck; and, somewhat later, some of them felt a delayed shock wave of intellectual guilt. Most of them thought that the course of history had now irrevocably changed. Perhaps Stalin knew better. When he was told about the atomic bomb during the largely inconsequential summit meeting at Potsdam, he said that he was pleased: and that was that. He was about to declare war on Japan anyhow.

When the Japanese surrendered the Americans found that they need not have been uneasy: the Japanese were pacific and obedient, willing to take all kinds of American leaves from American books, for their future benefit.

Yet winter was coming, and spring seemed far away. The Japanese huddled over their small brazier fires. The Russians were hungry still. Those who, inside and outside their vast country, hoped that after the war and its triumphs the dictator would allow for an easier life, were to be disappointed: Stalin was readying himself for what he saw as the American challenges of the cold war. Terms such as "cold war" and "iron curtain" were not yet current; United Nations Assemblies and Foreign Ministers' Conferences were still going on; the representatives of the Great Powers denied that a struggle of the Superpowers was about to open; yet there were many people who saw what was happening, and some of them, like Charles de Gaulle, began to chart their politics accordingly. Meanwhile the gelid winter cast its long shadow. The autumn rains came early in 1945. The liberation of the summer was past. The few white-coated waiters retreated to the bowels of Maxim's, waiting for Americans. The British people voted for Labour, less because they were hopeful of a socialist future than because they were worn and tired of the burdens of an imperial past. Except for a few fortunate men and women (actors, for the most part) who could make it to New York, the two coldest and grayest winters of an entire decade lay ahead of the English people, not behind them. The austerities of the war years were far from over. Hunger was widespread in Germany and in Central Europe. The war had ended; but reconstruction had barely begun. And people in both halves of Europe, including Germany, thought that for better or worse (most of them thought for the better) the future was with America; indeed, that their future depended on the presence of America. Their images were shaped accordingly. On those rainy and cold 1945 afternoons millions went to see American movies, warming themselves in the large cavernous cinemas that had survived from the thirties in their towns.

The movies: life was imitating art, at least on the level at which the forms of images take shape. Life in the United States was warm, crowded, automobile, and rich. In these movies women were beautiful, men were successful, houses and cars were shining with luxuries. The millions of American soldiers, sailors, and airmen saw their future in much the same way: they were going home to a paradise, the only material paradise known to man, to families designed by Norman Rockwell, and to endless rides and parties, with new cars and fizzy beer. America was an endless epic; unlike Europe there were no tragedies in America, except perhaps on the upper levels: in July a B-25 crashed into the Empire State Building, like a missile thrown by King Kong, life imitating the movies again. When in Europe the surviving Jews from Mauthausen or Belsen had lost their ragged hopes of finding their destroyed homes and their people, in America the title of Miss America was won by a beautiful Jewish girl from America, New York. When the first Jewish survivors of Auschwitz landed in New York, they found their American relatives getting ready for the winter season in Miami in the sun. The mass migration of entire peoples through the Germanies went on. By December there were more than six million refugees whom the American military bureaucracy designated as Displaced Persons. The only displaced persons in America were the victims of the postwar divorces; they were moving around the country in search not of food or shelter but of another version of a dream. In the hothouse climate of the Plaza sleek South Americans were wearing large flowers in their buttonholes: while Europe was still down and out, South America had been the surrogate destination of some of those dreams of innocents abroad. Nineteen forty-five went out in the grand ballrooms of New York to the music of Guy Lombardo and Xavier Cugat.

When Woodrow Wilson landed in Europe in December 1918, young girls in white dresses threw flowers from dainty baskets before his feet. No one strewed flowers in Harry Truman's path in 1945. Yet in 1918 probably less than half of the then two billion inhabitants of the earth knew the names of Wilson and Lenin, Lloyd George and Clemenceau. In 1945 almost everyone in this world had heard of Hitler and Roosevelt and Truman and Churchill and Stalin. In this book I devote certain chapters to each of them, since in 1945 great events were the results not so much of inevitable and relentless social forces as of the decisions and the ideas and the characters of these men. This is not a chronological history of that year, and it has no pretensions to completeness. It is about Hitler, Churchill, Roosevelt, Stalin, and Truman, about their vision of the future in 1945, and about their contribution to the world order (or disorder) that was to follow.

Nineteen forty-five was the last great turning point in the history of the world. I write "the world," because it was a decisive year for all kinds of people in faraway continents over whose heads 1914 or 1789 or 1776 had passed without much meaning at all. There was only one other year in the history of this century (indeed, perhaps in the history of the entire Modern Age) that measures up to 1945 when we contemplate its long-range consequences; that was 1914, the sudden outbreak of the First World War, which, as we all know, marked the end of an entire era. Or perhaps the beginning of its end: for what had started in 1914 was concluded in 1945. During those thirty-one years the two greatest wars in the history of mankind came to pass. Two world wars, the Russian Revolution, the world depression, Lenin, Mussolini, Hitler, Roosevelt, Stalin: there has been nothing even remotely comparable to these tremendous events during the thirty-two years that have passed from 1945 to the time when this is being written—an argument to which I shall return, in the next-to-last chapter of this book.

Nineteen forty-five was the end of an era, not only of Mussolini or of Hitler or of Roosevelt. It was the end of the era of world wars. It was the end of a united Germany. It was the end of European predominance in the history and in the political geography of the world. It was the end of something else, too. Hitler's death in 1945 meant the end of the mass appeal of what has been loosely called "Fascism"—an inadequate and imprecise term for a more complex, and more universal, phenomenon. We have been accustomed to look at the twentieth century as if it were marked by the struggle of two great world systems, Communism and Capitalism, or call it Communism and Democracy if you wish. Yet soon after the Russian Revolution, in the wake of the First World War, when it seemed that the great struggle between Communism and Capitalism had begun, there arose, in the center of Europe, a new force, which was both anti-Communist and anti-Capitalist, and which soon demonstrated its potential of powerful mass appeal. Consequently, during the quarter-century after 1920, there was a great confrontation between three forces, not two. This was especially evident in Europe, but it had powerful reverberations elsewhere, too. Because of one man, Hitler, all of this culminated in the Second

World War, beginning in 1939. During that war, again because of Hitler, Capitalism and Communism became allies. Before the end of the war, in 1945, Hitler, who was the living incarnation of National Socialism before his people, killed himself; and it was over the wreckage of his heritage, including the site of his suicide, that the confrontation of Communism and Capitalism, represented principally by the Soviet Union and the United States, was about to begin.

II. HITLER'S TESTAMENT

In the first hours of the year 1945 a goodly part of the world was burning. Old German cities, half battered down into ruins, were peppered by small flames. There was an irregular ripple of fire across Belgium and Alsace where the Battle of the Bulge was burning out. There were man-made stars in the cold sky above the Apennines in Italy. In the eastern half of Europe, where the vast Russian and German armies were resting face to face, the night was dark, ominous, and dull. The exception was Budapest, the largest city between Vienna and Moscow, on the edges of which dozens of houses stood in flames, since its siege had begun. There were thin fires across the jungles and on the river-banks of Burma. On New Year's Eve American Flying Fortresses had visited Tokyo and Yokohama and Yokosuka, where many houses were burning still.

The Russian empire lay swathed in darkness. The fires of war had moved beyond its borders in the west. Spared by war and by deprivation, the cities of America were lit in colors. Moscow was no longer singed by fire and New York not yet. (This was twenty-five or thirty years before houses in the city of New York would be set on fire, here and there, night after night.)

On New Year's morning there came a German blow from the air. Eight hundred German planes swept out from the east, low over the American and Allied airfields in Belgium, Brussels, northern France. They included dozens of the first jet planes in this war. The Allied ground crews and troops were dazed. Nearly five hundred American and American-made planes were destroyed on the ground. The Germans lost about one hundred of their own. It was the air equivalent of their stunning ground offensive that had been launched two weeks before, when the German army, counted down and perhaps out, had broken Eisenhower's battle line, grinding its way across Belgium toward the Channel. But a week later this German offensive was brought to a halt. On the first bright day since this Battle of the Bulge had started, thousands of American and hundreds of British planes could roam the Western European skies, shooting up the Germans without serious opposition. The German army may not have been down and out, the Allied generals thought; but the German air force surely was. They were wrong. Göring, whose star had set years before, rose out of nowhere, and with his young commanders prepared the secret strike. The blow was typical of the way in which the Third Reich fought this war: hard, unexpected, surprising, and painful. But Göring overdid it, again. He and his planners kept the secret only too carefully from their own army as well. The German planes, flying home, ran into showers of fire from stacks of German antiaircraft guns. More than two hundred of Göring's planes were blown up in the air, or crashed on the ground.

Like the Ardennes offensive, the valiant effort cost too much.

The first day of 1945 came and went. Few people, including Hitler, doubted that the war would end that year.

Hitler's temporary headquarters were in Ziegenberg, about twenty-five miles from Frankfurt, near the Rhine, in a solitary forest rising at the end of a silent valley. There was the usual New Year's celebration, of which event Speer's account survives. He had left the Western Front in the morning, driving all day. He reached Hitler's compound two hours after midnight. The mood was not very jolly, even though everyone had drunk a great deal of champagne. Hitler was sober, as usual, though he seemed (or, perhaps, he pretended to be) intoxicated with his own rhetoric. Victory was possible in 1945, he kept saying. After the low point in Germany's fortunes the German star was to rise again. He talked for a long time. He compared his situation with that of Prussia and of Frederick the Great near the end of the Seven Years' War. Alone, encircled by enemies, on the verge of complete defeat the great King remained tenacious and strong. And then Fortune turned, smiled at him, his perils melted away, and victory came. During the last eight months of the war this theme, the parallel with the Seven Years' War, with the year 1762, appeared more and more often in Hitler's discourse. His harangues about faith, faith in victory, too, would be repeated and repeated. They contribute to the prevalent impression: that Hitler, near the end of the war, was blind, on the verge of mental derangement, living in a dream world, commanding imaginary armies, unable to believe that the Third Reich could disappear, unwilling to face the prospect of defeat.

This impression is inaccurate. Hitler knew that his war was

lost. He knew it before 1945. Years earlier he knew that he could no longer win it. He mentioned this in passing to some of his generals in November 1941, when Bock's troops were still moving forward in an arc around Moscow: "the recognition, by both of the opposing coalitions, that they cannot annihilate each other, leads to a negotiating peace."[1]

General Jodl was Chief of the Operations Staff of the High Command of the Wehrmacht. Before his execution in Nuremberg in 1946, he dictated to his wife a memorandum about Hitler's strategy, the last paragraph of which read: Hitler's "military advisors—today one often hears it said—should certainly have made it clear to him earlier that the war was lost. What a naive thought! Earlier than any other person in the world, Hitler sensed and knew that the war was lost. But can one give up a Reich and a people before they are lost? A man like Hitler could not do it."[2]

A man like Hitler—the public Hitler—could not admit that the war was lost. Hitler was a secretive man. Yet the public and the private Hitler were not that different. Hitler believed in strength—or, more precisely, in the kind of conviction that, to him, resulted in strength; and in the kind of impression that, again to him, strength alone could give. If he were to admit to his people that the war could not be won, the war *would* be lost, in a matter of days. Not only would the morale of the German people be fatally shaken but their enemies would be instantly vindicated; they would know, finally and irrevocably, that they had won. Since November 1941 Hitler's strategy was essentially simple: to fight tough and split his enemies. The coalition between the Anglo-American capitalists and the Soviet Russians was an unnatural one. The tougher the German kernel, the more likely that the coalition would break apart. This strategy was essentially simple: but its execution was difficult. In Hitler's mind the issue included all kinds of considerations that he thought he alone understood. Ribbentrop, Goebbels, Göring, Mussolini, the Japanese kept asking him to consider negotiation with one side or the other. We might echo Jodl's words: What a naive thought! Hitler knew that the British and the Americans would not negotiate with him: not with Churchill and Roosevelt in power. He said this to Rommel in 1943, adding bitterly: now the West will have the war it wanted, till the end. What he did not tell Rommel or, indeed, any of his generals, was this: one unexpected German blow, one great German victory, might turn the trick. Hitler, who kept haranguing and inciting his generals to victory, victory at all costs, before and during decisive battles, seldom spoke to them about the *political* consequences of the outcome of the battles—probably because he did not wish to disturb or confuse the impression of the single-minded war leader with that of a calculating statesman.

This was the kind of calculation that lay behind Hitler's plan for the Ardennes offensive in December 1944. He did not go for Paris. He wanted to get to Antwerp, to the Channel, to cut off the northern American army in another Dunkirk so that the Americans would have second thoughts about trying to break Germany in the West. He knew something about certain divisions within American public opinion, and about the rising concern with Communism in certain quarters within the United States.

But his last attack in the West was failing: and now, in January 1945, he had but one hope left. As the end of the war approached, the American and the British misgivings about the Bolsheviks might mature; and the enemy coalition, already stretched and riven by unpublicized strains, might break apart while the fighting power of Germany was still largely intact. A forlorn hope, but a hope nonetheless: a hope that was not altogether irrational.

This calculation may have been involved with his temptation to remain at the front in the East. Eight days before his suicide, in April, when he had chosen to stay in a Berlin encircled by the Russians (the alternative would have been to go to Bavaria, to die or to fall into the hands of the Western Allies there), he said to Jodl: "I should already have made this decision, the most important in my life, in November 1944, and should have never left the headquarters in East Prussia." This would have achieved two things. One: Hitler, the *Feldherr*, would have died in battle, on the front, at the head of his battered armies, on the eastern borders of the Reich, breasting the Asiatic flood, an act with incalculable symbolic consequences for future German, and perhaps European, generations. Two: such an end of the Third Reich, in late 1944, would have meant the flooding of most of Germany by the British and the Americans, a great swirling confusion of Anglo-Saxon and German armies, the former wending their way eastward in the midst of a still largely intact German army and a still largely intact German people, eventually meeting the suspicious Russians somewhere in eastern Germany, Anglo-Saxons as well as Russians hoping, first nervously, then more and more determinedly, to get the Germans on their side during their developing confrontation.

After everything is said, Hitler was a statesman of sorts. The cunning of reason affected him, too. He could peer into the future, sometimes beyond the inevitable Götterdämmerung, the coming collapse of his Reich. He did not wish to contemplate that prospect: but he thought about it nonetheless.

So did the German people. In January 1945 they were not yet fatally divided; their spirit was not yet broken beyond repair. But like their Führer, they, too, were thinking of more than one thing, on more than one level of their minds.

What is more amazing, in retrospect, than Hitler's performance is the behavior of the German people toward the end of the war. They still fought. They would not give up. Their cities were destroyed. Their armies were retreating everywhere. Their conquests were lost. Their enemies had broken into Germany proper. The Germans were outnumbered five to one. For every German plane, tank, truck, gun, their enemies had ten or fifteen. Few Germans believed that they could still win the war. They spent night after night in their cellars while their cities were exploding over their heads. Yet they carried on. Much of their belief in Hitler remained. In March 1945 his minister Speer admitted to himself the thought that Hitler might have to be destroyed. Near the Western Front he overheard soldiers and workers talking about Hitler. Their faith was unbroken. The Führer knows what he is doing, they said. Speer relented. The German workers—the vanguard of the proletariat in what had been the fatherland of Marx—were wedded to Hitler still. Wedding, Red Wedding, was the name of a working-class suburb in Berlin, the gray citadel of Central European Communism, Socialism. In

February and March 1933 swastika flags had sprouted like large
vulgar flowers from the windows of those gray tenements. They
had outnumbered the red flags with the hammer and sickle,
hanging limp. The Marxists were bitter with the pain of jealousy. Those whom they had believed to be theirs had heard the
voice of Hitler, they had chosen to be married to Hitler. Wedding, 1933.

But this was 1945. The Germans were not simpleminded.
They were of two minds, like Hitler. They knew that they
could no longer win the war; but they were not certain that their
cause was irrevocably lost. Of course, "they" is an indefinite pronoun in this case. There were millions of Germans who knew
that the war was lost and who were even silently looking forward
to the end of the war. How many of them were? How were
the Germans divided? There was no Gallup poll in Germany
in 1945; and even the confidential opinion-surveys that Himmler's secret police had been conducting earlier in the war were
no longer made. But this is perhaps irrelevant. The most important division existed not among Germans but within their own
minds. The war was being lost because Germany's opponents
were superior—superior in numbers, superior in matériel. But the
Germans were still the defenders of European civilization; at least
some of their principal enemies were bound to recognize this;
German genius and German power would profit from this recognition, and from the irreconcilable differences among their enemies. Most Germans thought these things at the same time. This
was the real division within German minds in 1945, not some
artificial division between German militarists and German
pacifists.

Fewer and fewer Germans believed in man-made wonders, that some kind of mysterious and tremendous weapon would be brought out, the ace up Hitler's sleeve. Nor is it true that the Allied slogan of Unconditional Surrender—senseless as that slogan was—made the Germans stick together till the bitter end. It was Roosevelt and Churchill who proclaimed that principle, not Stalin: yet the Germans feared the Russians, not the Anglo-Americans. Indeed, the Germans were beginning to surrender: but there was calculation in that choice, inevitable as it may have seemed on occasion. After the Allies crossed the Rhine in March, certain German commanders would abandon German towns and cities to them without much fighting. In eastern Germany more than one million Germans were fleeing before the advancing Soviet armies, hoping to surrender to the Americans before the Russians could get to them. In the south, German commanders, including an SS general, were secretly negotiating their surrender to the Americans after January (negotiations which, contrary to the later claims of Allen Dulles, the American secret intelligence chief in charge, shortened the war there but by one or two days, not more).

Underneath these parleys ran the hope for a postwar American-German alliance against the Soviet menace. Heinrich Himmler, the most feared man in Germany, had been negotiating with international Jewish spokesmen through Switzerland for many months now. Near the end of the war he invited a Jewish spokesman, Herr Masur, to his headquarters, treating him as a Very Important Person, which the latter showed every sign of appreciating; through prominent Swedish personages Himmler was also trying to negotiate a German surrender to the

Western Allies. Hitler's most rigid and loyal follower, Ribbentrop, the Foreign Minister (one of the few who would still proclaim his unbroken loyalty to Hitler during his trial at Nuremberg), in February instructed all German diplomatic stations to try to initiate contact with the Western Allies and through careful language (the instruction was called a *Sprachregelung*) suggest the advantages of collaborating with Germany against the overwhelming danger of Russia in Europe.

There is no evidence that Hitler knew of these calculated attempts; but neither is it certain that he was wholly ignorant of them. They may have been conducted behind his back; but it is not unreasonable to think that he tacitly understood some of these things that were going on. He would order the demolition of buildings, the scorching of Germany before the advancing enemy; yet he would tolerate Speer when the latter, at least on one occasion, pleaded the necessity to preserve the livelihood of the German people for the time after the war. During his last days Hitler ordered Göring stripped of all his functions, titles, and honors. At the same time he dropped a remark: if Göring wanted to negotiate with the Americans, why not, since there was not much else left to do. He, Hitler, kept repeating that the English ought to see the light; yet when he received a report that certain English prisoners of war were willing to fight with the Germans against the advancing Russians, Hitler dismissed it as an insubstantial rumor (which it was). Like the German people, Hitler may have been of two minds. Unlike the German people, he had no illusions.

In early 1945 the German scene was not uniform. The previous November, Himmler had ordered the suspension of the gassing of Jews: but tens of thousands of Jews and other prisoners were beaten, killed, and starved to death until the very last days of the war. Some of the survivors of the July 1944 conspiracy against Hitler were treated with relative care, some of them (Goerdeler) were encouraged to compose speculative memoranda about alternative forms of government for Germany which Himmler, presumably, read with great attention. Still, before Berlin fell most of these political prisoners were executed cruelly, in a last cold wave of terror. In early April, American tank columns drove east along the *Autobahnen* with hardly any opposition. Still Field Marshal Model chose to shoot himself, rather than surrender, in the destroyed steel jungle of the Ruhr. In some ways life remained surprisingly normal: rationed food, for example, was available even during the last days of the battle of Berlin, and the advancing Americans and British and French were sometimes amazed to find quiet German towns, peaceful valleys, well-fed people, with the amenities of life hardly touched at all. In other ways and in other places the German scene was reminiscent of an apocalypse: burnt cities, veritable hecatombs of corpses (in Dresden they had to be burned in the open, stacked crosswise on steel racks after the terrible fire bombing), along the roads the frozen bodies of those who tried to flee the Russians, the twisted blackened steel girders of the cathedrals of German industry, the sense of occasional madness in the air—described by black humorists such as the French Céline who had moved along the edges of the exodus, and continuing to fascinate the inconsistent imagination of another generation of writers, such as the American Vonnegut or Pynchon, whose literary ambitions consistently outran their art.

No one, perhaps not even Hitler, understood this dual aspect of German reality in early 1945 as well as Joseph Goebbels. This little demonic figure, with his dark hair and face, his maddeningly attentive eyes, his large mouth with white snapping teeth, was a Rhinelander, a western German, born of Catholic parents. Small, almost but not quite gnome-like, filled with ambition, his very name sounding like the compressed energy of a rubber ball ready to jump—among all the Nazis Goebbels was perhaps the prototype of the *modern* German. He may have been the most brilliant journalist of the twentieth century. Goebbels knew how to play on the fears of the Germans about Communism and the Russians. In editorial after editorial he repeated the same themes: If Germany were to be defeated an iron curtain would descend over Europe (he used this phrase before Churchill was to make it world-famous). In the middle of Europe the Germans would be enslaved, the women raped, and millions of them deported. In Eastern Europe hundreds of millions of non-German peoples would be the subjects of brutal Bolshevization, "probably with the applause of the Jewish press in London and New York." The rest, Western Europe, "would be engulfed in chaotic political and social confusion which would only represent a preparatory stage for the coming Bolshevization . . ."[3] He orchestrated this theme in all kinds of ways. He was attempting to influence the remaining neutral nations of Europe.* No matter how powerful the orchestration, the music did not reach the outside world. But it was heard by the German people. Germany

* An editorial in *Das Reich* (4 February 1945) praised the Swiss Carl J. Burckhardt, a potential intermediary between Germany and the West.

belonged to the *Abendland*, to the West—meaning the anti-East. Germany was the bulwark of Europe, and perhaps of the world, against Communism: it was a tragedy, a pity, that the Western enemies of Germany did not want to understand this. After everything was said and done, the Germans and the English and the Americans had much in common. This is what most Germans thought in the last months of the war.†

But there was another side to Goebbels. Even more than Hitler, he was impressed by the spectacle of the German Twilight of the Gods. He was obsessed with the symbols of heroism shown in the face of overwhelming force. He kept insisting on how important that image was.‡

Even more than Hitler, Goebbels hated the bourgeois world. In more than one way, Goebbels hated the Western civilization. From the very beginning of his political career in Berlin, Goebbels favored Nazi collaboration with the Communists, if need be. During the war he was often in favor of a separate peace with Stalin. But there was more to that. Goebbels was not only the principal journalist of the Third Reich; he was not only its principal propagandist. He—far more than ideologues such as Rosenberg, far more than Himmler, the head of the SS—was its

† Some Americans did too—General Patton, for example, especially when German-Austrian officers presented him with a pride of white stallions, an event later immortalized by Walt Disney in Hollywood.

‡ In early 1945 the Germans were treated by Goebbels to a magnificent color movie, *Kolberg*, about an embattled Prussian fortress during the Seven Years' War. On one occasion he said to his circle: "We cannot capitulate. Imagine people watching us on a color film one hundred years from now. Do you want them to stand up and boo at us?"

principal revolutionary. In the last months of his life Hitler took some consolation from the fact that at least he had achieved one thing, the destruction of the Jews in Germany and in Europe. Goebbels took consolation from what he saw as the destruction of the bourgeois world and of bourgeois values, especially in Germany. The bombs of our enemies, he wrote at a high feverish pitch, have succeeded in but one way: they demolished the old buildings of our cities, the prison walls of our remaining bourgeois existence, so that we now live amidst the ruins of the nineteenth century. Our enemies are clearly the last obstacles for us. Now we will be forced to rebuild, from scratch. They think that they destroyed us, us who represent the future of Europe. What they are really destroying is what has been left over from the past. There was some truth to this, even as Goebbels was proven wrong: for the victory of the Western Allies in Western Europe, including western Germany, meant the restoration of bourgeois values, and ways of life, all of Goebbels' ideas and editorials (as well as those of *The Nation* or *The New Statesman*) notwithstanding—at least for one generation after the war.

During the war years Goebbels and Himmler were rivals for power in the Third Reich. The Reich Propaganda Minister and the Reich Security Chief were very different men; they pursued different goals, personal as well as ideological. Yet what Goebbels was saying corresponded to a significant, and often overlooked, political condition within the Third Reich during the last months of its existence. These last months *were* the last months of Fascism, of the Fascist era in the history of Europe, and of the world. Yet in many ways the Third Reich was already a post-Fascist state.** By 1945 the SS had become a veritable state within the state. It had its own army, its own police force, its own intelligence service, its own foreign service. Its leaders, men such as Himmler or Schellenberg, were well aware of the difficult situation of the Third Reich: as we have seen, they had been trying to negotiate with their opponents, including Jews, for months (indeed, on some occasions, years) before the collapse. What is more significant, there was a world of difference between their ideas and the ideas professed by different Fascists all over Europe. This condition went beyond the fact of national differences: that, for example, an Italian Fascist was usually more humane than was a German SS. The functionaries of the SS state were no longer ideologues. They gave little thought to the official ideology of National Socialism.†† They believed in power, in power alone: in the rule of the tough. They did not hesitate to employ certain criminals and convicts in some of their SS brigades. In the closed underworld of the concentration and extermination camps, too, they preferred to choose certain criminals to help them rule the mass of prisoners: the Kapos.‡‡ In the overworld of international politics the leaders of the SS state, too, would deal with those who

** "Fascist" is an inadequate blanket term covering all dictatorships of the so-called Right. There were considerable differences between Fascism and National Socialism. In 1934 Hitler was supposed to have told Rauschning: Fascism is only a half job.

†† As early as 1933–34 the young SS leaders did not take the official ideologues, men such as Rosenberg or Ley, seriously.

‡‡ It is in this respect that the SS state was a post-Fascist state, and the world of the concentration camps was part of the post-modern world. Its rulers knew that they were living in a world where the older standards of civilization had ceased to exist. The Kapos knew this even better. They

were the possessors of power. Himmler and Goebbels may have
been rivals in the entangled hierarchy of the Third Reich,* but
this they had in common: if, in the end, someone had to negotiate with the enemy, they would be the ones to conduct the negotiations. And in this respect they were in harmony with the
thoughts of the secretive Hitler who, in 1945, often expressed
his bitter hatred for remnants of the old order, regretting that he
had followed a policy of collaboration with opportunists such as
Pétain or Franco. At the very end of his life Hitler again acted
in harmony with this duality. In his last testament he made a
kind of balance in the composition of the new regime. Surprisingly, he appointed the "conservative" Admiral Doenitz to be his
successor as the head of the German state, while he made the
revolutionary Goebbels his successor as its chancellor. True to

---

were killers, murderers, thieves, rising—that is the proper verb—from the
ranks of prisoners. Compared to the latter, they were privileged persons.
But their privileged state was not the result of ideological preferences. It
grew out naturally, from the very condition of things. The SS administrators of the prison camps needed accomplices among their victims. The
most natural of accomplices were the criminals: because they were tough;
and because they had no convictions beyond the sense of the savage law
of the jungle. Precisely because of their brutal and savage kind of opportunism the Kapos were the natural allies of the SS administrators. A
new kind of feudalism: the tough ruling the weak. It was natural.
The Kapos were no longer criminals in the sense of pariahs, the lowest outcasts of civilized society. *This* society was something else. They
were no longer the lowest. They had slaves of their own. They were toughs.
In sum, a kind of tacit cooperation between criminals and the police, because the tough respect each other more than they respect the weak.

* There is some evidence that as early as in 1942 Goebbels pushed for
the complete extermination of Jews *against* some of Himmler's ideas. Cf.
F. Bramstead, *Goebbels and National Socialist Propaganda* (Lansing,
Mich., 1965), pp. 282, 384, 392.

their form (and, probably, to Hitler's expectations) Doenitz immediately attempted to bargain with the British and the Americans, and Goebbels with the Russians. Their attempts at bargaining soon ended, in vain. Goebbels and Himmler committed suicide. Doenitz survived his trial, imprisonment, and the war.

On 24 February 1945 Hitler held a reception for party leaders in Berlin. His appearance depressed some of the guests, most of them older party officials.† His face was ashen. He moved with difficulty. He dragged one of his legs. He was bent, his eyes were clouded. He said: "My hands may be shaking. My head might shake. But my heart will never tremble."

During the same month, February 1945, Hitler dictated his political testament—a document of great significance that perhaps has not received the attention it deserves. There were three testaments by Hitler. His will and testament for the German people, dictated the day before his death, and his personal will and testament, disposing of his material belongings, are well known. Less well known, except to historians and specialists of the Third Reich's history, are his political remarks dictated to Bormann in February 1945, including one last batch dictated on 2 April.

These remarks—or, rather, their record, their documentary residue—have an interesting history. They were a kind of table

† He had been ingesting an extraordinary number of pills. This contributed to, rather than caused, his condition of sickness, months before his suicide. During these months he abandoned his ascetic eating habits for one kind of indulgence: he kept devouring an extraordinary number of creamy cakes of the Viennese kind.

talk, reflective monologues addressed by Hitler to his closest circle of confidants, in the cellar of his headquarters. They were
authenticated, after retyping, by Bormann, who signed each
typed page. On 17 April Bormann gave the typescript to a
minister of the Reich government who took it with him to Austria, where it was deposited in the vault of a bank. After the collapse of the Reich this bearer wanted the manuscript destroyed.
Eventually a lawyer friend of the bearer made a photostatic copy
which then reached François Genoud, a French-Swiss lawyer,
an uncompromising votary of Hitler's cause and the chosen cus-
todian of more than one important Nazi personal document. It
was published in Paris (by Fayard) in 1959 and in London in
1961, but not in the United States. It is not impossible that
someone like Goebbels may have done a little editing here and
there; but otherwise the text is true Hitler.‡

And why is this text so significant? For three reasons at least.
It is the most detailed record of what Hitler said and what he
may have thought during the first months of the year 1945, the
last months of his life. It contains Hitler's retrospect of the war.
It also includes his prospect of the future, of the postwar world,
of the world after him. Ruminating about the causes of the German defeat, Hitler said many things about his decisions during
the war that he had merely suggested, hinted at, or left unsaid

‡ As Professor Trevor-Roper put it in his introduction to the English
edition: "To anyone who has studied Hitler's mind, the internal evidence
alone would be conclusive. These documents are, in a sense, Hitler's full
political testament, to which his official 'political testament,' signed on
29th April, together with his private will (which appointed Bormann as
his executor), is merely a brief, formal tailpiece."

before. He rationalized and explained his choices, wherefore these memoirs are of great value to the historian of the Second World War. Of course we must keep in mind that the bunker in Berlin was Hitler's St. Helena. Like Napoleon, he had to use whatever time was left in order to justify himself to posterity. There can be no question that his posthumous reputation played a principal role in his thoughts. Like the memoirs of any public figure, they must be taken with more than a grain of salt. The fascinating matter is not how Hitler lived near his end; it is, rather, how he saw the future—the future of Germany, of Europe, of America, of the world. What happens in the mind of a fanatical visionary when his faith in the actual power of his faith no longer works? What did Hitler think, what was going on in his mind not only when he realized that he could no longer win the war but when he knew and admitted that his Third Reich, and National Socialism with it, would soon be completely overrun, defeated, submerged, and lost?

These were thoughts that he would not admit easily, even to himself. Philosophically speaking, Hitler was an extreme neo-idealist. He believed in the power of ideas, of mind (or spirit) over matter. In this he was an extreme representative of a particularly German intellectual tendency. Again, in the German manner, his belief in certain ideas was rigid and categorical—which eventually proved to be his undoing. He believed that the idea of National Socialism was stronger and more dynamic than the idea of Communism (which was probably true)—and that, consequently, Germany was bound to defeat Russia (which was not necessarily true). He (as did Goebbels) regarded the war as but a repetition, on a larger scale, of the struggle for power in

Germany before 1933, when the originally few but strong National Socialists overcame all of their opponents, including the numerous Communists. So the Germans would overcome the liberal democracies in the West and the numerous but primitive Russians in the East. One National Socialist was worth two Communists in the streets or in the beer halls or on the podiums before German audiences before 1933. One German soldier was worth two Russians. Hitler was convinced of this. There was enough truth in this to bring him close to victory, and the world to the edge of a catastrophic change. Eventually he failed because Germany was one thing, and the rest of the world another. It was not only that the Nazis were more dynamic than the Communists in Germany; it was that, for Germans, they were more attractive: they appealed to certain atavistic German sentiments and ideas, which was not true of most other peoples in Europe and in the world. Hitler had won the Germans over not because one German Nazi was worth two German socialists or two German conservatives, but because inside every German socialist and inside every German conservative there was a German nationalist. Inside every English socialist or inside every Polish conservative there was a nationalist, too: but not a German one. By 1945 there were at least five enemy soldiers—two Russians, two Americans, one British—converging on every remaining German: and this was the end.

"If we are destined to be beaten in this war," Hitler said on 2 April 1945, "our defeat will be utter and complete." He had made such statements before, as a warning, a threat to the German people. But now he said it as a starting point for his speculations about the future. He was trying to peer ahead into the darkness, to look at the world beyond his death, which he knew was approaching fast.

He had always thought in terms of nations rather than in terms of classes (which was one of his main strengths). He found it difficult to believe that the German Third Reich could disappear. "As far as I personally am concerned I could not bear to live in Germany during the transition period that would follow the defeat of the Third Reich. . . . It is beyond comprehension that, after twelve years of National Socialism, such a thing could happen. My imagination boggles at the idea of a Germany, henceforth deprived of her elite which led her to the very pinnacles of heroism, wallowing for years and years in the mire." But now he had to face this prospect. His earlier occasional rhetoric about a gigantic Twilight of the Gods, the German people destroyed and consumed in flames together with him, now fell away. He speculated instead about the future of the German people after he would be gone. No doubt some of his statements were meant for their posthumous effects on the German people. Still Hitler's optimism about their long-range future was remarkable. "The German people is a young and strong people, a people with its future before it." Germany will rise again, and its people will live to know a glorious tomorrow.[4]

The Germans must never again allow themselves to be divided. Within Germany all particularisms must disappear: a strongly welded, united German people must remain.** Beyond

** Possibly this was Hitler's "minimum" goal: a unified state of all German-speaking people within Europe. It is interesting to note that, contrary to his objurgations against military retreats, he did not object to the westward migration of millions of German civilians from the eastern territories, including eastern Germany, during the last months of the war.

that, the Germans "must at all costs avoid" becoming the pawns
of either the United States or Soviet Russia, the two only remaining "Great Powers capable of confronting each other" in
the world. "The laws of both history and geography will compel
these two Powers to a trial of strength, either military or in the
fields of economics and ideology. These same laws make it inevitable that both Powers should become enemies of Europe. And
it is equally certain that both these Powers will sooner or later
find it desirable to seek the support of the sole surviving great
nation in Europe, the German people."[5] (His people did not follow his advice. For the next twenty-five years most of them favored an American-German alliance, with its attendant promises
and possibilities; this was the principal political idea in their
minds.)

"I have been Europe's last hope. She proved incapable of
refashioning herself by means of voluntary reform. She showed
herself impervious to charm and persuasion. To take her I had
to use violence."[6] Some charm! Some persuasion! For some of
the historic peoples of the continent Hitler had nothing but contempt. Throughout these last remarks he spoke of his dislike of
the Latin peoples. His dislike and contempt for the French went
back to his early childhood.†† Now, in these last talks, he would
say some terrible and unjust things against them. But he said
something else, too, which was close to Goebbels' ideas. He was
ruminating about a mistake he may have made. He, Hitler,
ought to have helped to make a European social revolution. For

†† "I have never liked France or the French, and I have never stopped
saying so" (15 February 1945).

the first and the last time in his life, he had some good things to
say about certain Frenchmen, especially about those who had
chosen to fight on the German side till the end. He also had
some good things to say about their working classes. "Our obvious course should have been to liberate the working classes and
to help the workers of France to implement their own revolution. We should have brushed aside, rudely and without pity,
the fossilized bourgeoisie."[7] He returned to this theme the next
day. "By not liberating the French proletariat at once in 1940
we both failed in our duty and neglected our own interests."[8]
He said similar things about Spain and the Spanish. He cas-
tigated Franco for his cautiousness, his slippery ambiguity during the war. Going further, Hitler said that he hated the Franco
regime, composed as it was of profiteers and clerical puppets. He
had some good words for the Spanish Communists: "I shall
never forgive Franco for not having reconciled the Spaniards
once the civil war was over . . . and for having treated like bandits former foes, who were very far from all being Reds. To put
half a country beyond the pale of the law while a minority of
pillagers enrich themselves, with the blessing of the priesthood,
at the expense of the rest is no solution at all. I am quite sure
that very few of the so-called Reds in Spain were really
Communists."‡‡ This was in harmony with some of his earlier statements: among his domestic opponents he preferred a
German Communist worker over a German bourgeois. It corre-

‡‡ 10 February 1945. Eleven years before, José Antonio Primo de
Rivera had said: "Inside every Spanish socialist there is a nationalist." His
interview in *Ahora*, 16 February 1934, cited in José Antonio Primo de
Rivera, *Selected Writings*, Hugh Thomas, ed. (London, 1972).

sponded, too, with his preference for Stalin over his other opponents: throughout the war he often privately expressed his admiration and respect for Stalin.

But there was a curious discrepancy—or, perhaps, disconnection—in Hitler's mind about Stalin and the Russians. He respected Stalin: and yet he was unwilling throughout the war, when it may still have been possible, to negotiate about a separate peace with him. In these last table talks Hitler, on one occasion, almost admitted that his war with Russia might have been avoided, that some kind of a rigidly defined coexistence of Germany and Russia could have been constructed. Yet he also returned, over and over again, to the argument that the war with Russia was inevitable; indeed, that he should have invaded Russia earlier than June 1941, in which event the war would have been won. On one occasion, late in April, Hitler said something to the effect that the outcome of the war demonstrated the power of the Russian masses, that the Eastern nation has proven stronger in the great contest. Yet in his last testament he repeated that the purpose of the German people remained the same: to secure land in the East. Hitler had two principal ideas: to get rid of the Jews (which, to him, was an unavoidable matter of internal sanification); and to gain more land for the compressed people of Germany in the East, at the expense of the culturally inferior Slavic peoples, Poles and Russians. But there was a difference. This self-appointed German prophet and statesman was much more obsessed with the Jews than with the Slavs, including Russians. The Jewish problem: Hitler *thought it through,* with a kind of categorical cruelty that never disappeared from his mind. But this same kind of obsessive determi-

nation is missing in his speculations about Russia.* Throughout
his career, Hitler made many brutal statements about Russia and
the Soviets; yet his general ideas about them were often
undefined, and his speculations about their future even uncertain on occasion. There was little or no duality in his ideas about
the Jews. But his duality about Stalin, for example, persisted till
the end. Better than any statesman in the West, including
Churchill or Roosevelt, Hitler comprehended something—not
all, but something—about Stalin's horrible purges. "I imagined
that after fifteen years of power, Stalin, the realist, would have
rid himself of the nebulous Marxist ideology and that he was
preserving it merely as a poison reserved exclusively for external
use. The brutal manner in which he decapitated the Jewish intelligentsia, who had rendered him such signal service in the destruction of Tsarist Russia, encouraged me in that belief. I pre-
sumed that he did not wish to give these same Jewish
intellectuals the chance of bringing about the downfall of the totalitarian empire which he had built . . ."[9] Five weeks later he
returned to this theme: "It is possible that under the pressure of
events, the Russians will rid themselves completely of Jewish
Marxism, only to re-incarnate pan-slavism in its most fierce and
ferocious form."[10] Yet, for Germany's interests, was a nationalist
and anti-Semitic Russia preferable to a Jewish-Marxist Soviet

* The difference may be attributable, at least in part, to Hitler's early
experiences. In Vienna he met numbers of Jews and Slavs. His deep-
seated obsession with Jews had crystallized then. He didn't like the
Slav population in Vienna either: but he had fewer encounters with
them. In short, the difference between the intensity of his Judaeophobia
and that of his Slavophobia was there from the beginning.

Union? Throughout his Russian war Hitler was ambiguous about this. He was loath to encourage Russian nationalism, including Russian collaborators with the Third Reich. He could not decide. Now, near the end: "At this juncture it is difficult to say which, from the ideological point of view, would prove to be the more injurious to us—Jew-ridden Americanism or Bolshevism."†

It is difficult to say. He could not make up his mind—a rare Hitler admission, this. He was not altogether ignorant of the United States. He had devoured popular literature about America during his youth. Later he devoted some attention to American institutions and American politics. About America, too, his mind was divided. On the one hand, he kept repeating the standard, and ignorant, Nazi propaganda slogans about the large, overgrown, spiritless and mindless mass democracy of the United States: "It may well be asked whether this is not simply a case of a mushroom civilization destined to vanish as quickly as it sprang up."[11] *It may well be asked.* He did not know. He was perplexed by the successful development of the United States. "This war against America is a tragedy." "It is illogical and devoid of any foundation of reality."[12] He blamed American intervention on Roosevelt and the Jews. "Without the Jews and without this lackey of theirs, things could have been quite different. For from every point of view Germany and the United States should have been able, if not to understand each other and sympathize with each other, then at least to support each

† Mussolini, at the same time, to a close collaborator: "What would you prefer Italy to become, an English colony or a Soviet Republic? I would choose a Soviet republic." E. Amicucci, *I 600 giorni di Mussolini* (Rome, 1948), p. 312.

other without undue strain on either of them." "Germany expects nothing from the United States, and the latter have nothing to fear from Germany. Everything combines to ensure the possibility of peaceful co-existence, each in his own country and all in perfect harmony. Unfortunately, the whole business is ruined by the fact that world Jewry has chosen just that country in which to set up its most powerful bastion. That, and that alone, has altered the relations between us and has poisoned everything." He and Roosevelt had come to power at the same time. But Roosevelt ruined it all. "Had Fate so willed that the President of the United States during this critical period were someone other than Roosevelt, he might well have been capable . . . of becoming the greatest President since Lincoln." And now Hitler was ruminating not about the past but about the future, about American prospects. "It will not be very long before the Americans realize that the Roosevelt whom they have adored is an idol with feet of clay and that this Jew-ridden man is in reality a malefactor—both from the point of view of the United States and of humanity as a whole." He was prepared "to wager that well within twenty-five years the Americans themselves will have realized what a handicap has been imposed upon them by this parasitic Jewry . . ." He was prepared to wager: but, then, he wasn't sure. "One thing is quite certain—within a quarter of a century the Americans will either have become violently anti-semitic or they will be devoured by Jewry." "If they do not swiftly succeed in casting off the yoke of New York Jewry (which has the same intelligence as a monkey that saws through the branch on which it is perching), well—it won't be long before they go under, before ever having reached the age of maturity."[13]

About the Jews there were no *ifs* in his mind. Seldom, if ever, did he make an exception or a qualification of his categorical conviction—conviction in both senses of the word—of the Jewish people. Entire libraries have been written about the horrible mass murders that Hitler's words and decisions created. Yet perhaps not enough attention has been paid to how Hitler himself saw the meaning of his acts, and how he saw the historical prospect. Ever since 1919 he had prided himself that he saw the Jewish "problem" in "a cold, scientific way." He now returned to this argument: "I am quite free of all racial hatred." "I have always been absolutely fair in my dealing with the Jews."[14] In his mind it was all very simple‡—simple enough to be categorical, in a frighteningly German way. The Jews were a virus, a bacillus, a dangerous element for any nation. He wanted to get rid of them within Germany—preferably through emigration.

‡ Except for one thing. Contrary to general belief, Hitler's attitude to the Jews was not exclusively biological-racial. He regarded the Jews as an insidious spiritual element. "We use the term of Jewish race as a matter of convenience, for in reality and from the genetic point of view there is no such thing as the Jewish race . . ." "The Jewish race is first and foremost an abstract race of the mind. . . . Nor does Jewry possess the anthropological characteristics which would stamp them as a homogeneous race. . . . It cannot, however, be denied that every Jew in the world has some drops of purely Jewish blood in him. Were this not so, it would be impossible to explain the presence of certain physical characteristics which are permanently common to all Jews . . ." But: "A race of the mind is something more solid, more durable than just a race, pure and simple . . . there in a nutshell is the proof of the superiority of the mind over the flesh!" (13 February 1945.)

He thought that the Jews were instrumental in egging men such as Churchill and Roosevelt against him. All right, then: if there was to be a Second World War, the Jews of Europe would be punished for it. "On the eve of war I gave them one final warning."** "I told them that, if they precipitated another war, they would not be spared and that I would exterminate the vermin throughout Europe, and this once and for all." (Would he have "spared" them if there had been no war?) The final decision to exterminate—exterminate, not merely expel—the Jews in Europe was taken around the time of Pearl Harbor.†† By that time Hitler knew that he could no longer win the war. Churchill and Stalin were supported by Roosevelt, and behind Roosevelt were the Jews. Against the Jews in America he could do nothing. But he would get rid of the Jews of Europe. This was one of his war aims, to which he returned over and over again, for the last time in his public testament where he admonished the German people to stay free of the Jews. He may have lost the war; but at least he eliminated the Jews "and . . . the future will be eternally grateful to us."[15]

About Jews, Hitler was consistent—fanatically consistent—until the end. About other peoples and races he was not. He paid little attention to Rosenberg, the official ideologue of the race myth of the Third Reich; indeed, he made jokes at Rosenberg's

** Reference to his speech of 30 January 1939. He would often mention this "warning" speech during the war, confusing its date, on occasion, with his speech of 1 September 1939.

†† The ominous Wannsee Conference in which bureaucrats and technicians of the Third Reich decided on the technicalities of the "final solution" was originally scheduled to meet on 29 November, postponed to 8–9 December 1941; it finally convened on 20 January 1942.

expense on occasion. He was far from consistent about the
Aryan race. He would ally himself, on occasion, with Italians,
Spaniards, Arabs, Afghans, Japanese; he would wage war on
Englishmen, Danes, Norsemen. Nor were these alignments
merely forced upon him by necessity. During the war as well as
near the end, Hitler expressed his high praise of the Japanese
and also of their enemies, the Chinese. He said that he was looking forward to the triumphant rise of the yellow and brown
races. He foresaw the "swift emergence of the Asiatic, the African and, perhaps, the South American nationalisms." He rumi-
nated over the fact that Germany's best friends in this war have
been the Islamic peoples. And, if the American people were not
able to change their mental habits, it was questionable whether
North America "will for long remain a predominantly white
continent." This "giant with feet of clay" may bring about "its
own downfall. And what a fine chance this sudden collapse will
offer to the yellow races!" Then they could invade the American
continent.‡‡

Such were Hitler's ideas about the world to come. True to his
character, there was a base substance of vulgarity and brutality
running through these last recorded remarks that is consistent
with his rhetoric and with his view of the world throughout his
political life. There can be little doubt that when he spoke of

‡‡ 2 April. And the only white peoples who have "any chance of survival and prosperity" are those who "know how to suffer and who still
retain the courage to fight, even when things are hopeless, to the death.
And the only peoples who will have the right to claim these qualities will
be those who have shown themselves capable of eradicating from their
system the deadly poison of Jewry."

the future of the German people he meant what he said. He might have even agreed with the slogan that the Soviets posted in the portion of Germany that they occupied: "The Hitlers come and go but the German people remains." Let me repeat: after all is said, Hitler was an extreme nationalist rather than an extreme ideologue. Of course Hitler also had posterity in mind. He chose to commit suicide at the end because he dreaded the prospect of falling into the hands of his enemies, with the result of a humiliating spectacle or, perhaps, with the necessity of defending, or even recanting, some of the things he had said or done. He spared himself this, and also spared his enemies. Churchill, for one, had no desire to capture him: he speculated on what would happen if Hitler, doing a Napoleon, were to fly to England at the end, saying: "Do with me what you want, but spare my unfortunate people." Hitler spared Churchill such an embarrassment.

Hitler's death, then, was curiously void of echoes. He prepared it well, ordered a very large mass of gasoline to be poured over his remains; he was determined that his body be reduced to ashes, that it disappear. When the news of his death finally came, there was little rejoicing among Hitler's victims, nor was there much rejoicing among his opponents: Churchill, worried about the future of Britain and Europe, reacted to the news with a kind of resigned indifference. About his followers: according to contemporary accounts the German people, in the depth of their trouble, felt a kind of numb relief. Few of the people in that cellar chose to peek out into the courtyard where the bodies of Hitler and Eva Braun lay burning for four hours, from 4 to 8 P.M., that day. A week passed between the news of the Führer's death and the German surrender, including a Sunday. Was there one church somewhere in a northern German town or village, as yet unoccupied by the advancing enemy, where some pale-faced nationalist Lutheran pastor preached a sermon on *Ehre* and *Volk* and the dead Führer to a congregation with frozen faces on a cool May Sunday? I somehow doubt it; but one would like to know.

Only a few intellectuals, scattered in the oddest places, admirers of National Socialism and of Germandom, were ready to make a gesture, for the record. There was a requiem Mass in a Madrid church. Knut Hamsun, in Norway, thought that he had to write a eulogy: "He was a warrior, a warrior for mankind and a prophet of the gospel of justice for all nations. He was a reformer of the highest rank, and his historical fate was that he flourished in a time of unexampled coarseness, which felled him at last." Justice for all nations? There is something very wrong with this.

More than thirty years have passed since Hitler's death and the world has not yet come to terms with his memory. Interest in him has ebbed and flowed (Hitler remains a far more interesting and frightening historical phenomenon than a Lenin or Stalin or Mao). Biographies of Hitler exist by the dozen, some very good ones, far more detailed and scholarly than were the biographies of Napoleon thirty years after his disappearance from this world. For most Germans, perhaps naturally, it has been easy to blame Hitler for their misfortunes and misdeeds, which is the course that most German generals have taken, and even some of the Nuremberg defendants, among whom few proclaimed their admiration for Hitler till the end. For the rest of the world the easy way out has been to think of Hitler as a madman, a terrible freak in the course of evolving history—which, of course, makes no sense at all (besides relieving Hitler of the responsibility for his acts). There remain admirers of Hitler here and there, particularly among Asians and Africans who regard him as a great national leader. But Hitler was quite unlike Napoleon. Nineteen years after Napoleon's melancholy death on that rock in the South Atlantic his ashes were brought back in an impressive ceremony to the majestic Invalides, where he rests. Less than thirty years after Napoleon's death there was a Bonapartist revival among the French, who chose a new Bonaparte to become their President, and Emperor. Hitler's ashes were scattered by the last winds of war, blown away; his remains disappeared from the face of the earth, a fact which is symbolic as well as real. The revival of interest in Hitler did not mean a revival of interest in his ideas. German National Socialism has not revived at all. Of course, everything is possible. If the civilization of the West were to collapse, there is a chance—a dreadful opportunity, this— that Hitler might appear, in the eyes of a future generation, as a kind of Diocletian, a determined upholder of what was once order and greatness. This has not yet happened. Let us hope that it never will.

In this book, the subject of which is the year 1945, we must not speculate about the meaning of Hitler, since his ideology, together with the structure of the Reich he personified, died with him. But, apart from his meaning, the enormous consequences of his career were there for everyone to see: a destroyed Berlin, a destroyed and divided Europe, and the end of a long era, the European era, in the history of the world. It was with these

consequences—with his estate, not with his will and testament—
that the statesmen and the peoples who conquered him had to
deal. They survived him. They were now the undisputed and
undisputable masters of the world. And to them we must now
turn—at least for 1945, Zero Year.

III. CHURCHILL: THE CHILL OF OLD AGE

Churchill was nearly fifteen years older than Hitler; and he would survive Hitler by nearly twenty more years. He belonged to another world, and to another generation. When Queen Victoria died he was twenty-six years old.* He was a man of the world, a public person, who had made his mark in political life and launched himself on a spectacular career at a time when Hitler was a forlorn waif, a sullen adolescent, a boy of twelve, indistinguishable among the cramped lives of the gray millions who constituted the lower middle classes in Central Europe. At one moment during the First World War, Churchill, a British officer, and Hitler, a German corporal, were but a few miles from each other, in the opposite trenches. Their lives moved in different spheres and different places. After the war Hitler entered on a political career. He knew Churchill's name before

* When Franz Josef died Hitler was twenty-seven. He felt no loyalty to the last Hapsburgs. Churchill's loyalty to his monarch was sentimental, deep, and unbroken. Certain Victorian institutions, amenities, and standards—standards, rather than ideas—left an enduring impression on Churchill, even though he was far more Edwardian than Victorian in character. Hitler was deeply influenced by Vienna, but at a time when the spirit of Franz Josef merely hovered above the city like an ancient specter, a respectable ghost.

Churchill heard of him. What he knew he didn't particularly like, even though he admired Englishmen. Hitler disliked the French; Churchill (a true Edwardian) liked them. He was the kind of aristocratic Englishman, Hitler thought, who did not want Germany to be powerful; he did not have sufficient understanding for the idea of German destiny. To the contrary, Churchill understood the German idea of German destiny only too well.

Churchill was also a romantic. He had a certain admiration for men who rise from nowhere, afire with the purpose of redeeming their downtrodden nation. He had heard of Hitler, an odd and rising figure on the German national scene. In the summer of 1932 their paths met. Motoring through southern Germany with friends, Churchill put in at Munich. At an evening party he met a well-bred giant of a Bavarian, "Putzi" Hanfstaengl, a kind of social secretary to Hitler at the time. Churchill said that he would like to know Hitler. Hanfstaengl rushed to Adolf, who was in a strange and sullen mood. He did not wish to meet Herr Churchill, he said. It was to be Hitler's loss, and not only in the short run. Hitler had a unique talent, perhaps the principal asset of his political genius. He had a powerful, an instinctive, understanding of men he met, no matter what their social or national background, an understanding especially of their weaknesses, a sixth sense in some ways similar to the way in which a dog smells fear in a man. Having failed to meet Churchill in person, Hitler failed to size him up in the way he would comprehend the character of other people he met, whether allies or opponents. On the other hand, Churchill understood Hitler rather well—because of his own genius, a kind of comprehension which was a historical, not an emotional one.

During the crucial summer of 1940 this kind of inner intelligence served Churchill very well. He understood Hitler better than Hitler understood him. He could anticipate some of Hitler's moves at the very time when Hitler was perplexed about the English, and had not quite made up his mind what to do. This kind of superior intelligence could be very important; yet it was not a substitute for power. Hitler bested Churchill in three momentous campaigns of the war: in Norway, in France, in the Balkans. Churchill bested Hitler in the Battle of Britain; but as late as June 1941 this score—3–1 in Hitler's favor—still reflected the realities of the war. Churchill's Britain could not defeat Hitler's Germany, certainly not without Roosevelt's United States and Stalin's Soviet Union. Once these powers entered the war, and once the Soviet Union survived the great German invasion of 1941, Hitler could no longer win it. In December 1941 the duel between Hitler and Churchill stood at a draw: 3–3. But it was no longer the original duel, no longer the original war. It had become a World War, with two superpowers, the United States and the Soviet Union, in it. Their weight and might would crush Hitler in the end.

Still Churchill remained Hitler's principal antagonist throughout the war. He and Britain fought the war from the very beginning to the end, for nearly six years; the United States and the Soviet Union for less than four. During the most crucial phase of the war, Britain, led by Churchill, defied Hitler's might and deviltry alone. Churchill had incarnated the struggle against Hitler from the very beginning. Consequently his prestige remained great till the end, and after. It was a compensation for the gradual erosion of British power. Churchill, of course, knew what this loss of power meant. This was one (though only one) of the reasons why he, the protagonist of the fight against Hitler, took little comfort from the final destruction of his opponent. On 1 May 1945 someone asked him in the House of Commons whether he had any statement about the war situation. He said: "Yes, it is definitely more satisfactory than it was this time five years ago." Yet, as Harold Nicolson remarked: "Generally, he is good at making this sort of joke. But he was feeling ill or something—his manner was languid and his face puckered and creased—it did not go down well."[1] And now contrast Churchill's own recollections, in his war memoirs, of May 1940 and of May 1945:

11 May 1940

[England at the gates of defeat]

. . . as I went to bed at about 3 a.m. I was conscious of a profound sense of relief. I felt as if I were walking with Destiny, and that all my past life had been but a preparation for this hour and this trial. Eleven years in the political wilderness had freed me from ordinary party antagonisms. My warnings over the last six years had been so numerous, so detailed, and were now so terribly vindicated, that no one could gainsay me. I could not be reproached either for making the war or with want of preparation for it. I thought I knew a good deal about it all, and I was sure I should not fail. Therefore, although impatient for the morning, I slept soundly and had no need for cheering dreams . . .

10 May 1945

[England in the hour of victory]

. . . there were few whose hearts were more heavily burdened with anxiety than mine. . . . I struck a sombre note. . . . I must warn you . . . that you must be prepared for further efforts of mind and body and further sacrifices to great causes. . . . You must not weaken in any way your alert and vigilant frame of mind.

Apprehension for the future and many perplexities had filled my mind as I moved about among the cheering crowds of Londoners in their hour of well-won rejoicing. . . . The Soviet menace, to my eyes, had already replaced the Nazi foe . . .

In his victory speech to the British nation, he said: "On the continent of Europe we have yet to make sure that the simple and honourable purposes for which we entered the war are not brushed aside or overlooked in the months following our success, and that the words 'freedom,' 'democracy,' and 'liberation' are not distorted from their true meaning as we have understood them. There would be little use in punishing the Hitlerites for their crimes if law and justice did not rule, and if totalitarian or police Governments were to take the place of the German invaders . . ."

He called the last volume of his war memoirs *Triumph and Tragedy* "because the overwhelming victory of the Grand Alliance has failed so far† to bring general peace to our anxious world." This was true, but only in a limited sense. No American (and no Russian) record or memoir of the Second World War would call itself *Triumph and Tragedy*. Their memoirists' titles are quite different: *Crusade for Europe, The Defeat of Tyranny, Victory over Fascism,* etc. The reason is simple: the triumph of the United States and of the Soviet Union in 1945 was complete, largely unmixed with tragedy, though of course not devoid of all kinds of consequences. Churchill thought and saw triumph *and* tragedy in 1945, not only because no general settlement of peace ensued, and not only because the British people voted him out of office that year. Triumph: because the purpose of the war had been accomplished, Hitler and the Third Reich were destroyed. Tragedy: because the result, in 1945, was the

† Written in 1953. Most of the volume had been completed two years earlier.

Soviet menace, with Soviet Russia "having established herself in the heart of Western Europe."‡ Double tragedy: because much of this could have been avoided, if he had had his way. Nor was this merely the argument of an aged statesman in retrospect. Churchill, tired and unwell as he was in 1945, saw things rather clearly. The Russian domination of Central Europe was a disaster not only for the peoples of that portion of the continent but for all of the continent, for a long time to come. It was also a menace to the rest of the world. The Russian domination of the eastern borderlands of Europe was one thing, but of Central Europe another. It meant the end of a certain kind of civilization, in the defense of which Churchill had gone to war. It meant that the kind of Europe which Hitler had attempted to replace by force could not be restored. The restoration of civilization, and of Europe: this was one of the purposes, and it was certainly the result, of England's exertions against Napoleon. It was, even more, Churchill's purpose in fighting Hitler: but now the results were different. The division of Europe with the Russians: it did not seem a disaster for Americans, even though they would become obsessed with Communism after the war. To Churchill *this* kind of division was a tragedy, the darkest possible result of the war.

He knew that the Russians would increase their dominions. It was the inescapable consequence of the gigantic Russian contribution to the defeat of Germany. Churchill thought that the

‡ From his introduction to *Triumph and Tragedy*. Berlin, Wittenberg, Prague, Vienna, Budapest: "the heart of Western Europe"? A little exaggeration but not much: at most, a geographical slip that shows whereto Churchill's mind kept wandering back, years after the war.

Russians deserved to regain the general influence in Europe and in the Far East, and many of the particular territories in Eastern Europe that their empire had possessed before the First World War and that Lenin had forfeited for the sake of proceeding with the grisly Communist experiment in what remained (it was still plenty) of Russia after the First World War. Unlike most Americans after 1945, Churchill was not unduly worried about Communism. Unlike many leading Americans in 1945 and before, Churchill never had any illusions about it: he saw its crude and backward nature from its very beginnings. He nurtured certain illusions about Stalin, precisely because he saw in him a profoundly unrevolutionary statesman, a national warrior, a leader. Consequently Churchill was not particularly concerned with the spread of Communism across that part of Europe that lay outside the reach of the Russian armies. He was concerned with how far the armed might of Russia would stretch at the end of the war. He believed that, whenever possible, the limits of Stalin's conquests ought to be defined, and agreed upon, before the end of the war. Stalin had indicated what he wanted to the visiting Anthony Eden as early as December 1941, when windowpanes in Moscow were still rattling from the echoes of German guns. Eden had come with the draft of an Anglo-Russian declaration. Stalin said that he wanted an agreement, not a declaration: "A declaration I regard as algebra, but an agreement as practical arithmetic." He produced a Russian draft agreement, replete with secret protocols, establishing his right to certain territories in Eastern Europe. Churchill was inclined to consider this, for two reasons. First, he feared that Stalin might be disappointed with his Western allies to the extent of seeking a separate peace with Hitler**—something for which there were many precedents in the history of Russia, ancient and modern. Second, he thought that it would be advantageous to reach a definite agreement on the western frontiers of the Soviet empire at the time when the Russians were still struggling for their lives in the midst of their vast country, before they would surge westward, flushed with their victory. He did not have his way. The Americans, for all kinds of reasons—mostly domestic—did not wish to make such a commitment. Eventually Stalin realized that he would profit even more from American algebra than from British arithmetic.††

As the war proceeded in the Mediterranean, Churchill had another idea. This was to extend the Anglo-American presence

** Conversation with General Sikorski, Prime Minister of Poland, March 1942. Churchill: "his own assessment of Russia did not differ much" from that of the Polish general; "however, he underlined the reasons which made it necessary to conclude the agreement with Russia. She was the only country that had fought against the Germans with success. She had destroyed millions of German soldiers and at present the aim of the war seemed not so much victory, as the death or survival of our allied nations. Should Russia come to an agreement with the Reich, all would be lost. It must not happen. If Russia was victorious she would decide on her frontiers without consulting Great Britain; should she lose the war, the agreement would lose all its importance." *Documents on Polish-Soviet Relations, 1939–1945* (London, 1961), Vol. I, pp. 297–98.

†† This was especially true about Poland. At the end of the war the Russian armies would surge through Poland; under no circumstances would Anglo-American troops arrive there. Churchill hoped to save the Polish state and nation by trading off land for the sake of its freedom: to agree that Russia obtain eastern Poland, approximately up to the so-called Curzon Line, in exchange for Stalin's acceptance of a pro-Russian, though non-Communist, national government in the rest. He failed in that, too.

from Italy northeastward. Again he had two main reasons for this. First, he wanted to profit from Anglo-American naval superiority, by opening up more fronts against the Germans, reducing thereby the mass of available German troops against the eventual Allied invasion in Western Europe. Second, he hoped to establish an Anglo-American presence in Greece, Yugoslavia, Austria, western Hungary perhaps. Again he did not have his way. The Americans were opposed to this kind of strategy: first, because they believed that it would weaken the force of the single main thrust from Normandy to Germany; second, and more significant, because they were suspicious of Churchill's political motives. After the end of the North African campaign Churchill had trouble enough in convincing the Americans that the Allies should go on to Italy from Sicily. Eventually they did: but the entire Italian campaign no longer had much sense; it was not much more than a long cul-de-sac. Throughout 1943 and 1944 the Americans turned a deaf ear to Churchill's urgings. There was not a single important American personage, either in Roosevelt's circle or among the American military, who would listen to Churchill, eloquently as he argued for the advantages of exploiting the Italian campaign. They suspected Churchill of having political purposes, especially when he—aware as he was of these suspicions—did not openly reveal them. He preferred, instead, to advocate his strategy on military grounds alone. In the summer of 1944 these things came to a head. The Allied plan for the great invasion of Western Europe—which Churchill had accepted loyally the year before—called for a secondary landing on the French Riviera, ninety days after the Allied establishment of the bridgehead in Normandy. As that time was approaching the Germans were moving out of France fast. The Russian armies were now converging on the Balkans. Churchill was convinced that the divisions destined for the empty beaches of southern France ought to be thrown forward in Italy. The liberation of Italy would be speeded up, wherefrom they would advance rapidly to the northeast. Again the Americans refused. The landing on the Riviera took place in a vacuum. It was of no military import whatever. Churchill was now deeply worried, and embittered.‡‡ There would be no Anglo-American presence in the Balkans, none in Hungary, perhaps not even in Austria. He thought he had now no option left except to sit down with Stalin and divide the Balkans. There was no time to spare.

So he flew to Moscow in October 1944. This conference with Stalin was perhaps the most important, because the most consequential, meeting during the entire war, more important than the famous summits in Teheran or Yalta or Potsdam. "The moment was apt for business," Churchill said, and he wrote out "on a half-sheet of paper":

Rumania	
The others	10%
Russia	90%
Greece	

‡‡ He no longer felt it necessary to keep silent about political purposes. The memorandum of General Brooke at the Quebec Conference, in September 1944, openly admitted that the plan for an Anglo-American advance through Istria "had not only a military value but also political value in view of the Russian advances in the Balkans."

Great Britain	90%
(in accord with U.S.A.)	
Russia	10%
Yugoslavia	50–50%
Hungary	50–50%
Bulgaria	
Russia	75%
The others	25%

"I pushed this across to Stalin, who had by then heard the translation. There was a slight pause. Then he took his blue pencil and made a large tick upon it, and passed it back to us. It was all settled in no more time than it takes to set down . . ."

". . . After this there was a long silence. The pencilled paper lay in the centre of the table. At length I said, 'Might it not be thought rather cynical if it seemed we had disposed of these issues, so fateful to millions of people, in such an offhand manner? Let us burn the paper.' 'No, you keep it,' said Stalin."*

Churchill had no other option. His hands had been bound for some time. He had done what he could. This arrangement saved Greece,† where British troops put down a Communist insurrection in December 1944, an intervention that the Americans

* *Triumph and Tragedy*, pp. 227–28. In the case of Hungary there was more haggling between Molotov and Eden, with the result that the formula was revised to 75–25% of Russian preponderance.

† Churchill to Eden, as early as 7 November 1944 (nearly a month before the Communist insurrection in Athens): "*Having paid the price we have to Russia for freedom of action in Greece,* we should not hesitate to use British troops to support the Royal Hellenic Government . . ." (My italics.)

protested, while Stalin looked away.‡ In November 1944 Churchill revealed his view of these events to De Gaulle in Paris, even though he did not tell De Gaulle about the Percentages Agreement. De Gaulle was critical of the Americans: they were letting the Russians into the middle of Europe. Churchill admitted that this was wrong. Russia is a great hungry wolf, he said, full of appetite; she is advancing now in the midst of her victims. "But after the meal comes the digestion period." Russia would not be able to digest so many Eastern European nations.

Churchill was to be proven right. But we only know this from retrospect. In early 1945 the prospect, to Churchill, was ominous. He had hoped for a working relationship, indeed for a lasting relationship, with Stalin. So far as Eastern Europe went, he hoped that the Russian victories would make Stalin sufficiently secure, that Stalin would take comfort from the fact that much of Eastern Europe was in the Russian sphere, so that he would not feel compelled to force the grim, and unnatural, Communist system on these peoples, with the result of cordoning them off and separating them from the rest of the continent. Soon after the Yalta Conference, Churchill saw that this was an illusion. The time had come—finally—to make a stand. It was not only that time was pressing; the Americans and the British had certain advantages now. They were advancing rapidly toward the heart of Germany, while the Russians were slogging it out, more

‡ Thirty-three years have passed since Churchill's Percentages Agreement with Stalin in Moscow. Surprisingly enough, it has lasted till this day: Greece non-Communist; Yugoslavia half here, half there; Hungary not entirely Sovietized; Rumania not entirely subservient to Moscow; etc., etc.

slowly. He wanted to make an issue of Poland. The Americans refused, again. Meanwhile the Germans gave way almost everywhere in the West. Stalin was worried. Churchill wanted the Anglo-American armies to push into Berlin before the Russians. Eisenhower refused.** In sum, Churchill's arguments were sound; his rhetoric was impressive; but they exhausted his resolution; and he gave in. This momentous sequence of events was typical of his relationship with the American leaders throughout the war. It was, sadly enough, symptomatic of the relative weakness not only of British, but also of his own, strength.

At the end of the war in Europe the Russians were in Berlin, Prague, Vienna. Still the Anglo-American armies had met the Russians nearly one hundred miles within the territory that had been allotted to the Russian zone of occupation in Germany. Churchill believed that they ought to stay there until Stalin turned more amenable, that they should not move back to the previously designed demarcation lines save in exchange for

** On 28 March Eisenhower, *on his own* (the exact circumstances and the motives of this decision remain unclear to this day) sent a message to Stalin, informing him that the Western armies were not going to move toward Berlin but would make their principal thrust further to the south. Churchill was upset but, as so often before, remonstrated with Eisenhower on a purely military basis at first. A few days later he changed his mind. On 2 April he sent a message to Eisenhower, taking issue with the latter's statement that "Berlin has lost its former strategic importance." To the contrary, "I deem it highly important that we should shake hands with the Russians as far east as possible." But he could not shake Eisenhower, who had marshaled the support of Washington. On 15 April the Ninth American Army was across the Elbe, in some ways even closer to Berlin than the Russians at that moment. Churchill tried again, but in vain. (He contented himself with having Montgomery make fast for Lübeck, to seal off the Danish peninsula from the Russians.)

substantial Russian concessions. Again Washington rejected his ideas; and by the time of the last summit meeting in Potsdam it was too late.

We have to carry this story a little further. In 1945 Churchill found himself in a situation which was distressingly similar to his situation a decade earlier, during the Locust Years of the Thirties. He was out of office before the Second World War began; now, when it ended, he was out of office again. His warnings against the German menace were unheeded then; his warnings against the Soviet menace were unheeded now. Again he saw the disastrous consequences of lassitude and selfishness and of false illusions assemble before his eyes; again he was largely powerless to do anything about it, except to speak out. There was a difference, however. The appeasers of Hitler, mostly British politicians then, had been sticking to power, unwilling to change their ideas until Hitler attacked Western Europe; but by that time British public opinion had turned in Churchill's direction. The appeasers of Stalin, mostly influential Americans, began to change their ideas after 1945, even though Stalin had ceased to advance toward Western Europe; within a few years they became doctrinaire anti-Communists, almost to a man.

There was a positive and a negative consequence to this for Churchill, and for the free world at large. The Americans eventually committed themselves to the defense of Western Europe and of certain other parts of the world, which was all to the good. They did this in the name of the ideology of anti-Communism, which was not so good. They thought, or at least some of them acted as if they thought, that the main danger and the main issue was the spread of Communism. Churchill, on the other hand, continued to believe that the main issue was not ideology but territory: not Communism but the presence of Russia in the middle of Europe. In 1951 he became Prime Minister again. In 1952 his wartime ally Eisenhower was elected President of the United States. In March 1953 Stalin died. Churchill thought that this was the time to try to correct, and to renegotiate, the division of Europe. He rightly estimated that the new leaders of the Russian empire were worried men, unsure of themselves, aware of their own problems that their swollen empire created in Eastern Europe and particularly in Germany. Again Churchill did not have his way. The Americans refused even to consider his ideas. The same Eisenhower who in 1945 would deal with the Russians, such splendid fellows, over Churchill's head if need be, by 1953 had become a prime anti-Communist, following the advice of John Foster Dulles: Churchill was all wrong, there was nothing to be gained by talking to the fiendish Russians. In 1945 Churchill was too anti-Russian for American tastes; by 1953 he was not anti-Russian enough. In reality it was Churchill, not Eisenhower, whose convictions, including his view of the Russians, had not changed. The essential principles of his thinking remained the same, while people such as Eisenhower had no principles except for certain ideas that they proclaimed as principles when this seemed both opportune and popular. Eisenhower's uneasiness vis-à-vis Churchill: it was not only an unedifying spectacle, but full of dire consequences in retrospect. Eventually, forced by circumstances, the erstwhile opponents of Churchill's ideas would adopt them, years after Churchill had proposed them in vain; but by that time, in one way or another, it would be too late.

Compared to such people as Eisenhower or Dulles or Chamberlain or even Roosevelt, Churchill was almost always right. But he had many faults.

Churchill was a quintessentially English character, except for one thing: he had a very quick mind. This, of course, was a great and even profound advantage on occasion: he could see things quicker, farther, and often deeper than most of his countrymen as well as his political contemporaries. A quick mind, which is not necessarily a shallow one, is, however, prone to suffer from two conditions: impatience and boredom. Because of his impatience, allied with his impetuosity, Churchill had alienated many of his countrymen before the Second World War. This condition, more than often, was their loss not his. During the war, however, his impatience, compounded with boredom, compromised the standards of his personal diplomacy.†† Like many of the great masters of language (who, to their good fortune, did not have to make their mark in politics and statecraft), Churchill was inclined to trust the influence of his expressions unduly. He would often mistake his own words for action. He would dictate a message to Roosevelt or Stalin, or he would make a statement at a conference with them, putting his best efforts into phrasing his propositions strongly and clearly. He would take good care to make his message or his speech all-

†† The exception was his first three months as Prime Minister. He hit his stride so well that his timing, too, was perfect—not only in regard to Hitler but also in regard to Roosevelt.

inclusive, including every possible argument to sustain his thesis. Having expended his energy, care, and concentration on the statement of his propositions, he would sit back, willing to listen eventually but already half tired of the whole thing. But the recipients of his messages or of his rhetoric did not read or listen to his prose accordingly. They were seldom moved by it: especially during the pell-mell conditions of talk at the large conference tables they were, at times, visibly bored with Churchill's lengthy rhetoric. Eventually they found that they could profit from the condition that it was, more often than not, a one-shot affair, since Churchill usually said everything he wanted to say in one big sweep, after which it was not only that he had few strong points in reserve but that he himself was bored, since he disliked to repeat himself. Again there was a great difference between 1940 and 1945. In 1940 Churchill's rhetoric was the best thing that was. But in 1945 the circumstances, the audience, the problems were quite different. In 1940 he had an appetite for details which was astonishing. In 1945 he was bored with details, especially when these involved chronic and painful problems such as that of the Poles.‡‡ At Yalta, and even more at Potsdam, he came to the conference tables ill prepared about many matters, some-

‡‡ On the other hand, his mind would still light up strong and clear when certain matters of honor were involved, which, for him, were always matters of substance not symbol. Example: his message to the Foreign Office and War Office about the Polish general Anders on 31 May 1945: "This gallant man has long fought with us. I am not prepared to allow our distribution of military honours to be overshadowed by Bolshevik prejudices. I should propose that General Anders should receive a decoration for his long fighting services."

times with portentous consequences.* All of this made him, on many occasions, a poor diplomat at the tables. At times he could still make himself heard as the greatest speaker of the war; at other times he would give the impression of an old man who could be formidably voluble but not much more.†

He also had certain illusions. He kept them up, unwilling to abandon them for a long time, since they gave sustenance to his philosophy of the war. His attitude toward Russia, and especially toward Stalin, was an extraordinary compound—compound rather than mixture—of extraordinary realism with extraordinary illusions. I have suggested his realism a few pages earlier: Churchill instantly understood that Stalin was a statesman, not a revolutionary, a man unhampered by doctrinaire thinking. He consequently concluded that he could deal with Stalin: but his impetuous and recurrent optimism in this regard was both right and wrong. It was right in the sense that Stalin, a realist, would consider real issues, not ideological categories. It was wrong in the sense that Stalin's realism made him more dangerous as a partner, not less. Stalin's realism had an Oriental

---

* At Potsdam, Stalin, who was probably baffled about British noncommittalness about Hungary, asked Churchill a point-blank question about that country. Churchill was unprepared for an answer.

† Truman's reminiscences of the Potsdam Conference: "Churchill always found it necessary . . . to make long statements like this and then agree to what had already been done. . . . On several occasions when Churchill was discussing something at length, Stalin would lean on his elbow, pull on his mustache, and say, 'Why don't you agree? The Americans agree, and we agree. You will agree eventually, so why don't you do it now?' Then the argument would stop. Churchill in the end would agree, but he had to make a speech about it first." *Harry S. Truman: Memoirs* (New York, 1953), Vol. I, p. 363.

streak in it: it was narrow, cynical, cruel, and suspicious. Stalin and the Soviet leaders had a deep-seated complex of inferiority in front of the Western world. Churchill understood this: but he was unable to turn it to his advantage. His own impetuousness baffled Stalin, rather than impressing him. They would make quick deals about important matters, after which Churchill felt relieved, while Stalin was surprised that there had been no real haggling. As late as 1945 Churchill kept repeating to his closest confidants that if anything happened to Stalin this would be a "disaster." When Churchill wrote his auto-history of the Second World War, during the dangerous years of the cold war when Stalin was at his worst, paranoid, crude, cruel, Churchill would still include many passages in these memoirs that showed not only his wartime respect for Stalin but also the satisfaction that he, Churchill, got from Stalin's occasional expressions of respect for him. To Churchill, Hitler was a greater danger than Stalin. An Edwardian aristocrat would get along better with a Caucasian bandit than with the ugly genius of an Austrian demagogue.‡ Also, the German domination of Europe presented a greater, and clearer, danger to Britain than the Russian domination of the eastern part of the continent. Half of Europe was better than none. Most Englishmen would agree with that. Only Churchill also had certain romantic illusions about this Caucasian bandit that were not altogether unlike the

‡ He had a high opinion of Stalin's, and a low opinion of Trotsky's, abilities (reflected in his biographical sketch of the latter, reprinted in *Great Contemporaries* in 1937, both brilliant and prophetic). This was understandable: but he carried it too far, as in December 1944, when he referred to the Greek Communist insurrection as "terrorist" (true) and "Trotskyite" (untrue).

illusions of other latter-day Edwardians such as T. E. Lawrence about gallant and dependable Arabs, or those of some of Saki's figures. Churchill had been right about almost everything before the war, with one major exception: he believed that at the time of the Munich crisis Stalin would have fought Germany on the side of the Western democracies, which was not the case.** Caucasian bandits, no matter how impressive, were also prone to think in ways that were cruel and warped and, more than often, sordid. Poles knew these things by experience; but the English would not listen to them. Churchill heard them; he would agree, on occasion; but in the end, his impetuous nature would carry him away. He did not feel like haggling with Stalin. He was satisfied when he felt that the two of them understood each other, that somehow they were getting along, that Stalin would not betray him and drop out of the war, that Stalin would get what he wanted but not at Britain's expense. He thought that the core of realism he saw in Stalin was evidence of the latter's moderation, instead of what it was: a kind of Oriental caution cloaked by aggressiveness and inspired by fear.

In sum, Churchill was not very wrong about the Russians and Communism and Stalin. Even when some of his illusions about Stalin may have compromised his perspective, his essential vision of the Russian problem was largely reasonable and correct. Surely he saw things about Stalin and the Russians better than Roosevelt and the American establishment saw them. But this advantage turned out to be of little or no benefit to him in the

** He believed this as late as 1948; witness the first volume of his *History of the Second World War.*

end. One of the reasons, if not the principal reason, for this was that he, Churchill, had certain illusions about the United States: and that was a very great matter. It included his entire political life, the course of the twentieth century, and the entire prospects of Western civilization. I shall take but one paragraph to suggest that this is not a grandiloquent assertion.

Churchill's father was English, his mother was American. Theirs was a bad marriage. They were not very good parents either.†† No matter: Churchill loved them. He dwelt on their characters and backgrounds throughout his life. He wanted to reconcile them within himself; and he largely succeeded. This was in perfect harmony with his political aspirations; more important, with his vision of the future of the world. He wanted an ever closer union between Britain and the United States, eventually a kind of confederation of the English-speaking nations of the world. This was not only his avowed desire during the Second World War when Britain was in mortal peril, and when she depended so much on her alliance with the United States. Churchill believed in this from the earliest beginning to the very end of his political career, from the age of twenty-four, in 1898, when he first spoke of this, and when he counseled his mother who had embarked on the publishing of an *Anglo-Saxon Review*, to the age of eighty-one, in 1955, when, racked with illness and feebleness, he resigned his last political office. And indeed, it was exactly from 1898 to 1955 that the closeness of Britain and the United States *was* the principal reality in the

†† As in Hitler's case, Churchill's strong love for his mother was an important factor in his personality. But these sons sublimated their filial affections in very different ways.

politics of the globe. Only they were not close enough. Churchill wished that they would grow closer, merging along the edges.
He knew that a close alliance between Britain and the United
States would have prevented the First World War—which, in
turn, would have precluded the Second World War. A confederation of the English-speaking nations would have been the
greatest power in the world. Few would have dared to challenge
its might. Such a Pax Anglo-Americana would have extended
the rule of Western civilization for at least one or two centuries.
Churchill's writings, very much including his four-volume *History of the English-speaking Peoples,* were devoted to the fur-
thering of this aim.‡‡ "People," Dr. Johnson said, "need to be
reminded more often that they need to be instructed." Churchill
wanted to remind the English-speaking peoples of their common
heritage; and to eventually translate this into a permanent association.

But this did not come about. It was not to be. There were all
kinds of reasons for this. For one thing, during Churchill's lifetime the character of the American people changed. They were
no longer predominantly of Anglo-Saxon ancestry. Their institutions were still Anglo-Saxon in form, less and less so in content.
Churchill knew this, but perhaps he did not give it sufficient
thought. He took great satisfaction from knowing that the leading classes and the governing figures of American politics and

‡‡ There are innumerable examples of this in his writings. One of them
is his brilliant tour de force, an article written in the twenties about what
would have happened "If Lee Had Not Won the Battle of Gettysburg,"
in a volume of collected historical speculations, edited by J. C. Squire,
and entitled *If: or History Rewritten* (New York, 1931).

society, the people whom he knew and cultivated and who, in turn, respected and often even admired him, came from the same background in 1940 as they had come from forty years earlier, in Edward's or even in Victoria's days. He should have known that the power of this predominantly Anglo-Saxon elite, largely of the eastern seaboard, their power in governing America, their ability in committing Americans to certain actions and to certain preferences, was no longer what it had been before. In 1900, when England and the United States were still eight days apart by the fastest of ships, when their alliance was still beyond the horizon, the desirability of some kind of an Anglo-Saxon union was a respectable idea, almost an *idée reçue,* to which many of the elite of the Republic would, and indeed did, respond. In 1945, when England and America were but eight hours apart by the speediest of military airplanes, and when their alliance had been victorious in two world wars, the idea of an Anglo-American union evoked no response in American minds and hearts; it all seemed somehow limiting and backward compared to such things as world government or the United Nations.*

This was certainly true of President and Mrs. Roosevelt. And here we come to the essential, and paradoxical, nature of the Churchill-Roosevelt relationship. Churchill's illusions, his expec-

---

* Churchill had a justifiable skepticism about the United Nations. To Eden (in San Francisco), on 11 May 1945: "The Russians may remain with hundreds of divisions in possession of Europe from Lübeck to Trieste, and to the Greek frontier on the Adriatic. All these things are far more vital than the amendments to a world constitution which may never come into being . . ."

tations, his rather magnanimous sentiments concerning Roosevelt were but a paradigm of his illusions, his expectations, his rather magnanimous sentiments about the United States and the American people at large. Essentially they were simple. Americans were a great and generous people. They came to the aid of Britain and of the cause of freedom. They were slow to react; but once they understood what it was all about their energies were boundless. Their cause and the cause of Britain were essentially the same. Their relationship was not a temporary liaison out of calculation, but an alliance with a broad prospect for the world. This is how certain Americans and, what was more important, their President reacted in 1940. For this Churchill remained forever grateful. It seemed to confirm to him that his view about Americans, about their sentiments and their thinking, was largely correct. Yet the American people at large, and Franklin Roosevelt in particular, were not simple. Roosevelt liked the English: but he did not like the idea of their empire. Roosevelt liked Churchill: but he did not like listening to him. Churchill could exhilarate Roosevelt on occasion: but Roosevelt would also be bored with Churchill, beyond reason. With all of his patrician self-confidence, Roosevelt reflected the complex sentiments of most Americans toward the British at the time: a mixture of inferiority and superiority. Roosevelt was vainer than Churchill; Roosevelt knew that Churchill was the smarter of the two; he also knew that he, Roosevelt, was more powerful. By knowing that Churchill was smart, Roosevelt mistakenly deduced that Churchill was also cleverer, that is, more calculating. To the contrary, Churchill was open with Americans, thinking—wrongly—that his warmth and frankness would instantly melt away American suspicions, which was not the case. Churchill was impatient; Roosevelt's attention-span was limited. Their correspondence and the records of their conversations attest to this. Churchill, unlike Roosevelt, was a master of English prose: yet in his letters and in his talks it was Churchill who was long-winded, verbose, prolix, outtalking and outwriting Roosevelt four words to one. Churchill knew better how to talk to his own people than how to talk to Americans. On occasion he would attribute to Roosevelt, and to the Americans, an inability—hopefully a temporary one—to see things in the way he saw them. In reality, the matter went deeper: Roosevelt, like most Americans, was unwilling—unwilling, rather than unable—to listen to all that Churchill had to say.

In sum, the record of Churchill's warnings, and of his foresight, was impressive. His resolution, and his ability to influence Americans, was not. For them their relationship to Russia in 1945 had become more important than their relationship to England.† To Churchill the relationship between England and

† There was something pathetic in the tone of Churchill's letters to Roosevelt during the last winter and spring, 1944–45. He would write, for example: "I was much hurt [about a State Department communiqué in December 1944, criticizing British actions in Greece] . . . I am sure such things have never been said by the State Department about Russia . . ." After Yalta: "I do not wish to reveal a divergence between the British and the United States Governments, but it would certainly be necessary for one to make it clear that we are in presence of a great failure and an utter breakdown of what was settled at Yalta, but that we British have not the necessary strength to carry the matter further and that the limits of our capacity to act have been reached . . ." Roosevelt's answer was cold and unfriendly: "I cannot but be concerned at the views

America had the absolute priority at the end of the war, as much as, if not more than, at its beginning. His mistake was to base everything on this priority, perhaps beyond reason. Of course, he was right about this at the beginning of the war and even later, when Hitler came close to winning: he would rather transfer the British Empire bit by bit to the Americans than keep the Empire by agreeing to the Germans' mastery of Europe—something that Hitler would not understand, at least not for a long time. But Churchill should have given more thought to what this priority of America over Europe would mean for Britain at the end of the war, and after. In 1945 Britain, because of her prestige alone, could have obtained the leadership of a united Western Europe for a song. The British people, and the Labour government that they had elected, were wholly uninterested in this.‡ Churchill, who throughout his life was far less insular, and more farsighted, than the immense majority of his compatriots—it was, after all, his deep comprehension of European realities that had made him the great protagonist of the struggle against Hitler—was not much interested in it, either, at least not in 1945: a failure of vision with all kinds of consequences. The

expressed [in your message]." "I am surprised at your [message]." "I do not understand what you mean by a divergence . . ." Etc., etc. *Roosevelt and Churchill: Their Secret Wartime Correspondence,* Loewenheim, Langley, and Jonas, eds. (New York, 1975), pp. 621, 671, 674.

‡ They, however, instinctively felt—like Churchill—that they must "avoid stepping on American toes. Whenever, for example, bored American soldiers have become rowdy and made themselves unpopular in a provincial town, it has been the timid custom of the papers merely to print the mayor's indignant denial that anything happened." Mollie Panter-Downes in *The New Yorker,* 14 January 1945.

principal reason for this failure was his continued illusion about the uniqueness of the Anglo-American alliance.

The trouble behind this failure of vision was the failing of his strength. He could no longer impose his will on others; as a matter of fact, he could not even make them see things his way. He sensed this about his own people, too. Well before his electoral defeat he was worried about their insular mood, about their lassitude. In his victory speech in May he not only warned and exhorted them about further difficulties, about necessary sacrifices that still lay ahead; he also told them ". . . not to fall back into the rut of inertia, the confusion of aim, and the craven fear of being great." Much like the Americans, the British people were unwilling to listen to much that Churchill had still to say. They reverted to their pattern of the twentieth century, during which the Churchillian spirit was of course the exception, not the rule. Democracy was doing them in.** When the British people—somewhat shamefacedly, it is true—had refused Churchill and the Conservatives in the July 1945 election, some of Churchill's friends and associates muttered something about the ingratitude of the people. With his natural magnanimity Churchill said that the British people were entitled to their

** The first sentence of the second volume of Michael Foot's biography of Aneurin Bevan—written nearly thirty years after these events—reads as follows: "No Socialist who saw it will forget the blissful dawn of July 1945." With all of the allowance due to the electoral joys of the Labour Party, how smug and parochial and stupid this is! July 1945: half of Europe and England in ruins, the Soviets astride half of the Old World, the peoples of the Continent starving and shorn, the burst of the first atomic bomb, the ominous beginnings of the cold war between the superpowers, England sliding down to the status of a second-rate power and state: Some bliss! Some dawn!

choice: they had had a very hard time.†† ("If a man is genuinely superior to his fellows," Chesterton once wrote, "the first thing he believes in is the equality of man.") Years later Churchill would say that during the Finest Hour he was not the lion: the British people were the lions, he only gave the roar. In reality he had been both lion and roar in 1940. In 1945 the British people were not only tired of lionship and of roaring: they preferred to close their ears, and drop their eyelids as well.

They were tired, rather than exhausted. There is a standard, a hitherto unchallenged, explanation of their condition. Their finances were exhausted, they were on the verge of bankruptcy: a hard economic fact. They had spent most of their money in the Second World War; consequently they could no longer afford to play the role of a great power. Allow me to challenge this hard economic fact. When people say that they cannot afford something, this usually means that they don't want to afford it—a truism as valid in the lives of nations as in the lives of individuals, perhaps even more so. Germany in the 1930's could not afford to spend money on armaments: Hitler gave this economic condition not a thought. In the summer of 1940 the British could nary afford to fight Hitler, low as they were in cash, and devoid of guns, rifles, tanks: they gave their economic condition not a thought—rightly so.‡‡ In the lives of individuals as well as

†† He did say, however, in a private letter to Alexander Cadogan (5 August 1945): "A very formidable event has occurred in Britain, and I fear it will diminish our national stature at a time when we most need unity and strength."

‡‡ Churchill himself knew this. In 1940 he worked mightily for American material help. But he knew that even more important than the ma-

in the lives of nations economic considerations are seldom more
than rationalizations of deeper and stronger purposes: and consequently the Hard Facts of Economics turn out, especially in
retrospect, to have been the softest facts of all.

"The craven fear of being great": in 1945 Churchill's phrase
may have been too much. The English people did not respond.
But his own strength was going, too. "What we call genius is
the ability to invent one's own occupation," Ortega y Gasset
once wrote. During the 1930's Churchill, angry, alone, betrayed,
Cassandra as well as Demosthenes, took relish in his self-appointed task. He shone with vitality, in spite of his indulgences,
including alcohol: his mind, and perhaps also his body, were
younger than his age. In 1945, in the seventieth year of his life,
he was an old and tired man. Two serious illnesses, a minor
stroke, and the six years of immense concern with the survival of
his nation had taken their toll, to say the least. He commanded
the ship of state throughout the war, assisted by his personal
genius, which made this task more bearable than it would have
been for lesser men. So far as his body went, he organized his
daily life in accord with certain highly individual preferences
and comforts; and his quick mind enabled him to take many
shortcuts that would have been beyond the compass of lesser
men. But by the end of the war much of his strength had faded;

terial coming from America was the commitment of the United States on
the side of Britain: the impression, rather than the goods. This was certainly true of the destroyer deal. When Roosevelt, departing from neu-
trality, offered to Britain fifty overage destroyers in the late summer of
1940, this was an important event: its symbolic meaning counted more
than the actual ships.

and, what was worse, his resolution faded with it. His mind was worn.* The incomparable rhetoric still flashed here and there; but behind the phrases there was less and less resolution, less and less strength of purpose. The British people may have chosen to close their ears and drop their eyelids as well; so did Churchill, on many occasions, during cabinet meetings and during the two summit conferences.

His perspective of the world scene remained farsighted and brave. He was so aware of the Soviet danger that in May and in June he, of all people, ordered the British military authorities to stop the disarming and the reduction, not only of certain British armed services but even of certain German units,†—a preparation against the prospect of Soviet armed aggression. In so doing he again showed his true mettle, his willingness to take unpopular measures when he thought that this was needed, and his capacity to comprehend the imminence of danger for Europe. Yet in other matters he was losing some of the courage of his convictions. He would rather not quarrel with the Americans. He would gather his energy and compose farsighted warnings in his messages to President Truman: but then he would, and could, do little to translate his long-crystallized convictions into actions. Not only were the people of Britain tired and worn;

* Cadogan's diary during the Potsdam Conference, 18 July 1945: "The P.M., since he left London, has refused to do any work or read anything."

† As he himself said, his hate for the Germans had died with their surrender. During his desultory visit to the ruins of Hitler's Chancellery someone showed him two Iron Crosses found there. "Poor devils," he said. *Churchill: Taken from the Diaries of Lord Moran*, p. 291.

so was Churchill. The cheer of life was fading; the chill of old age had come.‡

‡ On 26 March 1945 he had clambered across the Rhine at Wesel, while a few German shells fell in his vicinity. General Brooke: "I honestly believe that he would really have liked to be killed on the front at this moment of success. . . . I rather feel that he considers that a sudden and soldierly death at the front would be a suitable ending to his famous life and would free him from the never-ending worries which loom ahead with our Russian friends and others . . ." Cited in R. Parkinson, *A Day's March Near Home* (London, 1974), pp. 462–63.

IV. ROOSEVELT NEAR DEATH

The victory of those who are armed to defend a just cause is not necessarily a just victory; it is not the cause for which men took up arms that makes a victory more just or less, it is the order that is established when arms are laid down.

> —Written during the first year of
> the Second World War by Simone Weil

In 1945 there was no world power comparable to the United States. There had been nothing like it since the Roman Empire. Great Britain after Napoleon, the France of Louis XIV, the Spanish empire in the sixteenth century had been first among equals, *primus inter pares*. The vast Eurasian empire of the Soviet Union was a superpower because of her size, not because of the extent of her sway. Stalin did not have the slightest inclination to challenge the American dominion over the Atlantic and the Pacific. He was anxious to keep American influences out of his Eurasian domains, no matter how widespread these influences might be elsewhere in the world.

As the war was coming to an end, the President of the United States was a sick man, close to death. His mental capacity had weakened. He had been crippled by polio, dependent on his wheelchair for more than two decades. Apart from his legs, his body and his mind had remained powerful for many years. Sometime after 1939 Roosevelt began to weaken. It is impossible even now to determine the exact beginnings and the nature of this change. He developed an inclination for protracted periods of rest. There were lengthening periods of weariness and lassitude. Unlike Churchill, who in 1940 was in top form, exhilarated in body and mind, Roosevelt had slipped from the peak of his powers when his country was catapulted into the war, even though he was not yet sixty years old. Among his contemporaries, Stalin and Churchill at sixty were as strong as ever.* At sixty, Roosevelt's arteries were those of a man ninety years old; they had narrowed and hardened, constricting the natural course of his blood. His heart was enlarged. His entire body had become flaccid, including the hitherto unaffected torso, of the strength of which he had been more than ordinarily proud. In 1941 Roosevelt began to take longer and longer vacations. His ability to concentrate was impaired. He required ten or twelve hours of sleep. In May 1944, the month before the invasion of Europe, Roosevelt was "out of bed no more than six hours a day, on his back eighteen."† By January 1945 he could no longer sign his name without difficulty. Throughout the war Churchill's entourage had to keep him from plunging into all kinds of

---

* Mussolini and Hitler had aged rapidly during the last years of their respective lives. The former was removed from power in July 1943, four days before his sixtieth birthday.

† J. Bishop, *F.D.R.: The Last Years* (New York, 1974), p. 18. This work by a popular journalist includes many minor details that professional historians chose to ignore, with no peril to their reputations whatsoever.

strenuous and dangerous activities in quest of adventure. Roosevelt's problem was the opposite one. He enjoyed the restfulness of small talk, undemanding friends and favorites, the American domesticity of the cocktail hour. He could still flash his famous smile; his willpower still sufficed to raise his spirits and his voice, impressing people on occasion. But he could concentrate for shorter and shorter periods. (At Quebec, when Churchill kept talking, Roosevelt's head was dropping. At another time Elliott Roosevelt shouted at his father: "For God's sake, tell him you're tired. You work all day while he takes naps." This was both untrue and unfair.)

The American people knew nothing of this. Most of them believed that their President was a vigorous man, a happy husband, a relentless worker, a powerful mind, until he was suddenly felled by a stroke, like a tree in full leaf. There were two reasons for the extent of this kind of national and popular ignorance. First, the deterioration of the physical condition of Franklin Roosevelt was kept from the people through all kinds of intricate public relations shields. Second, people did not want to think otherwise. Close to the President hovered dozens of newspapermen who could see his deteriorating condition with their own eyes. They would not report, or even suggest, anything about it to the American people; as a matter of fact, most of them would not think much about it at all. There was the case of Admiral McIntire, the chief physician in the White House. (Like Woodrow Wilson, Roosevelt had thought it proper to elevate his doctor to the rank of admiral.) McIntire's main concern seems to have been to keep the seriousness of the President's condition from the public, from the President's family, indeed from everyone, including himself. In March 1944 when his family thought that Roosevelt looked awful, Admiral McIntire told them that it was an influenza bug. At the insistence of Roosevelt's daughter, the Admiral ordered a young cardiologist, Dr. Bruenn, to examine the President in the Bethesda Naval Hospital. The results of the examination were most disturbing and ominous: a prematurely aged body, approaching death. McIntire did not seem to be unduly disturbed. He arranged for Dr. Bruenn to be posted as the President's attendant physician. He would be under the Admiral's orders. He was forbidden to discuss the President's condition with anyone, including the patient himself or his family. It was indeed like the ancient (or, at that, the modern Communist) court in China, with the ruler's chief physician unwilling to admit bad news, satisfied as he was with his position: Poo-Bah.

The President was still capable of being his old self. He seems to have been aware of his condition. He knew that he was weakening, perhaps even that death was not far away. There was a grain of honesty in this kind of self-knowledge. It enabled Roosevelt to rise above the prison of his body. During the last months of his life he could be cheerful, jaunty, self-possessed, and not merely for the purpose of striking a pose; he could enjoy what life still had to offer him, which was no mean thing. There was more than a grain of vanity in this, perhaps, and a sense of duty. Only this sense of duty was often employed in the ephemeral cause of publicity. On 21 October 1944 Roosevelt was driven through the streets of New York in an open convertible in a cold downpour, for four hours, through a tour of the city amounting to fifty-one miles. He had thought this was imperative for the purposes of the coming election, in which he sought the support of the American people for an unprecedented fourth term. The route had been publicized for weeks beforehand. He went through with it, at the cost of very great strain and risk to his health. It did not seem to have done him much harm; but there is something awful in the spectacle of this sick man, with rain pouring down his hat and cape, with a relentlessly large smile on his face, propped up by his concerned and stern-faced minions, because of the unbreakable traditions of a presidential motorcade, for the sake of impressing the American people with the unbroken continuity of an image.

There was a brave kind of nonchalance in Franklin Roosevelt's makeup that persisted till the end. Oliver Wendell Holmes was supposed to have said that Roosevelt had a third-rate mind and a first-rate temperament. The statement reflects the New Englander's typical division of reason from emotion, of mind from temperament—but there is enough truth in it to be worth quoting. Roosevelt's temperament was generous, strong-willed, and vain—altogether not an unattractive combination, and rather fortunately suited for an American President in his circumstances, in his times. His mind was both broad and superficial. His temperament had some of the engaging qualities of the American spirit at its best; his mind accepted, and reflected, the prevalent consensus of American enlightened opinion of his times.

Roosevelt's view of the world was Wilsonian. So was that of most Americans who were concerned with international affairs. Woodrow Wilson bequeathed to the American people a philoso-

phy of internationalism that has dominated American public
thinking for most of the twentieth century. The extent of this
posthumous influence has never been adequately limned. Wilson
was a Democrat: yet such Republicans as Herbert Hoover, John
Foster Dulles, Richard Nixon were avowed Wilsonians. Wilson
was born in the South; yet his philosophy of world affairs had all
the marks of the New England mentality, legalistic and moralis-
tic—in one word, unreal. Wilson was a very complex person,
who committed the United States to intervention in a European
war in 1917—one of the greatest turning points in American and
world history, an event that, in the opinion of this writer, was
more consequential than the Russian Revolution in that year,
both in the short and in the long run. Both his principal political
rivals, Theodore Roosevelt and Charles Evans Hughes, had a
more realistic view of the world than did Wilson; but Wilson's
electoral fortunes prevailed, and his particular advocacy of internationalism, a kind of worldwide projection of his liberal progressivism, had an intellectual appeal in the long run. In the
short run, Wilson was repudiated. After their emotional participation in the First World War, the American people had a kind
of national hangover. They were convinced that they were the
greatest power in the world;‡ but they were not at all sure that
they wanted new kinds of unaccustomed responsibilities. They

‡ They indeed were. In terms of relative power the United States was
even more powerful after the First World War than after the Second
World War, when she had to share the dominion of Eurasia with the
Soviet Union. After the First World War she shared the dominion of the
seas with the British Empire; but the British, unlike the Russians, would
give way to American wishes in almost every instance.

felt that Professor Wilson's diet of internationalism was too much. Yet in the long run they would swallow it all. During the Second World War, Wilson seemed vindicated. If only the American people had listened to him! If only the United States had not refused to be part of the League of Nations! Hitler, Mussolini, the Second World War could all have been avoided. This is what most Americans came around to thinking, even though it was a myth. In 1944 and 1945 millions of them saw the movie *Wilson*, in which their former President was portrayed as the prophet of the century, a martyr. It was a maudlin kind of Hollywood confection, but a box-office success nonetheless, since it showed what most people had come to believe at the time. Their enlightened minority had, of course, never relented in their advocacy of the Wilsonian ideals, of an American kind of internationalism that was enlightened, liberal, and progressive. Men and women such as Franklin and Eleanor Roosevelt had believed in it from the beginning. In reality Wilson's view of the world was as limited as that of, say, Calvin Coolidge, though on a different plane—just as in the Tennessee monkey trial Clarence Darrow's dogmatic belief in Science was as narrow as William Jennings Bryan's literal belief in the Old Testament. Yet these were just the kinds of thoughts that enlightened Americans preferred not to entertain.

Franklin Roosevelt may not have had a third-rate mind. What is certain is that the second-rate idealism of Wilsonianism appealed to him. At the same time there was a pragmatic side to Roosevelt's mind that ought not be underrated—even though, as we shall shortly see, this enabled him to achieve a kind of mastery in domestic affairs rather than international ones. His temperament, at any rate, was more attractive than Wilson's. Roosevelt was much more sure of himself than Wilson had been. His American patrician background was invaluable in this regard. He also knew much more of the world. Franklin Roosevelt's naval experiences, his travels in Europe, his acquaintance with members of the English and continental social and political elites over many years, resulted in a knowledge of Europe that was much superior to Wilson's. Indeed, it was rare among American Presidents. All of his vanity and jealousy notwithstanding, Roosevelt was at ease with Churchill, as well as with members of European royalty who lived in the United States or in Canada during their wartime exile. They were unanimous in paying their respect to his charm. In one significant case he was inclined to pursue a policy different from Wilson's. He seems to have believed that the destruction of the Austro-Hungarian monarchy after the First World War might have been a mistake. He espoused the independence of Austria, even though at the end of the war he did not protect the independence of Hungary. About Russia, Wilson's attitudes and ideas oscillated wildly. At first he welcomed the Russian Revolution as one of the greatest events in the history of freedom in the world, but he soon became the bitterest enemy of the inheritors of that revolution, the Bolsheviks. Roosevelt was not a dogmatic anti-Communist; he was typically inclined to think that the enemies of freedom came from the Right rather than from the Left. In the end he was willing to divide Europe as well as the Far East with Stalin. It would be a mistake, however, to ascribe these deals with Stalin to Roosevelt's pragmatism alone. His overriding belief in the virtues of an international organization, of the United Nations, was profoundly Wilsonian in its idealism.** Wilson made all kinds of compromises with the British and the French for the sake of getting his League of Nations; Roosevelt made all kinds of allowances to the Russians for the sake of getting them to take part in his United Nations. Neither realized that their compromises were not worth the trouble; neither of them would live to see that the League of Nations and the United Nations were of little or no help in maintaining even the rudiments of an international order, that they were useless against aggressive national ambitions. Nor did they realize that their broad-minded general concepts for a Parliament of Man were, in reality, projections of a rather narrowly American concept of parliamentarism. "To make the world safe for democracy" was Wilson's phrase. Roosevelt believed in it as much as had Wilson; indeed, he thought that something could be done about it, after the war. Yet, after all is said, To Make the World Safe for Democracy is an ideal not much different from What Is Good for America Is Good for the World.†† There is a difference in tone; there is not much difference in substance.

This mixture of broad-minded, as well as narrow-minded,

** The fact that Roosevelt, in 1932, was elected espousing a platform that preached a kind of isolationism rather than internationalism does not vitiate this argument. His isolationism of the early New Deal years—if that was what it was—was also of the liberal, progressive, left-of-center variety. His recognition of the Soviet Union in 1933, his revision of the American contractual relationship with Cuba and the Philippines in 1934, are evidences thereof.

†† De Gaulle on Roosevelt: "It was true that the isolationism of the United States was, according to the President, a great error now ended. But passing from one extreme to the other, it was a permanent system of intervention that he intended to institute by international law."

idealism was not merely a mental attitude. It had all kinds of pragmatic consequences. Roosevelt and his circle would preach and believe in the virtues of American non-involvement, when this suited their minds. On the other hand, they also believed in American omnipotence. Throughout 1944 and 1945 Roosevelt and the high officers of the American government would tell their critics, and also themselves, that there was no way in which the United States could (or should) "impose its will" on Stalin when it came to such touchy problems as that of Poland. On the other hand, the United States must not be left out of any arrangement between Churchill and Stalin. When Churchill, exasperated with American noncommittal attitudes in regard to Eastern Europe, flew off to deal with Stalin in Moscow, Roosevelt cabled Stalin that it was a pity that the two of them were meeting without him. "While appreciating the Prime Minister's desire for such a meeting . . . you, naturally, understand that in this global war there is literally no question, political or military, in which the United States is not interested." It was not enough to be broad-minded; one must be high-minded as well, especially in public. Not to bother about Bulgaria or Rumania when, in exchange, one could get a free hand in Greece was Churchill's old way of doing business. Not to bother much about Poland but concentrate, instead, on the higher purpose of establishing the United Nations was Roosevelt's way of proclaiming virtue as if it were necessity. Unless "the Russians can be persuaded or compelled to treat Poland with some decency there will not be [a United Nations] that is worth much," Anthony Eden said (in his private record). Churchill thought, and on occasion said, much the same; so did a lone American, George Kennan, a junior diplomat who wrote courageously from Moscow that Washington was being "negligent in the interests of our people if we allow plans for an international organization to be an excuse for failing to occupy ourselves seriously and minutely with the sheer power relationships of the European peoples." Perhaps none of them realized at the time that Roosevelt was not merely being naive. The advocacy of high ideals was the most practical way to win friends and influence people, especially in America. His speech writers and his circle of advisers understood this to the core. In 1944 Benjamin V. Cohen, one of Roosevelt's close advisers, suggested that Roosevelt not run for a fourth term. He knew that Roosevelt was ill but did not dare refer to this in his nine-page letter. In the true liberal-progressive way he suggested that the President renounce a fourth term "for a higher calling." He should become "the Chief Executive Officer" of the new international organization to maintain the peace. That is: from President of the United States to President of the World, in order to make the world safe for democracy, for what was good for America must be good for the world.

Roosevelt would rather be President of the United States. He thought he could influence much of the world from Washington. He believed in some of the virtues of the old American patronizing and missionary attitude towards the Orient. China, India, eventually Japan, ought to follow the American example. The United States would teach the world how to be democratic, independent, prosperous, educated. Roosevelt had the usual American prejudices against the surviving British, French, and

Dutch empires.‡‡ Like most Americans, he had fewer scruples in dealing with Asian than with European politics. Consequently he was more confident, and also more successful. At Yalta he would divvy up Manchuria and North China with Stalin, with no trouble either to his conscience or to his calculations. At Yalta, too, he would be eloquent on the virtues of the American, as distinct from the British, view of the world. He proposed a toast: "You see, Winston," he said, "there is something here that you are not capable of understanding. You have in your veins the blood of tens of generations of people accustomed to conquering. We are here at Yalta to build up a new world which will know neither injustice nor violence, a world of justice and equity." Stalin pretended to be moved to tears. (Or perhaps he was really moved. God alone knows.)

Stalin had reason to be moved. Roosevelt and the Americans, for whom, like most Russians, he had enormous respect, were not necessarily on the side of Churchill and of the British; they were plunking themselves down in the middle. Unlike Hitler, who had known since the thirties that Roosevelt and Churchill were in cahoots, Stalin could profit from their differences—especially since Roosevelt did his best (or, rather, his worst) to demonstrate these differences to him. Roosevelt snubbed Churchill at Teheran and at Yalta, in plain view of everyone.

‡‡ His much-vaunted, and well-known, dislike for General de Gaulle was not only the result of liberal and democratic prejudices against a rigidly authoritarian personage. Roosevelt (as indeed most Americans) wanted to restore the Third Republic in France. To say that they wanted a weak rather than a strong France would be too much; but it would not be too much to say that he did not relish the idea of a France that would be independent and strong enough to be recalcitrant.

Even apart from its consequences, there was something slightly obscene and cruel in this spectacle: a public demonstration of new interests at the expense of the old and faithful friend or consort. Roosevelt thought himself a man of powerful charm, an experienced and insouciant seducer. He kept telling his friends, including Churchill, that he knew how to charm Stalin: "I think I can personally handle Stalin better" than anyone else. He did not understand that Stalin was more than willing to respond, but out of motives that had nothing to do with patrician insouciance and American charm. When an American seductionist goes to the Caucasus he'd better bring plenty of money.

Roosevelt's misreading of Stalin was not the solitary source of future troubles. His misreading of Russia was involved with his misreading of the historical situation of his own country—a misreading which many Americans shared at the time. He saw the world in terms of a progressive democratic evolutionism. Hitler, Mussolini, and the Japanese represented the reactionary forces from an atavistic past. Churchill was admirable in many ways, outdated in others: a Dickensian figure, Tory England, Old Roast Beef and all that. Stalin and the Bolsheviks were moving crudely toward the future, rough and ready Siberian pioneers that they were, both prophets and pioneers of the collective state of the people. The United States, with its progressive liberalism, was midway between the British and the Russians, slightly left of center (that was Roosevelt's favorite expression of his political bearing). There was some truth in this progressive vision of the world, but not much. In reality it was Hitler who incarnated the most radical revolutionary force of his times, whereas in many ways Stalin's rule was reminiscent of that of Ivan the Terrible. More important, the liberal progressivism that formed the substance of Roosevelt's political philosophy was almost wholly outdated. It rested on a view of human nature and of the nature of politics that was a compound of Franklin and Jefferson and Gladstone and Wilson, very much of the nineteenth century, and in many ways more backward than Churchill's. Even more important, Roosevelt's view of the relative positions of Britain and the United States in relation to the Soviet Union was the reverse of the truth. Already during the war Britain was less capitalist, more collectivized, more of a regimented welfare state than the still considerably capitalistic United States. The power that was destined to become the principal opponent of Russian imperialism after the war was not Great Britain but the United States.

Roosevelt could be high-minded and low-minded at the same time. He was both an idealist and a pragmatist; more accurately, he was an idealistic pragmatist rather than a pragmatic idealist— not the best of possible combinations. He was a master of political expediency to the point where his art of compromising would eventually lead not only to the sacrifice of principles but sometimes to that of expediency itself. He saw in Stalin a figure reminiscent of the powerful political bosses of the Democratic Party with whom he had had to deal. There was some truth in this assessment; what was wrong with it was that the deals he would make with Stalin were more harmful, and more consequential in the long run, than the deals he had had to make with a Hague, a Farley, a Pendergast. His concern with the few million Polish-American voters who, in his estimation, could swing the 1944 election against him in certain principal states, is amazing in retrospect. He subordinated the entire issue of Poland not only to the cause of the future world government but also to this pragmatic concern with the Polish-American vote. He tried to impress this repeatedly upon Stalin,* as if to make of this necessity a virtue—the occupational disease of pragmatists, who are wont to sacrifice their much-vaunted realism for facts that in the end do not amount to much. At the same time Roosevelt wanted to maintain his image of the high-minded statesman. He wanted to impress not only Polish-Americans but all kinds of people that he was doing the best he could for Poland. Toward this end, he would often ask Stalin to make small concessions re Poland, for the purpose of domestic politics. (When he was asking Stalin to consider a new three-power summit conference, he wrote: "Such a meeting would help me domestically.") He thought that such frank admissions of political realism would impress Stalin and thereby strengthen his own position.† It may or may not have impressed Stalin; it certainly did not strengthen Roosevelt's position.

His approach to the Pope was also in this vein. He cultivated a well-publicized approach to Pius XII from the beginning of the European war because of his concern with American Catholic voters, most of them Democrats, many of them also isola-

---

* By the time of Yalta, Stalin grew restless with this argument. He said that he doubted the figure of five to seven million Polish-American voters.

† It must be said that at Yalta Churchill would, on occasion, stoop to the same low stratagem, even though more subtly than Roosevelt; he would suggest to Stalin that an agreement on Poland would silence critics of his alliance policy in the House of Commons.

tionists, and anti-Communists almost to a man. After Hitler's invasion of Russia, Roosevelt wrote to the Pope that Communism was less dangerous than Nazism (something that may well have been true at the time), and that there was less persecution of the churches in the Soviet Union than in the Third Reich (which was not true). Again, he wanted to commit the Pope against Hitler not only for the sake of principle. Again, as with Stalin, Roosevelt was less than subtle; he instructed his envoy to the Vatican to tell the Pope that he was worried about the Catholic isolationists in America (". . . there is a Catholic minority in the United States" who are causing trouble because of their inability to distinguish between Russia and Communism; "in order to avoid a deep schism among American Catholics a clarification from the Holy See would be necessary"). Monsignor Tardini, the Pope's principal adviser, understood. In a memorandum to the Pope he wrote that the President's letter "reveals clearly what Roosevelt wants from . . . the authority of the Holy See— he wants to obtain a large advantage in American internal politics."[1]

Roosevelt need not have been concerned. He had a large advantage in American internal politics, without the help of Stalin or the Pope. He was unduly anxious about the Polish-American vote, about Irish Democrats in Massachusetts, because of his tendency of overestimating the appeal of isolationist sentiment among the American people. Consequently he found it necessary to use all kinds of political and rhetorical tricks, including double-talk on occasion. This suggests how Roosevelt, this seigneurial figure towering over American politics, was far from being immune to not only the temptations of political prevarication but also that most corrupting inclination to which so many high-minded and high-talking Americans have been prone: in this republic, established upon the principle that the common people can be trusted, they end up underestimating, rather than overestimating, the native intelligence of the people. Whatever is worst in American life, the practices of advertising, of publicity, of public education, for example, derives from this fatalist inclination that, instead of being the result of a healthy conservative skepticism, is in reality the result of cynicism cloaked by sentimental rhetoric: in sum, the easiest way out. The easy way out: it works, in the short run. I repeat: Roosevelt need not have been concerned. He had all the domestic support he needed, especially in 1945. The chorus of the American press, of public opinion, of public figures, after Yalta was deafeningly uniform. Yalta was the greatest hope of the world; "no more appropriate news could be conceived to celebrate the birthday of Abraham Lincoln"; it was "the greatest United Nations victory of the war," "a landmark in human history," "a complete success." These were not only paeans of praise from liberal newspapers and commentators. *Time* magazine wrote: "All doubts . . . seem now to have been swept away." Even Herbert Hoover, who grew more and more crabby as the year 1945 went on, saluted Yalta: "a great hope to the world." Senator Vandenberg, the chief Republican in the Senate, and until 1945 an isolationist, stated that Yalta affirmed the "basic principles of justice" in the world. Like Leninism-Stalinism, Wilsonianism-Rooseveltianism seemed triumphant in 1945. Vandenberg was on the way to his public conversion to internationalism. It was the avenue of public remuneration, in more than one way.

Roosevelt was a leader, a leader-President such as the American people had wanted since Theodore Roosevelt. He produced the leadership that the American people needed in 1933, and for many years afterwards. His career as the leader of the American nation was, in many ways, parallel to Hitler's career as the Führer of the German nation. They came to power at the same time, in the winter of 1932–33. Hitler was appointed Chancellor on Franklin Roosevelt's birthday, 30 January 1933. Both were officially invested with power in March 1933. Both ruled for twelve years, of which the first six were years of relative peace, the last six the years of a world war. Both Roosevelt and Hitler were more successful in governing their own peoples than in imposing their designs on the world. Both died in April 1945, before the end of the war, only eighteen days apart. Whatever these coincidences, Roosevelt and Hitler were very different men. Whatever his shortcomings, Roosevelt was an American gentleman, incarnating some of the best features of the American character. Whatever his genius, Hitler was propelled by hate, incarnating some of the worst features of the German-Austrian national character. Hitler's tragedy issued from the depths of his tortured soul. Roosevelt's failures grew from the blandness of his mind. His character was exceptional, original, in more than one way. There was nothing exceptional, nothing original in his ideas. His relationship with his wife was unusual in this respect. His temperament, his nature, his humors, his personal preferences, were quite different from Eleanor Roosevelt's; so

was his approach to people, his entire *modus operandi*. Yet his
political ideas, his views of the world were hardly different at all.
It was not that he followed her advice in political matters
(though he often did), nor was it that Eleanor was necessarily
the stronger of the two. It was simply that she was an intellectual, and a vocal representative of the liberal-progressive
world view, which was the *only* view of the world to which
Franklin Roosevelt was accustomed, and to which he could not
conceive of any alternative. In this respect he was no leader at
all.

Most Americans loved to listen to him. His speeches projected
much of that first-rate temperament of his: his voice was warm
and strong and convincing. Reading them, they are all blan-
diloquent; his phrases taste and look like oatmeal, with perhaps a
little cocoa powder or sugar on top, but oatmeal nonetheless. His
speeches were written for him by a group of people who represented a consensus of those liberal categories that were to be
found in the Sunday supplement of *The New York Times* or in
the *Saturday Review of Literature*. They were different men:
Jonathan Daniels (a Southern liberal), Lauchlin Currie (a
crypto-Communist), Robert Sherwood (a successful playwright),
Samuel Rosenman (a judge). No matter—their minds ran in the
same grooves. So did the minds of those few men on whom
Roosevelt depended for intellectual sustenance: Judge Rosenman and Justice Frankfurter, for example. They, too, thought in
the same ways, as did Harry Hopkins, Roosevelt's closest aide
and troubleshooter during the war years. There is something depressing in this. On the one hand, the United States was a free

country, amazingly free in 1945, so free of bureaucratic regimentation that this alone filled many Europeans with admiration, envy, and wonder. On the other hand, the categories of intellectual discourse were deadeningly uniform. Liberal progressivism in the United States had a monopoly of accepted ideas to which public homage had to be paid, not altogether unlike Marxism-Leninism in the Soviet Union. Unlike in the Soviet Union, in the United States there was open, and sometimes vocal, opposition to this philosophy, voiced by certain Republicans and isolationists. Yet they were incapable of producing an intelligent alternative. *Their* ideas were not broad and flat, they were narrow and flat, like the voice of Senator Taft, their most esteemed spokesman.

And the trouble was not only that Roosevelt's speech writers and advisers and friends would not think except in certain categories. They also kept telling the President (and each other) what he (and they) wanted to hear. This kind of habit eventually spares men much of the necessity of thinking for themselves. It certainly does not accustom them to think ahead. And here it is no longer possible to rely on the standard argument, to distinguish between Roosevelt's temperament and his mind. Let me repeat: Franklin Roosevelt was not a naive man. But he was a master of taking the easy way out. When he knew that he was up against a difficult problem his natural inclination was to postpone facing it. This is natural for us mortals, and we must make allowances for Roosevelt's encroaching illness. Surely his habit of procrastination grew worse during the war, and especially during the last months of his life. But it was not only a habit; there was method to it. He did not merely procrastinate; he refused to admit the existence of certain problems as such.‡ Both his denial of the existence of the problem and his procrastination were the results not of naiveté or of feebleness but of calculation —not of his inability but of his unwillingness to recognize them. He was—very much unlike Churchill, but very much like the entire circle of his friends—loath to change his mind.

There is the accepted legend according to which Roosevelt was on the verge of changing his mind about Stalin, of getting tough with Stalin, when death cut him down. There is very little evidence for this. Most of the evidence, literal and circumstantial, points to the contrary. During the two months following Yalta, Stalin showed that he interpreted the declarations about Poland and about "Liberated Europe" in one way: they amounted to a Russian-American division of Europe, no more and no less. Because of certain circumstances, foremost among them the rapid advance of the American and British armies across Germany, Churchill thought that the time was ripe to make a fuss about this; but Roosevelt refused, even when Stalin

‡ Again the Polish example. In August 1944 the Polish Home Army rose against the Germans in Warsaw. Stalin stopped the advance of Russian columns before Warsaw, preferring to see the Polish resistance bleed to death. He refused British and American planes permission to fly on to Russian airfields after dropping supplies on Warsaw. Churchill was desperate. On 5 September Roosevelt replied to Churchill: "I am informed by my Office of Military Intelligence that the fighting Poles have departed from Warsaw and that the Germans are now in full control. The problem of relief for the Poles in Warsaw has therefore unfortunately been solved . . . and there now appears to be nothing we can do to assist them." This was untrue. Not wishing to deal with this problem, Roosevelt selected the appropriate kind of information—or, rather, misinformation —that relieved him from having to deal with it.

had showed himself to be fearful and nasty, accusing the British and the Americans of talking surrender with the Germans behind his back. He did send off an indignant reply to Stalin; but, for all of that reputedly first-rate temperament, his indignation fizzled out in a day or two; it would not last. Stalin sent off a complicated answer, without much of an apology. Roosevelt thanked him for his "frank explanation." "There must not, in any event, be mutual mistrust, and minor misunderstandings of this character should not arise in the future." Harriman, from Moscow, suggested to Roosevelt that the word "minor" be deleted, "since I confess the misunderstanding appeared to me to be of a major character." Roosevelt told Harriman to leave the text as is, since it was his "desire to consider the . . . misunderstanding a minor incident." It was his last message to Stalin.**

Those who believe—and they include most of his sympathetic

** It was dated the day of his death. That day he sent, too, his last message to Churchill: "We must be firm . . ." but: "I would minimize the Soviet problem . . . our course thus far is correct." In 1954 Harriman recorded certain reminiscences, according to which Roosevelt may have had "a change of heart" about Stalin's trustworthiness in late March 1945. The evidence is not convincing.

The attitude of the State Department (often the *bête noire* of the American Left) was identical with Roosevelt's. At the time of his death his officials prepared a "position paper" for the new President. This said, among other things, that "the British government has been showing increasing apprehension of Russia and her intentions. Churchill shares this government's interpretation of the Yalta Agreement on Eastern Europe and liberated areas. He is inclined, however, to press this position with the Russians with what we consider unnecessary rigidity of detail." Considering the allotment of half of Europe to the Russians, "unnecessary rigidity of detail" and "minor misunderstandings" are champion exemplars of bureaucratic waffling.

biographers—that Roosevelt, had he lived, would have as acutely, and swiftly, responded to the Soviet menace as he had to the Hitlerite menace, are talking through their hats. Everything indicates the contrary. Whether Roosevelt would have changed his mind is not for us to tell. He may have had to change, indeed he might have eventually changed, the course of the giant American ship of state: but everything indicates that he would have changed its course more reluctantly, and more slowly, than his successor, Harry Truman. The latter was, after all, less encumbered with the ideological categories that ruled Roosevelt's view of the world. In this respect the Missouri background was preferable to Groton and Harvard and New York and Washington.††

Roosevelt's death came before the end of the war, before the American confrontation with the Soviet Union over Europe had crystallized, a confrontation that he had avoided at almost any cost, for many reasons, including his own mental comfort. The fact of his death, at the relatively early age of sixty-three, was a tragedy for those who loved him. Yet it may have been a blessing for his posthumous reputation. In April 1945 the war was

†† Because Roosevelt in 1943 and 1944 had, by and large, agreed with Churchill in not sharing the secret of the atomic bomb with the Russians (they rejected the rather harebrained idea of Professor Niels Bohr at the time), there are certain historians who claim that the conflicts of the cold war had begun as early as then, under Roosevelt's direction. We do not know what Roosevelt would have done with the atomic bomb during the crucial summer of 1945 and after. But the abovementioned argument has little substance. It was not only that Roosevelt depended, to a considerable extent, on Churchill's assent about what to do with the atomic bomb. Roosevelt also knew that including the Russians could have meant trouble in domestic politics.

nearly over, but ominous clouds were approaching fast. It was better that Roosevelt went before the sky got darker, before the living appreciation of his leadership faded in the minds of a generation for whom he had meant so much.

After the genuine and tremendous national experience of mourning passed, there was a strange reaction. It was not quite like the national hangover that followed the era of Wilson; it was a kind of queasy uneasiness about Roosevelt's place in history. The American people somehow found it awkward to come to terms with the memory of this President. Soon after his death millions of his followers, huge groups who had been the mainstays of his Democratic Party, deserted it. Most American Catholics voted Republican in the 1950's, and so did many Southerners. Hundreds of thousands, perhaps many millions, of working-class people who had followed Roosevelt as late as 1945 supported Joseph McCarthy a few years later. In 1947 Congress proposed a constitutional amendment (ratified by the required three-quarters of the state legislatures) restricting future Presidents to two terms—obviously a reaction against the memory of Franklin Roosevelt. Yet no one would admit this openly. The American people were confused—about the recent past, rather than about the then present. During the late forties and the fifties anti-Communism became not only *the* accepted ideology but the main ingredient of American patriotism. This obsession with Communism included a reaction against the Second World War. For America to have been allied with Communism had been a mistake. This was the opinion—sometimes hinted at, though usually unspoken—held by such diverse political personages as John Foster Dulles, Robert A. Taft, Joseph

McCarthy, John Kennedy. By the time the last-named was elected President in 1960—an event that Eleanor Roosevelt witnessed with great bitterness—things were beginning to change. Kennedy's avowed opinions had changed accordingly. People's memories are short. Roosevelt's image was sliding into the safe past. He belonged to a period about which many people were becoming nostalgic: he was a large piece of it, like streamlining, the Twentieth Century Limited, big bands. Nostalgic musicals were produced about the late Fiorello La Guardia and plays about the early Franklin Roosevelt. Slowly, gradually, a consensus about his place in American history began to emerge. The last President who had a strong personal memory of him was Lyndon B. Johnson. When he was a young man, in Texas and in the Congress, he had been profoundly impressed by Franklin Roosevelt. His Great Society was to be the natural consequence, the logical completion, of the New Deal. He thought that in struggling against the opponents of the war in Vietnam he was fighting Roosevelt's struggle against the isolationists of the thirties all over again. It was a tragic misreading of history.

Roosevelt was much concerned with his place in history. He was the first President to design his own memorial library during his lifetime—a regrettable practice that was followed at great expense after him by every President, including some who read and wrote practically nothing. About Franklin Roosevelt hundreds of books were written after he died. Half a dozen history professors made very profitable careers as his biographers. With all of their research apparatus they were little more than hagiographers, especially when it came to Roosevelt's last years, to the war. In spite of the mountain ranges of accumulated papers, in spite of the Franklin D. Roosevelt Memorial Library, much remained (and remains) unknown. The fact that Roosevelt had a love affair that lasted for years, the fact that during the final momentous year of the war Roosevelt was a dying man, were left unmentioned for decades, until popular journalists came around to writing books—sympathetically, and with understanding, it must be said—dealing with these previously unmentionable subjects. By the late 1970's the practices of publicity changed. There was little left that was unmentionable. Decaying harridans climbed on the publicity bandwagon, coyly suggesting that Franklin Roosevelt had taken them to bed. Assistant professors on the make climbed on the revisionist charabanc, composing books with theses such as that Roosevelt failed to share atomic knowledge with the Russians or that he failed to rescue the masses of European Jews from Hitler's clutches during the war. Probably all of this matters little. Probably the memory of Roosevelt will not suffer from these "revelations"; probably the contrary will be true. There was something deadeningly funereal in his image for a long time, like one of those Washington monuments cut in unearthly white, looking from a distance as if they were made of Alvastone. Plainly, he was too large for many people. By now the alternating lights and shadows that have passed across this national monument have softened some of its features, making it more real.

Many things were large about Roosevelt: his voice, his shoulders, his face. His face had, like Wilson's, a peculiarly American, preternatural nakedness about it, a dentist's expansive dream; but unlike Wilson's face, long and narrow and puritanical, Roosevelt's was large and fleshy, at times avuncular; his pince-nez was stuck on it like a monumental twinkle in his eye. He was a monumental figure, after all. He had become President at the right time: had he not been elected, in 1933 the United States may have faced the prospect of a social revolution. Many of Roosevelt's domestic reforms were inevitable. What was not inevitable was that the United States should enter the Second World War against Hitler, a war that Britain and Russia could not, and perhaps would not, have fought without the prospect of American support. Before this fact even Roosevelt's dubious arrangements with Stalin pale. Had someone like Hoover been President in 1940 Hitler would have won the war.

V. JOSEF VISSARIONOVICH
DJUGASHVILI "STALIN"

Nomen est omen. There is a meaning in names. Consider *Bismarck:* how the tone, the sound, the shape of the name fit the man! (Two-fisted, heavy, strong, German, imperious, declarative, determined.) Or *Mussolini.* (Muscular and Italian, masculine and operatic at the same time.) Or *Churchill.* Stalin's entire name matched his personality. *Iosif, Josef:* breathing a dark and squat virility, the mustachioed blacksmith, the Orthodox seminarian. *Vissarionovich:* Vissarion's son: the homage paid by a low Georgian peasant family to the name of a Byzantine saint. *Djugashvili:* the Caucasian family name, faintly Oriental, faintly ridiculous. No wonder that Josef Vissarionovich took a pen name at an early stage of his life even though he had no inkling that he would be the ruler of Russia before the age of fifty, just as Herr Alois Schicklgruber had no inkling of what would become of his Adolf one day. *Habent sua fata nomina,* there is a destiny in such things: had Schicklgruber not changed his name to Hitler there is some reason to doubt that his son could have risen to the leadership of the entire German nation, and there is some reason to doubt whether all of the Russias would have submitted to the reign of a man by the name of Djugashvili. He took the cover name of *Stalin:* man of steel. Oddly, it fit him better later rather than earlier in his career. The cunning, slow-spoken Bolshevik conspirator in the Caucasus was a wildcat, a lynx rather than a steel-man. But by the time he was the chief of the Soviet Union and their war leader, he was a man of steel. No one in the West had trouble pronouncing his name. *Stalin* was easy to say, it was pronounced uniformly, by bankers as well as bohemians, on two continents. *Stalin:* steel, like so many Russian words in the Petrine age, coming from the German *Stahl,* but also with a Near Eastern touch to it, *Stalin,* like *Stamboul,* a short-legged strong man with a big black mustache. People made fun of Hitler's mustache, yet the mustache belonged to Stalin's personality even more than to Hitler's. *Il Baffone:* the big-mustached one, Italians called him. *Uncle Joe:* his nickname in America and England, including Roosevelt's and Churchill's correspondence, was half wrong, half right. There was little that was avuncular about him, he was not much of an uncle. But he was Joe all right, perhaps especially to Americans, among whom there survives a medieval streak, an inclination for the popularization of the sacred, a people who speak with familiar ease of "St. Pete" and "St. Joe." The St. Joe of the Soviets: Stalin. Compared to that name, Trotsky sounded less substantial. Hundreds of books have been written about the conflict between Trotsky and Stalin. Few of them put their finger on the essential factor, which had nothing to do with ideology. Trotsky was Jewish; his pen name, too, sounded faintly Jewish. The Bolshevik government—including the Jews among them: Zinoviev, Bukharin, etc.—were aware of the dark Judaeophobia of the Russian masses. They knew that putting Trotsky in the ruling seat of Soviet Russia would be courting disaster. Had Trotsky become the successor of Lenin he would not have lasted long. The Steelman vs. the Speaker, *Stahl gegen Trotz,* it all fit into the Soviet twenties, with their German undertones, years before Hitler was to come to power in the fatherland of Marxism.

Stalin was a master of endurance. He outlasted his enemies. He also learned more and more about the world. He started out as a revolutionary, like Lenin; but by 1939, at the age of sixty, Stalin was no longer a revolutionary. He had become a statesman. Under Lenin's rule Russia had lost many of her former provinces and borderlands; she was diminished in size, and much diminished in power; she retreated into revolutionary isolation, licking her wounds. In 1939, under Stalin's rule, Russia began to regain these provinces: by the end of the war she had grown as big as the Tsar's empire had ever been, and the greatest power on two continents. By 1939 Stalin realized something that went contrary to everything that Marx had been teaching and that Lenin had been preaching. States were far more important than classes. The international solidarity of the working classes was not much more than a myth. The international Communist movement did not amount to much. Where Communists were useful, they were useful as instruments of Russian interests, not as agents of world revolution. The principal matter of business was the relationship of the Soviet Union to Germany, Britain, the United States, Japan. The destiny of the Soviet Union was not determined by the struggles between

Communism and Capitalism. It was to be determined by the struggles of the great national states of the world. These struggles involved territory, not economic systems. The greatest asset of the Soviet Union was not that she was the unique focus of world revolution; the power and security of the Soviet Union resided in the enormous extent of her territories. The more land, the better. This is what Lenin had not understood, whereas Stalin felt it in the marrow of his bones.

Classes were abstractions. The state was a reality. Stalin gradually learned to comprehend this. The realization rose to the surface of his consciousness. It explains much of his otherwise senseless and Byzantine purges during the thirties. They were not the results of an internal struggle within the Communist Party of the Soviet Union. They amounted to a drastic revamping, to a change both in the composition and in the purpose of the state apparatus. The purpose of the party was to serve the state, and not the other way around. From 1936 to 1939 the leading cadres of the party, of the army, of the government were replaced through a brutal purge that was both Draconian and senseless in its methods and in its extent; but it was not altogether senseless for Stalin's purposes. He replaced entire groups of people with men and women who knew nothing beyond their subservience to the Soviet state. He got rid of the Old Bolsheviks, just as Hitler had got rid of the Old Guard of the SA in 1934. Hitler's purge lasted two days, Stalin's three years. The latter was impressed by the former. The results were similar: the solid entrenchment of the national leader at the top not only of his party but of the state and the army as well. The fact that during the Russian purges many of the victims were Old Bolsheviks, international revolutionaries, Jews, etc., was significant, since their elimination corresponded with Stalin's inclination toward being a national dictator, rather than a world revolutionary figure. The elimination of the victims was also significant in view of certain of Stalin's decisions—his anti-Semitism, his wish to come to an arrangement with Hitler, for example. Yet it was not the most important outcome of the purge. The most important outcome was the formation of a Soviet state bureaucracy, of which a most important part was that of the police. The age of aristocracy was not followed by the age of democracy; it was followed, rather, by the age of bureaucracy—both in the so-called Capitalist West and in the so-called Communist Soviet Union. By 1939 the official Soviet vocabulary reflected this primacy of the state. Terms such as "state matters," "state police," "state interests" became sacrosanct, in a stiff parvenu sense. When a high Soviet official would use them it was instantly recognized that these were the matters of the highest importance, while references to the class struggle or to the cause of the revolution belonged to an older category of accepted pieties.

Until 1941 Stalin had but one official position in the Soviet Union: that of Secretary of the Communist Party. In May 1941 he found it necessary to elevate himself to be Chairman of the Council of Commissars, the equivalent of Prime Minister. For the first time in the history of the Soviet Union the same person was the head of the party and the head of the government. During the war he bestowed on himself the rank of marshal, and of generalissimo. He had had less military experience than Mussolini or Hitler or Churchill; yet he would command the Soviet armies and make all kinds of strategic choices. Stalin knew and understood that war was but the continuation of politics by other means. During the last year of the war he made many decisions, advancing or restricting the movements of Soviet armies because of his considerations of political expediency. He learned much during the war. In 1941 he would issue certain orders that were so categorical as to be both reckless and senseless; by 1945 his orders were marked by deliberation and caution.

At the end of the war he was the head of the party, of the state, of the army: a tremendous combination of jobs, but one made easier by the national habit of unquestioning authority. He was sixty-five years old. His health was, as yet, unbroken; but he had heart trouble. He was not an attractive man, especially not from close up: squat and hunched, his pockmarked face white, not ruddy, his teeth yellow or blackened. His looks, as the Yugoslav Djilas saw him at the time, reflected much of the crudeness of the man and of the brutal suspiciousness that governed his mind. Djilas was sufficiently perceptive and, what is more important, honest enough in retrospect to see another side of Stalin: "Still the head was not a bad one; it had something of the folk, the peasantry, the paterfamilias about it—with those yellow eyes and a mixture of sternness and roguishness." The paterfamilias was contemptuous of his mild son Yakov, who was captured by the Germans early in the war and died later in one of their prison camps. He was more indulgent to his younger son Vasili, a drunkard and braggart who rose high in the ranks of the Soviet air force because of his father. He was alternately kind and stern to his daughter Svetlana, who married a Jewish Russian during the war: thereafter her father grew more and more critical of her and saw her seldom.

He was a lonely man, by choice rather than by his nature, which was sufficiently gregarious. His working habits, strange to us, were typical of the Kremlin hierarchy during the 1940's. He rose late in the day and worked late into the night, often retiring well after dawn. His main indulgence was five- to six-hour dinners, night after night. Like Louis XIV, it was during these dinners that he conducted and discussed most of the important business with his close confidants; like the Sun King, he was the undisputable and undisputed master of his empire and of his table. At the Kremlin dinners there was much drunkenness, belching, and coarse jokes, more than often about bodily functions. When Stalin met Churchill and Roosevelt he was careful to refrain from some of these habits, although there was much gorging and drinking on those state occasions, too. At times perceptive foreign visitors, such as De Gaulle, would glimpse the awesome powers of the tyrant even at the dinner table. The fear with which his minions cowered before Stalin's slightest whim was worthy of the pen of a Shakespeare. This was true in more than one way: when Shakespeare was born Russia was ruled by the Terrible Ivan.

Unlike Ivan the Terrible, Stalin was locked in a grand alliance with Great Britain and the United States. About these countries Stalin was at least as ignorant as Ivan had been of Elizabethan England, even though in 1945 London and Washington were but a day or two away from Moscow by fast plane. Yet the power and the geography of the Soviet Union were such that this relative ignorance harmed Stalin but little. In any event, he was not much of a dreamer. He knew his limits. In this respect he resembled Bismarck rather than Hitler. In 1945 he almost overreached himself—almost, but not quite. In a way this corresponded with the side of his character that Djilas glimpsed and that appears, here and there, in the autobiographical reminiscences of his daughter Svetlana. Stalin was modest in his personal wants.* He accepted the Byzantine adulation that was being heaped on him, even as he was contemptuous of much of it. He liked a certain kind of domesticity, playing "Little Papa" with his daughter, at least before that daughter grew up to be a woman of eighteen. He insisted that she study seriously, and often took time to look at her homework and grades. Like that of many Russians of his generation, Stalin's concept of culture was of the German kind. His children had nurses and governesses who taught them manners, mathematics, piano, German. (Later Stalin realized that English was even more important, and ordered that his daughter take English lessons.) There was a musty scent of Russian-German *Bürgerlichkeit* in that overheated Kremlin apartment for a long time, with its embroidered tablecloths, carved heavy furniture, wood paneling, oil-painted walls, window pillows, antimacassars. Underneath the rough Caucasian and Russian habits there lived in Stalin's mind a respect for *Kultur,* in the peculiar Russian sense of that word which is both Germanic-serious and naive-sentimental, redolent of the respect that certain peasants have for their betters.

On a larger scale this kind of duality was perhaps typical of his mental attitude toward the world at large. His crude realism about the powers of this world, realizing the limitations of Rus-

* One exception was his predilection for Dunhill pipes.

sia and himself, was complemented by the driving necessity to be the absolute master of his house and empire, to the point of compulsive near-paranoia. He had enough self-confidence to know that he towered in strength over his subordinates, and over many other people besides: and yet there was in Stalin a sense of relative inferiority; a streak of unsureness. As Djilas wrote years after the war: ". . . he regarded as sure only whatever he held in his fist, and everyone beyond the control of his police was a potential enemy."[1]

His Western allies did not sufficiently understand this. They did not realize how unsure Stalin was in spite of the resounding Soviet victories in the war. He knew, better than many others, that his country and its peoples were bled white by the enormity of four years of war. In early 1945 he was often apprehensive about the age-old Russian problem: the Russian soldiers might not fight abroad with the discipline and the determination with which they had fought on their own soil. At the end of the war discipline in the Soviet armies was far from perfect. In many places it was a flushed horde rather than an army. There may have been more than one hundred thousand deserters roaming around eastern Germany and Eastern Europe. At the same time Stalin was tremendously impressed by the freshness and the material wealth of the American armed forces. Again, better than anyone else in the Politburo, Stalin knew how weak was the appeal of Communism in the part of Europe that the Soviet armies were conquering. His armies were in full control of much of Eastern Europe; yet in most of these countries there were but a handful of Communist émigrés, imported from Moscow, whom he could trust. There was a personal element in his unsureness. His first meetings with Churchill and Roosevelt were like a rich peasant's first meeting with the town bankers. After each of the summit conferences Stalin came home satisfied and relieved. He was relieved that the conferences had gone well, without a serious gaffe on the Soviet part, and that he had not been forced by Churchill and Roosevelt into too many concessions.

He overestimated American and British power, resolution, and cunning. The accepted view, according to which in 1945 Stalin, alone among the statesmen of the Great Powers, had a clear design, unrelenting in its purpose of extending and establishing Communist rule whenever and wherever possible, is both simplistic and exaggerated. There are many evidences to the contrary. He waited for long months in the autumn and winter of 1944–45 before he gave his orders for the last great offensive thrust toward Germany; he advanced the date of his offensive in January, partly in response to Churchill's and Roosevelt's urgings. In early February he ordered Marshal Zhukov to stop along the Oder River and not push further toward Berlin —a move with political considerations in mind (he may not have wanted to alarm Churchill and Roosevelt before their imminent meeting at Yalta) but also including military considerations: he feared the risk of losing a battle in Germany, a kind of Battle of Moscow in reverse. His entire strategy, and the tactics of the Soviet armies in 1945, were marked by his caution. Throughout April, Stalin was extremely vexed and worried as he saw the Germans surrendering entire provinces to the Anglo-Americans when they were struggling bitterly to hold the Russians from town to town, village to village. He correctly attributed to the

Germans their preferences to surrender to the Anglo-Americans; but he also believed—unreasonably, suspiciously, fearfully—that Churchill and the Americans were parties to this game. This alone explains the unusually effusive nature of his message to Churchill when, at the end of April, the latter assured him that he would not accept a unilateral surrender from Himmler: "Knowing you, I had no doubt that you would act in this way." (Churchill was charmed.) He continued to be worried about the presence of American and British armies in the middle of what had been allotted as the Soviet zone of occupation in Germany. In early July he allowed the British and the Americans to introduce their occupation troops into Berlin and Vienna, after he had been relieved to see that they were retreating to the previously established zonal boundaries—that is, that they kept their word.

Throughout 1945 Stalin gave no support to the local Communists in Greece: he did not want British and, possibly, American repercussions. In May 1945 Tito's troops were attempting to prod their way into Trieste, threatening a conflict with the Anglo-American armies occupying northeastern Italy: Stalin told the Yugoslavs to pipe down; he would not risk a conflict with the Anglo-Americans over Trieste. The Russian army was in total control occupying Hungary, a country about which the British and the Americans failed to say much in 1945: still Stalin was not sure about his possession: he queried Churchill about it at Potsdam, and in October and in November he felt compelled to permit something like free elections (the Communist vote came to be only 17 percent). Even in Rumania and

Bulgaria, which had been largely allotted to him by Churchill, Stalin deemed it necessary to cloak Communist police control by maintaining the front of coalition governments, with officially non-Communist figureheads as Prime Ministers. Because of American protests, he ordered the Rumanian government to include a few unimportant non-Communists in the revamped cabinet as late as in December 1945; because of American protests, he told the Bulgarian Communist government in August to postpone a rigged election.

He would not run the risk of antagonizing the Americans and the British unduly. This appears clearly from his treatment of Finland; even though his armies had fought and defeated the Finns twice within five years, Stalin chose not to occupy that country, aware as he was of the special sympathy that Americans had for the Finnish people. In Austria, Stalin first allowed the establishment of a democratic coalition, presided over by Renner, a non-Communist Social Democrat, in April; in November he consented to a nationwide election, in which the Communists got 2 percent of the entire vote.† In the Far East Stalin preferred a territorial deal with Chiang Kai-shek to a deal with Mao Tse-tung. He tried to wangle an agreement from President Truman that the Russians be allowed to occupy a portion

---

† These Austrian elections were significant. The Communist Party got most of its vote (4 percent) in the westernmost provinces of Austria, in the French zone of occupation; it received hardly more than 1 percent of the vote in the Russian-occupied provinces. This was proof of the general tendency across Europe: the closer people were to Russia and to the Russians, the more they found Communism to be repellent.

of the northern island of Hokkaido in Japan; but his language was remarkably sheepish‡ and he gave up without much insistence. Beyond those lands in Eastern Europe and the Far East that his armies occupied, Stalin showed little interest in Communist parties. He gave little or no support to them even where these had emerged as major political forces during the difficult and restless period at the end of the war in Italy or France, for example.

Stalin's principal aim was to consolidate his conquests, rather than to expand them further. Military geography, not ideology, counted foremost. What counted was whose armies stood where at the end of the war. He told this to his subordinates: each of the victorious Allies would rule the region that had fallen to them at the end of the war. "Everyone imposes his own system as far as his army can reach. It cannot be otherwise."[2] *It cannot be otherwise:* words of caution—caution, rather than moderation. Stalin in 1945, like Bismarck in 1871, knew that his empire had reached something close to its maximum tolerable limits. Unlike Bismarck, who had no compunctions or premonitions about the

‡ Both before the Russian declaration of war on Japan and after the Japanese surrender to the United States, Stalin appealed to Truman to consider Russian public opinion—a somewhat strange procedure by a Russian tyrant. ("The Russian public opinion would be seriously offended if the Russian troops were not to have an occupation region . . ." etc.) There are reasons to believe that Stalin was not altogether disingenuous in this respect. He was profoundly aware of the war-weariness of his people. He felt that he needed to justify to them the decision to intervene against Japan after the war against Germany was over. Somewhat like Roosevelt, Stalin may have overestimated the isolationist sentiments of his people.

absorption of Schleswig or Alsace-Lorraine by the Reich, Stalin was not quite sure about the very countries that his army had conquered and occupied. Yet it remains true that Bismarck ought not to have taken Alsace and Lorraine from France, since French enmity became in so many ways the Achilles' heel of Germany's position in Europe. So Eastern Europe was, and still remains, the Achilles' heel of Russia's position in Europe, a potential powder keg, the Alsace-Lorraine of the world order in 1945 and after. Stalin was worried about this in 1945. In practice, Britain and the United States had written Eastern Europe off: but he could not quite believe it.

The Russian victory did not make him feel more secure; rather, the contrary. Roosevelt and his friends believed that the Soviet Union would gradually mellow, as it was becoming a respected Great Power, a charter member of an international organization; that Russia's entrance into the United Nations would be but the first step of her successive participation in international institutions; that more and more Russian officials, functionaries, artists, performers, scholars, eventually tourists would visit the Western world and vice versa; that the suspicious isolation that had marked the relationship of the Soviet Union with the rest of the world before the war would soon melt away; that within Russia, too, the confidence brought by victory and the healing of the terrible wounds of the war would produce a more open and liberal atmosphere, more hospitable to outside visitors and to certain outside influences. The very opposite happened. Stalin feared not only the potential enmity but the actual friendship of his allies.** He chose to isolate the Soviet Union from the rest of the world as completely as possible. Visiting the Soviet Union was discouraged, except in those few instances where such visits served state political purposes. Within the Soviet Union the flush of victory brought no mellowing of the regime; to the contrary, a narrow kind of Great Russian nationalism was encouraged. It was on the increase, it aimed not only to stifle the faintest stirrings of popular or intellectual dissatisfaction (these were few) but to crush the spirit and to restrict the very existence of non-Russian nationalities— Jews, Crimean Tartars, etc.—whom Stalin did not consider reliable. In 1945 his Foreign Ministry was run by a troika of isolationists who were largely ignorant of the Western world: Molotov, Dekanozov, Vyshinsky, the first two having been advocates of the alliance with the Third Reich before 1941.

It is significant that Stalin isolated†† the Soviet Union not

** Stalin had made two mistakes: he let Europe see the Russians, and he let the Russians see Europe—an aphorism current in 1945. The first part of this aphorism was truer than the second. The behavior of the Russian armies in Eastern and Central Europe shocked millions of people, including previous sympathizers, Slavs and Communists. What shocked them was not only the brutal behavior of a conquering army; the Russians appalled people by their primitiveness. But it was because of this primitiveness, too, that, save for individual exceptions, Europe made no great impression on millions of Soviet draftees. Among the hundreds of thousands of roaming soldiers, including deserters, remarkably few were sufficiently impressed or attracted by the European amenities of life to desert to the West.

†† Stalin to Harriman, 25 October 1945: The Americans were high-handed in Japan. All right, then: "The Soviet Union would not interfere. For a long time the isolationists had been in power in the United States. He had never favored a policy of isolation, but perhaps the Soviet Union

only from Western Europe but even from his newly acquired satellite states. Behind the "iron curtain" there was a "brass curtain" along the state frontiers of the U.S.S.R., along its borders with Rumania, Hungary, Czechoslovakia, Poland, Finland. It was (it still is) even less penetrable than the iron curtain further to the west. In 1945 millions of Germans and so-called displaced persons could still move across zonal boundaries without much difficulty, it was still relatively easy for citizens of Eastern European states to cross frontiers; but very few citizens of the Soviet Union were permitted to cross the Soviet borders westward, not even to the new Russian-occupied satellite states.

The events of 1945 confirmed Stalin's low estimation of foreign Communists. In 1918, Russia had been defeated in the First World War and Lenin expected the revolution to break out across Europe "in a matter of months, perhaps weeks." In 1945, in spite of the tremendous Russian victory, there was not a single country where a successful Communist revolution occurred, where Communists came to power on their own.‡‡ This included the very countries that the Soviet armies had conquered. Stalin concluded that, as in Russia, it would be best to

should adopt such a policy. Perhaps, in fact, there was nothing wrong with it." W. Averell Harriman and Elie Abel, *Special Envoy to Churchill and Stalin, 1941–1946* (New York, 1975), p. 519.

‡‡ Partial exceptions to this rule were Yugoslavia and Albania in Europe, and China in the Far East. Still, had Yugoslavia been invaded by British and not by Russian armies, and had the Soviet armies not invaded Manchuria at the end of the war, there are many reasons to believe that Tito would not have been able to establish his complete Communist dictatorship in Yugoslavia and Mao would not have been able to wholly defeat the Nationalists in China.

give local authority and power not so much to old and tried Communists as to people whose subservience to Moscow would be assured by their opportunism and/or their rootlessness. There were men and women who, for a variety of personal reasons, were willing to act as Russian—Russian, rather than Communist —agents, assuring the Russians of their complete subservience. Stalin favored such people over many of the local Communists. Among the latter he chose to favor those who had been for long years émigrés in Moscow over those Communists who had lived as clandestine revolutionaries in their own countries during the war or before. This explains the apparent contradiction of Stalin, the anti-Semite, putting Jewish Communists such as Ana Pauker in Rumania or Rákosi in Hungary into power. Because of their background, because of their rootlessness, such people were entirely dependent on him. He held them in the palm of his hand.

Many people have thought and said that because of the brutality of his policies in Eastern Europe Stalin had made a great mistake in 1945 and afterwards. He alienated the local peoples; and he frightened the West. Had he been less brutal, had he allowed a minimum of traditional liberties, had he been satisfied with the existence of pro-Russian, and not necessarily Communist, governments in Budapest or Prague or Warsaw, the cold war could have been avoided, and the attraction of Communism as well as the prestige of the Soviet Union would have been immeasurably greater throughout the world. This argument overrates Stalin's paranoia while it underrates his realism. At the core of the latter stood his contempt for international Communism, together with his understanding of the backwardness of his own Russia. The prospect of Eastern European non-Communist regimes that would follow a pro-Russian foreign policy while their peoples maintained all kinds of cultural and financial and economic contacts with the Western world did not appeal to him. Under such conditions Moscow would be the loser sooner or later, since Russian influence would naturally, and inevitably, decrease. His was the ancient conservative preference for the bird in one's hand—in his case, rather, in one's fist.

His conservatism was the suspicious and obstinate conservatism of the peasant. It was both cautious and radical: for the sake of preserving what had come to be his, everything was permitted; the end justified any and every means. He was a conservative in another sense, too: his war aims were nearly identical with those of the Tsarist empire during the First World War. He wanted to recover most of the territories that Russia had lost, because of her revolutionary weakness, at the end of the First World War.* He made few pretenses about this when he sent

* It is seldom recognized that the actual extent of the Soviet Union in 1945 was, and remains, smaller than that of the Russian Empire before 1917. Unlike the Tsar's empire, the Soviet Union does not include all of Poland and all of Finland. In three minor instances Stalin extended his state frontiers to include portions of Eastern Europe that the Tsars never had possessed. He took a portion of East Prussia, including the ancient city of Königsberg; he took a portion of Bukovina from Rumania; he took the Transcarpathian Ukraine from his Czechoslovak allies. There were both strategic and political considerations behind these accretions. In the case of Königsberg-Kaliningrad, Stalin wanted a further Russian access to the Baltic. In the case of the Transcarpathian Ukraine he achieved three things—a Russian foothold beyond the ring of the Carpathians, at the edge of the great Hungarian plains; a common frontier with and access to Hungary; and the union of all Ukrainians within one state, for the first time in history.

Molotov to negotiate with Hitler or when he was dealing with Churchill and Roosevelt. When in August 1945 he ordered the Soviet armies to attack Japan across Manchuria and Korea, his Order of the Day referred to the Russian defeat in the war with Japan under the Tsars and exhorted his soldiers "to efface the shame of forty years before." (Lenin, in 1905, had welcomed that Russian defeat by the Japanese.) Beyond these imperial re-acquisitions there was the larger issue of Russia's position in Europe. Before the Russian Revolution of 1917 the diplomats of the Tsar had told their Western allies what Russia wanted out of the First World War: an Eastern Europe dominated by Russia, a Western Europe dominated by Britain and France, and a weak and divided Germany in between. That was exactly what Stalin wanted in 1945 and after. Had Stalin read the record of Sazonov's negotiations thirty years earlier? It is doubtful; but, then, he probably had not read Marx either. He was conservative because of circumstances, not because of principles.

So far as Stalin's political philosophy went, he had little in common with a Bismarck. He had much in common with Hitler. Like Hitler, Stalin was a radical nationalist. Hitler, the Austrian, identified himself with the cause of Greater Germany; Stalin, the Georgian, with that of Greater Russia. Stalin's respect for Hitler increased during the thirties. He was impressed by Hitler's capacity to create a formidable sense of national unity; he was impressed with the way in which Hitler eliminated those who may have opposed some of his policies. As in Hitler's case, Stalin's nationalism and his dislike of Jews were closely connected in his mind; there are many evidences that, as with Hitler, anti-Semitism was not a minor but a major element

in Stalin's thinking; instead of a prejudice, it was a growing conviction. Stalin's respect for Hitler continued through the war,
notwithstanding the tremendous brutalities that Hitler visited
on the Russian people. He had a kind of sympathy for Hitler
until the end. To De Gaulle in December 1944 he dropped a
remark: he pitied Hitler. ("The poor wretch, he won't escape
from this one!" he said.) In one sense Hitler's ideology won out:
later, by 1945, Stalin had become a national, instead of an international, socialist.

Underneath these attractions flowed the current of the peculiar Russian love-hate relationship with the Germans (a kind of
parallel to the German love-hate relationship with the English).
The Russian people respected and hated the Germans at the
same time.† Like Hitler, Stalin disliked the French (though he
was somewhat impressed with the stubbornness of De Gaulle
when the latter visited Moscow in December 1944). In 1945
Stalin also realized the increasing weakness of England. His esteem for the United States was nearly boundless. He was not
surprised at anything Americans were capable of producing, including the atomic bomb. On several occasions he told his
confidants: the United States is the strongest state in the world,
the greatest power in the world. He was loath to risk a war with
the United States, on any issue. The American possession of the

† The Soviet government, for twenty years after the war, made strenuous and exaggerated efforts to propagate the record of Nazi war crimes;
yet it said little about the most terrible evidence of these crimes, the mass
extermination of the Jews. There was a reason for this: the concern that
the dark Russian masses might admire the Germans for their resolution
in getting rid of the Jews.

atomic bomb did not seem to have changed either his mind or his politics; it merely confirmed his already existing views on the immense power of the United States, for which he had a healthy respect at times amounting to fear.‡

Especially after Roosevelt's death and the end of the war, he considered that the Americans might be having second thoughts about the Yalta agreements that, according to him, amounted to a tacit American acceptance of the division of Europe. During the second half of 1945 American journalists and congressmen

‡ There was, in this respect, a connection between his anti-Semitism and his fear of American influences. He regarded Jews as being cosmopolitan by nature, and attracted to the United States, where many of their relatives were influential and well off. He, who was worried about any kind of contact between Americans and Germans during the war, was aware of the secret negotiations (whose record is still extant) that certain American officials held with Himmler's men in 1944 for the sake of ransoming Jewish lives. In November 1944, twenty million Swiss francs were to be paid to Himmler's special representative in Switzerland in exchange for Himmler's *written* promise to close down the gas chambers and to spare the remaining Jews in Hungary. As one of the Hungarian-Jewish personages involved in this deal wrote in his memoirs: "From a strictly formal point of view . . . this constituted, it is true, a violation of the Teheran agreement whereby the Allies had made an accord with Stalin that the Third Reich should be absolutely boycotted. For this reason no doubt the Americans up to this day will make no revelations about these contacts." A. Biss, *A Million Jews to Save* (New York, 1975), p. 160. In January 1945, immediately after the liberation of Pest from the Germans, the Russians took the Swedish Wallenberg, who had volunteered to protect Jews in Budapest before and during the siege of the city, to a prison in Moscow, wherefrom he disappeared without a trace. Stalin's daughter wrote in her memoirs that her father "never liked Jews, though he wasn't as blatant about expressing his hatred for them [in the thirties] as he was after the war." Like Hitler, he believed that the Jews put their hopes in the United States, both during and after the war.

were traveling in Eastern Europe. The presence of the small American military missions in Hungary and Rumania was influential beyond their numbers. In November 1945 anti-Communist demonstrators in Bucharest shouted: "Long live the atomic bomb!" Mark Ethridge, a journalist and representative of the American Secretary of State, composed a report about the evidences of Russian and Communist police rule in certain Eastern European nations. None of this was the official policy of Washington, but this Stalin did not know for certain. Impressed with and fearful of American power, he found it quite probable that sooner or later the Americans would try to shake his domination of Eastern Europe—the domination which, after all, was the most important of his war aims, more important than the prospects of Communism in Western Europe, including the western portion of Germany, more important to Stalin than the Far East, including Japan. In his negotiations with Harriman and Byrnes in the autumn and winter of 1945, Stalin suggested one of his typical trade-offs: he would be reconciled to the monopoly of American control over Japan if the Americans would not interfere in his Eastern European domain.

Eventually this was what happened: but not because of any clarity of vision of either side. Here was the basis of the cold war. By the end of 1945 Stalin feared that the Americans, who won the war with relative ease, and who established themselves as the dominant power in Western Europe, were ready to challenge the Russian domination of Eastern Europe. The government of the United States, at the same time, was beginning to fear that after the establishment of victorious Communism in Eastern Europe, the Red flood would threaten to engulf Western Europe. In reality, neither was the case. It was a gigantic misunderstanding. Not until the autumn of 1956, after the Hungarian Revolution, did the Russians realize that the United States had no real intention of intervening in Eastern Europe, of correcting the division of the continent that had been arranged in 1945. By that time Stalin was dead, Nikita Khrushchev was in power, who was inclined to get on good terms with Americans anyway.

Stalin had both reasons and justification for extending his Russian empire to the west, wherefrom Russia had been invaded so often and with such terrible results. He made a mistake in swallowing more than what Russia could eventually digest. During the twentieth century the peoples of Eastern Europe had matured, they had come into their own. In spite of the terrible sufferings imposed upon them by Germans or Russians, the nations of Eastern Europe survived the world wars and their foreign occupations. Stalin's conquest of Eastern Europe made the Soviet Union the greatest power in Eurasia: but all of their terror and police rule notwithstanding, Stalin and his followers would never be sure of their domination of the nations of Eastern Europe. In 1956 the Hungarian revolutionaries demolished Stalin's giant monument in the first hours of their rising. Russian rule over Hungary was reestablished after ten days of fighting: Stalin's monument was not.

Within the Russias his reputation lived on. It is beyond the compass of this book to describe the ups and downs of his reputation, profoundly interesting though this is from a psychological viewpoint, since there is reason to believe that the Russian people, not to speak of his native Georgians, continue to admire him** in many ways, not despite but because of his tyrantship. The mills of gods grind exceedingly slow, and the minds of great masses of people even slower, especially in the age of universal education. The Russian people—Stalin's victims as well as his beneficiaries—must yet come to terms with the meaning of his rule, with their own history.

This is what the self-imposed lifework of Alexander Solzhenitsyn is all about.

** The only instance of popular demonstration against the Soviet government in fifty years of Soviet rule occurred in March 1956 in Georgia, when students and other people demonstrated *against* the news emanating from Moscow about Khrushchev's decision to downgrade the reputation of Stalin.

VI. TRUMAN AND HIS CIRCLE

"Providence," Tocqueville wrote at the end of the last chapter of *Democracy in America*, "has not created mankind either wholly independent or wholly enslaved. True, around every man there is a fatal circle beyond which he cannot go; but within the vast sphere of that circle man is powerful and free . . .". *Un circle fatal* sounds less severe in French than in English—an important nuance, since Tocqueville rejected not only fatalism but the kind of theoretical determinism that is often but a "scientific" version of the former. He also denied the factor of accidents in history. There is no such thing as a pure accident; every event has myriad causes, on all kinds of levels and in all kinds of ways; we are not God, we cannot know them all. History is not ruled by mechanical causality; sometimes the strangest events lead to the strangest results; and the most unlikely candidates become the carriers of the greatest events.

It was almost by accident that Harry S. Truman became the Vice-President of the United States in 1944—almost, but not quite. He did not have the slightest inkling that he would be nominated for the post of Vice-President before the Democratic Party convention opened in Chicago in July 1944. There was a powerful movement to deny the vice-presidency to the incumbent Henry Wallace, an honest man with an addled and confused mind.* Roosevelt thought it politic to keep his hands clear: he would not oppose Wallace but he would not help him either. He may have been too tired to fight for his choice; and he did not want a break with the strong-man bosses of the Democratic Party. He preferred William O. Douglas—like Wallace, a western progressive, a radical Jeffersonian, and a Sovietophile. It would have been a national catastrophe. Bismarck—or was it Lord Bryce?—was reputed to have said that God takes special care of children and of the United States. A Wallace or Douglas presidency in 1945, at the beginning of the confrontation with Russia, would have torn the nation apart. Eventually Truman became a national blessing. Robert E. Hannegan, a Missouri Democratic politician and Democratic boss, put Truman's name up even as Truman was wholly unaware of this; indeed, he had committed himself to support James F. Byrnes of South Carolina. Truman did not like to go back on his word: he accepted the fact that he was one of Roosevelt's preferences—the preference had been suggested to the President by Hannegan—only reluctantly. The politicians wanted a safe, colorless, decent, and reliable vice-presidential candidate. Truman was far from being colorless: but people would not learn this until he was President, indeed not for many years.

His limitations were the limitations of his circle. It was not that Harry Truman liked low company; he was one of the least corruptible of Presidents. Too much has been said about his

---

* He was Mrs. Roosevelt's favorite candidate.

Missouri cronies whom he kept inviting for poker parties in the White House. Some of them were low-minded and far from being incorruptible. "It is a rare prince who, like Shakespeare's Hal, can bear to rid himself of his Falstaffs, Bardolphs, Pistols, Shallows, and Snares."[1] Too little has been said about his relationship with the greats of the eastern establishment with whom he had to work, especially in world affairs. The same Truman who was sufficiently strong-minded to put Molotov and Byrnes and MacArthur in their places, in some instances as early as a few days after becoming President, accepted the alternatives put before him by Stimson or Marshall or Acheson for many years. He depended on their advice, even though he understood much about the world. ("We all understand more than we know," Pascal said.) *This* was the circle beyond which Harry Truman seldom stepped, not some kind of fatal limitation imposed by the limited radius of his mind.

More than perhaps any President since Theodore Roosevelt, Truman was a man of his own mind. The strength of his mind had two sources: one of them was that solidity of character without which intellectual power tends to be either useless or corrupt. The other source was his knowledge of history. Among the benefactors of the United States and the Western world in the twentieth century, two unknown women ought to be given places of high honor. They are Miss Maggie Phelps and Miss Tillie Brown, two teachers in the Columbian High School in Independence, Missouri, who inspired the boy Harry Truman's interest in history and biography. He felt it proper and just to record his debt to them in the political biography of his presidency. "My debt to history is one which cannot be calculated," he wrote.† Our debt to his knowledge of history cannot be calculated either. Few American Presidents knew as much history as Harry Truman. Few Presidents understood it better. His understanding of history was the traditional biographical one, exemplified by writers such as Plutarch (whom the young Truman had read with great profit): men made history rather than history made men. This is what he learned from the history of the Old World. From his avid interest in the history of his own country he came to understand the meaning of its Constitution better than the entire slew of high-powered constitutional lawyers who were swarming around Roosevelt. It was Truman's greatest asset.

One of the reasons why he was tapped for the vice-presidency in 1944 was that he was not a doctrinaire liberal or progressive. Men such as Hannegan probably understood as early as 1944 that the mood of many Americans—who later would be called "the silent majority"—was turning in a direction that was anti-Communist. An early statement by the then Senator Truman kept coming back to haunt him, especially through some of his liberal critics. After Hitler had attacked Stalin in June 1941, Truman made one of his then rare statements regarding world affairs. He disliked Nazism as well as Communism. On 24 June

† Harry S. Truman, *Memoirs* (New York, 1955), Vol. I, p. 119. He also bequeathed us a simple but profound aphorism: "The only thing new in the world is the history you don't know." Cited in Merle Miller, *Plain Speaking: An Oral Biography of Harry S. Truman* (New York, 1974), p. 146, a particularly valuable but generally dubious source.

he said: "If we see that Germany is winning we ought to help Russia and if Russia is winning we ought to help Germany . . . although I don't want to see Hitler victorious under any circumstances." Next day the isolationist Senator Taft said that "the victory of Communism in the world would be far more dangerous to the United States than the victory of Fascism . . ." Taft regarded Communism from faraway Russia as far more dangerous than Nazism, incarnated at the time by a triumphant Germany rampant across Europe; Truman did not.

Here was the latent origin of the struggle that Truman had to wage with the Republicans: the conflict between two different kinds of anti-Communism in 1945 and after. Just as Truman's liberalism was less abstract and more generous than the liberalism propagated and professed by the doctrinaires and bureaucrats in New York and Washington, his conservative side, too, was different, less cramped and less fear-ridden, than that professed by the Republican conservatives. Truman understood the limitations of American isolationism—because of his knowledge of world history, because of his experiences during the First World War, because of the natural and spontaneous generosity of his character. He understood not only the narrowness but the meanness of the isolationist mind; he also understood the inclinations of certain people to propagate anti-Communism and super-patriotism at the cost of many traditional decencies and freedoms in American life. This understanding, too, issued not merely from Truman's good-naturedness but from his knowledge of American history. He was well aware of past precedents of populist hysteria, of the super-patriots of the

1790's, the 1850's, the 1920's, from the Alien and Sedition Acts through the Know-Nothings to the Ku Klux Klan.

Six or seven years after the war, when the Truman presidency had already lasted many years and was in its decline, Churchill summed up the momentous period at the end of the war. He wrote about the Truman of the late spring and early summer of 1945: "In these early months his position was one of extreme difficulty, and did not enable him to bring his outstanding qualities fully into action." "The deadly hiatus," Churchill wrote, "which existed between the fading of President Roosevelt's strength and the growth of President Truman's grip on the vast world problem."[2] Yet Truman came to grips with the awesome problems confronting his office quickly and energetically. The source of the "deadly hiatus" was not so much time as it was place: it was the then pervasive spirit in Washington. "The United States stood on the scene of victory, master of world fortunes, but without a true and coherent design."[3] But there *was* a coherent design: to maintain the alliance with the Russians, if necessary, at the expense of the close American partnership with Britain—a design incarnating the ideology that was also the dead President's legacy: progressive America moving between Britain and Russia, in the democratic evolution of the world.

Writing about 1945, Churchill later wrote that "neither the military chiefs nor the State Department received the guidance they required. The former confined themselves to their professional sphere; the latter did not comprehend the issues involved . . ." The second half of the statement was truer than the first. Eisenhower, for one, surely had not confined himself to his "professional sphere."‡ He took it upon himself to send a message to Stalin, above the heads of Churchill and Roosevelt, at the end of March, to the effect that the Anglo-American armies would not move toward Berlin but would pursue the Germans further to the south. Two weeks later the American Ninth Army crossed the Elbe at two points; there stood not much between them and Berlin, which the Russians had not yet invested; Eisenhower ordered General Simpson not to advance further, a decision that the latter regretted ever after. Another ten days later the road was clear for the American Third Army to roll into Prague. Churchill asked Eisenhower to go ahead, but Eisenhower refused, again in agreement with the Russians, who became the eventual liberators of Prague. What would have happened if the Americans and not the Russians had arrived in Berlin and in Prague at the end of the war? The postwar realities of Europe, and of the world, may have been different. It is not the business of the historian to speculate about ifs—at any rate, not much. It is his business, however, to examine the purposes of certain men, and make certain corrections of accepted matters when these are both necessary and supported by evidence. The accepted view, shared by his supporters and even many of his critics until this day, is that Eisenhower was a sim-

‡ Writing in 1951, Churchill did not want to be too hard on Americans, specifically not on Eisenhower. He was Prime Minister again; and everything pointed at Eisenhower's election as the next President of the United States. When Eisenhower became President he showed not the slightest appreciation either for Churchill's magnanimity or for his view of world affairs. He found it both more politic and more convenient to rely on the anti-Communist opinions and objurgations of John Foster Dulles.

ple and good-natured American soldier, with a mind devoid of ruses and complexities. This was the Eisenhower of the famous grinning smile, the Eisenhower who after the war said to a reporter of the New York *Times* that Russians were very much like Americans, "very friendly," and that his contacts with them were "heartwarming"; the Eisenhower who said that the race for Berlin made no sense, since the German capital had "no tactical and strategic value . . . who would want it?";** the Eisenhower who in August opined to Harriman in Moscow that his friend Zhukov was going to succeed Stalin, and that the United States would have no major difficulties with the Soviet Union, "he was confident that a new era of friendly relations lay ahead."⁴ Again we encounter a mixture of calculation with naiveté. It was the same Eisenhower who had already confided to Harriman (in November 1944) that he had presidential aspirations.†† In sum, Eisenhower's military decisions during that momentous time in 1945 were not devoid of political considerations. The strategy that he was directing accorded perfectly with the ruling public ideology in Washington and in New York.

When he became President, Truman had no occasion to doubt Eisenhower's judgment. He had been kept uninformed by Roosevelt about world affairs—an astonishing hiatus in ret-

** Whereupon Patton is supposed to have answered: "I think history will answer that question for you." From the diary of one of Patton's officers, cited in John Toland, *The Last 100 Days* (New York, 1971), p. 371.

†† "He said that some of his friends had come to him and said that he ought to be President. He seemed torn between becoming President and playing the role of an elder statesman after the war." W. Averell Harriman and Elie Abel, *Special Envoy to Churchill and Stalin, 1941–1946* (New York, 1975), pp. 374–75.

rospect. Roosevelt had met him but eight times in eight months. At best Truman was patronized by the President, his family, and his circle. There was a patronizing tinge even in the kind phrase with which Eleanor Roosevelt answered his condolences in the hour when the news of the President's death came to the White House.‡‡ Now he had to depend on Eisenhower, Mac-Arthur, Hopkins, Marshall, Rosenman, Stettinius, Stimson, Leahy, men whose opinions he had no reason to doubt, even as sooner or later he became conscious of the inadequacies of some of them. He certainly did not lose time. His sprightly personality emerged on the very first day of his office. He wanted to be informed on the exact nature of the arrangements and commitments to the Russians. He got a long paper from the State Department; he called in Harry Hopkins; he told Jimmy Byrnes, his rival in 1944, that he wanted to make him Secretary of State. (He was already aware of Stettinius' shallowness of mind.) His natural inclination was to be businesslike and tough-minded with the Russians. He believed that the issue was simple: Stalin had not lived up to the Yalta agreements—a point that he would repeat years and decades later, in his *Memoirs* during the fifties, and in his interviews during the early sixties. Whether he understood that the Yalta agreements, especially regarding Eastern Europe, were a sop for public opinion, is difficult to tell. Within two weeks things came to a head. Molotov was in Washington, on his way to San Francisco. Truman spoke to him sharply about

‡‡ " 'Is there anything I can do for you?' I asked at last. I shall never forget her deeply understanding reply. 'Is there anything *we* can do for *you?*' she asked. 'For you are the one in trouble now.' " Truman, *Memoirs,* Vol. I, p. 5.

the Polish issue. "I have never been talked to like that in my life," Molotov said. "Carry out your agreements and you won't get talked to like that," Truman said—a retort of which he was sufficiently proud to include it in his memoirs and to repeat it later. It certainly reflected his own attitude toward Stalin and the Soviets, an attitude quite different from that of both his predecessor and his eventual successor in the White House. Yet changes in attitudes do not automatically involve changes in policies. Contrary to appearances, and the accepted view of revisionist writers, this noteworthy exchange did not mark a change of American policy toward Russia at the time. Truman continued on the course of appeasing Stalin until Potsdam, in some ways even after—mostly because of the influence of his eminent advisers.

The record of his cabinet meeting of 23 April—after Truman's first and before his second interview with Molotov—is important in this respect. Unlike other Presidents and heads of state, Truman prepared well for this encounter. He met with his advisers before it and after. The morning after the first conference with Molotov, Stettinius reported that the Russian attitude had stiffened further. Truman said that he was going to insist that the Russians live up to their agreements; if not, "they could go to hell." His advisers—including many later famous anti-Communists—waffled. Admiral Leahy (noted for his belief that supporting De Gaulle meant supporting the cause of Communism in France) and General Marshall (noted later for the Plan with the aim of solidifying Western Europe against Communism) said, in effect, that nothing much could be done with the Russians. Henry Stimson (the proper Bostonian, eloquent founder of the Doctrine according to which the United States should not recognize the results of international aggression anywhere in the world) said that since the Russians would not give an inch on the Polish question, the United States should not demand that they do. Harriman rather agreed with Truman but he was worried about the latter's peppy impatience. The only cabinet member who supported the tough stand against the Russians was Forrestal (another bantam rooster in the eyes of some), who put his finger on the essential issue: "He felt for some time the Russians had considered that we would not object if they took . . . all of Eastern Europe into their power."[5] He was convinced that on this issue it would be better to have a showdown with the Russians now rather than later. His opinions did not carry the day. Truman himself, in conclusion, reassured a rather anxious Harriman that "he had no intention of delivering an ultimatum to Mr. Molotov" but only to make the American position clear.

Molotov and Stalin thought that the American government would do little or nothing to challenge their own interpretation of the Yalta deal regarding Eastern Europe: but they were not quite sure. Stalin also thought—and not without reason—that he was being pressured to give up what was properly his. He did not consider the Yalta agreements to have superseded his percentages deal with Churchill. On the morrow of Truman's talk with Molotov he sent a message to Churchill and to Truman. He did not interfere in Belgium or in Greece; the Western Allies ought not to interfere in Poland. He did not know whether the Greek or Belgian governments were genuinely democratic or representative, and he did not care. "The Soviet Union was not consulted when those Governments were being formed, nor did it claim the right to interfere in those matters, because it realizes how important Belgium and Greece are to the security of Great Britain." He was ready to "do all in my power to reach an agreed settlement. *But you are asking too much.* To put it plainly, you want me to renounce the interests of the security of the Soviet Union."[6] (The italics are mine.) This was exactly what the majority of Truman's advisers said: Churchill and Truman must be restrained; they were asking too much. The advisers had their way. Truman, like Churchill, remained content with the record of his words. He did not press Stalin unduly on Poland or on Eastern Europe. In early May he decided to send two personal and special emissaries: the Sovietophile Joseph Davies (a very poor choice) to talk with Churchill in London, and Harry Hopkins to talk with Stalin in Moscow. Hopkins and Stalin laid down the basis of the forthcoming Potsdam Conference. By the time that conference assembled, the Anglo-American armies had moved back to their zonal boundaries in Germany, and the United States and Great Britain recognized the Polish government in Warsaw.* Stalin was more and more assured that his monopoly over Poland and Eastern Europe would not be shaken; that American remonstrances were not to

* Meaning that they withdrew their recognition from the legitimate Polish government in London. Stalin had agreed in his talks with Hopkins to include token personages from the erstwhile legal government in London in the pro-Communist government in Warsaw. It was a token compromise, with few or no effects at all. Yet it suggests that Stalin was far from having been impervious to American pressures.

be taken unduly seriously. On the way to Potsdam three of Truman's close aides, including Judge Rosenman, a holdover from the Roosevelt White House, gave him a brief memorandum on the important issues that were to be decided in Potsdam. There were six major items and many sub-items. Neither Poland nor Eastern Europe was included in this agenda—an amazing omission, in retrospect. It ended with the following, slightly ungrammatical, sentence: "In other words, we think that as a well-known Missouri horse trader, the American people expect you to bring something home."[7] By that time Stalin must have been aware that in America horse traders were one thing, politicians were another.

The first item on the agenda prepared for Truman on the way to Potsdam was Russia's entry into the war against Japan. This was understandable. No one knew how long the Japanese would continue to fight. They fought and struggled bitterly as the war crept closer to their home islands. No matter how great the superiority of the United States was, on the sea and in the air, thousands of American soldiers and sailors were being killed every day. On his first day as President, Truman was informed of the secret commitments in Yalta between Roosevelt and Stalin: the Russians would regain some of the territories and the influence they had in the Far East before the revolution; they would enter the war against Japan three months after the end of the war against Germany. Harry Truman instantly understood: this was a deal. The Russian attack on Japan would hasten the end of the war; it would spare the lives of tens of thousands of Americans who would have to subdue the fanatical Japanese, fighting tooth and nail in their home islands. This was one of the reasons why Truman had to tread cautiously in his dealings with the Russians. In this he had the support of everybody. Not only Leftists and Russophiles but Anglophobes such as Admiral King, later extreme anti-Communists such as General MacArthur and Ambassador Hurley, and members of the well-endowed China Lobby urged Russian participation in the war against Japan.

This concern with getting Russia to fight Japan was exaggerated. The Japanese government had been thinking about negotiating some kind of an honorable capitulation months before the Russians entered the war. There was no longer much need to bribe Stalin into attacking Japan.† Yet there is another side to this story. Stalin was willing, though not over-eager, to get involved in another major war. He was aware of popular sentiment among Russians: many of them were worn out with war. In his victory speech in June he announced a remarkably low figure for the Russian losses in the war against Germany. He went to unusual lengths to justify to the Russian people the reasons for going to war with Japan. He also kept his word. On

† An interesting consideration that has escaped the attention of most historians is the Far Eastern element in Molotov's first meeting with Truman in April. Molotov wanted to ascertain whether the Far Eastern agreements reached at Yalta between Roosevelt and Stalin were considered valid. The President said, "Of course," and inquired, somewhat anxiously, whether the Russians meant to keep the bargain. Molotov said yes. Next day his attitude toward American demands on other issues, notably Poland, stiffened. He, and Stalin, had been relieved to find that the Americans were even more anxious than they in seeing that the Yalta deal on the Far East would be carried out. This was an asset for Moscow which it could employ for different purposes.

several occasions he informed Americans that his troops would be ready to move across the Manchurian and Korean borders on 8 August, exactly three months after the end of the war in Europe. That this day came but two days after the atomic bomb had been dropped on Hiroshima was a coincidence, not the result of a hasty Soviet decision to cash in on the impending collapse of Japan.

The Japanese showed little of the political capacity of some of Germany's erstwhile allies, Italians, Finns, Rumanians, for example. Their very entry into the Second World War had showed their colossal misunderstanding of the global situation, as it was the result of their colossal mistake in timing. (They agreed to sign an alliance with Germany *after* Hitler had failed to invade Britain; and they chose to attack the Americans and the British *after* the Germans had failed to knock Russia out of the war.) It is true that in the early summer of 1945 they made all kinds of signals to the effect that they were willing to negotiate peace with the United States. But "they," in this instance, is an indefinite pronoun. The Emperor, and the conservatives in his circle, did not have their hearts in the war against the Americans and the British. Many Japanese officers and officials, especially the younger members of the military, were for battling to the end. Even after the two atomic bombs had been dropped on Japan, even after Russia had declared war on Japan, the Emperor and his circle had to face the grim opposition of many of the military leaders, including an attempted coup d'état by fanatical nationalist officers in Tokyo. There are few reasons to argue that President Truman should have, there are no reasons to suppose that he could have, dissuaded Stalin from fulfilling the Russian side of the bargain, from declaring war on Japan according to the previous agreements. There are more reasons to argue that Truman should not have ordered the dropping of the two atomic bombs on Japan, perhaps especially not the second one on Nagasaki. Yet Stalin was probably right when he told Harriman on 9 August: "he thought the Japanese were looking for a pretext to set up a government that would surrender and he thought that the atomic bomb might give this pretext."[8]

Harry Truman never regretted the dropping of the bombs. The atomic bomb, he kept telling people who asked him, over and over again, shortened the war and saved perhaps more than a half million lives, American as well as Japanese. The reasons for this argument ought not to be underrated. The atomic bombs helped the Emperor in Tokyo to win his case for peace. Also, the total number of those unfortunates who were killed and maimed in Hiroshima and Nagasaki was less than the numbers of those killed in the fire bombings of Dresden or Tokyo. The atomic bomb was a big bomb, and a new bomb. It would have gone against the American grain not to try it out, at least once. There is merit (though no certainty) in the arguments of those who say that the atomic bomb should have been demonstrated first to the Japanese in order to impress them with its awesomeness. There is no merit in the arguments of those who claim that there was a dual purpose in dropping the bomb: that Truman and his advisers wanted to frighten the Russians as well as the Japanese, that they wanted to bang the latter out of the Second World War while they wanted to scare the former with the prospects of a Third. There were a few men, such as Byrnes and Stimson—the South Carolina Irish politico and the proper Bostonian, otherwise different as night and day—who believed that the American possession of the atomic bomb could be translated into all kinds of advantages when negotiating with the Russians: but neither Byrnes nor Stimson understood Russian psychology, or the limitations of military technology.‡

There are few reasons to believe that Truman shared these thoughts. He was glad that the United States had the atomic bomb before anyone else; and he was loath to share it with the Russians. But that was it. Those who berate him with duplicity should consider the duplicity of the so-called idealistic atomic scientists. Not only did most of these liberals and humanitarians take pleasure in the profitable character of their work with the powerful military—the latter taking it upon themselves to deliver on the Japanese the fruits of the labor of the former, a fact that most of the scientists could square with their troubled consciences without undue effort—but their ideas about the political meaning of the bomb were no less illusory than the supposedly hardheaded calculations of Jimmy Byrnes. They, including most of those who had associated themselves with James Franck (one of the few attractive personalities among them) in opposing the use of the bomb as a military instrument against Japan, wanted to use the bomb as a political instrument: to impress the Rus-

‡ Stimson on 14 May 1945 to John McCloy: ". . . this was a place where we really held all the cards. I called it a royal straight flush and we mustn't be a fool about the way we play it. They [the Russians] can't get along without our help and industries and we have a weapon coming into action which will be unique . . ." Cited by Lisle A. Rose, *After Yalta* (New York, 1973), p. 74.

Truman was more skeptical. In October he indicated his doubts whether atomic bombs could ever be used in the future.

sians, not with American power, but with the American willingness to cooperate with the Soviets in the cause of World Government, Science, and Progress.** In 1946 George Kennan was speaking to atomic scientists in Berkeley. "The exact nature of their views," he wrote, "is still nebulous to me; they seemed to combine a grudging approval of Mr. Baruch's proposals for an International Atomic Energy Authority with an unshakable faith that if they could only get some Soviet scientists by the buttonhole and enlighten them about the nature of atomic weapons, all would be well."[9]

When the news of the Hiroshima bomb reached the President at sea, on his way back from Potsdam, he exclaimed: "This is the greatest thing in history." For once Harry Truman's understanding of history deserted him. Had the atomic bomb not been invented, the history of the world in 1945 and after would have been largely the same. Japan would have capitulated sooner or later. A Third World War with Russia was unthinkable, atomic bombs or not. This does not mean that Stalin was not impressed. He was: but the American atomic bomb only strengthened his belief that the United States was the most powerful country in the world. He understood that at the end of the Second World War the Pacific became a vast American lake, and that there was little that the Russians could do about it.

** This was typical of their leading sachems earlier in the war: "Convinced that the British attitude toward the bomb would undermine any possibility of postwar cooperation with the Soviet Union, Bush and Conant vigorously continued to oppose any revival of the Anglo-American atomic energy partnership." Bush to Hopkins, 31 March 1943, quoted by Martin J. Sherwin, "The Atomic Bomb and the Origins of the Cold War," *American Historical Review*, October 1973, p. 952.

True to his Caucasian ancestry and to age-old Russian diplomatic practices, he tried a bit of haggling, making high initial demands for bargaining purposes. He did want a Russian share in the occupation of Japan, a zone on the island of Hokkaido. Upon the news of Japan's surrender he told Molotov to request from Harriman that, together with MacArthur, a Russian general should sit in the Supreme Command over Japan. Harriman took it upon himself to tell Molotov that "this was absolutely inadmissible."†† Within two hours Stalin gave in. His idea seems to have been to trade off this request for an American agreement to a Soviet zone in Hokkaido. Having failed in this gambit, he now addressed Truman directly about the latter. He called this demand "a modest suggestion"; indeed, there was a plaintive note in his request. Harry Truman would have none of this. Stalin kept his peace. He was satisfied with the Soviet-American deal over China, the future government of which did not particularly preoccupy him.‡‡ As often before in the history of American foreign relations, Americans were more sure of themselves and more determined in dealing with affairs in the Far East than with those in Europe. The Russians, on the other hand, were much more concerned with their sphere of interest in Europe than with the Far East. In September, Stalin obliquely suggested to Harriman the terms for the larger trade-off:

†† Harriman and Abel, *Special Envoy,* pp. 499–500. The quickness and energy of Harriman's response were admirable, especially since the danger existed that a query to Washington might have resulted in tergiversations and delay, all of which would have served Stalin's purposes.

‡‡ All that he wanted to be sure of was that the U.S. Marines who occupied Tientsin after the Japanese surrender would leave soon. They did.

he was quite reconciled to the American rule over Japan if the Americans were to stay out of Eastern Europe.

Let me, for the last time, plead the importance of Eastern Europe. It was the faraway, the backward, portion of Europe, the darker, the less important part—especially to Americans. Those Americans who were looking out towards Europe saw first the recognizable old shapes and names of England, France, Scandinavia, the Lowlands, Italy: more familiar, and more meaningful than the obscurer shapes of Czechoslovakia or Yugoslavia—less real, less familiar, names with a slight Graustarkian flavor, peoples with which most Americans had but the vague associations and images of dark-faced immigrants with their round-faced women in kerchiefs. Had Hitler contented himself with dominion over Eastern Europe, the United States would not have elected to fight him. Not until Hitler smashed into Western Europe in 1940 did the United States begin to arm herself in earnest. Washington was concerned about Western Europe even in 1943 and 1944, all ideological and pro-Russian inclinations notwithstanding: Washington in 1943 and 1944 wanted to be certain that the Communists would not achieve undue influence in France or in Italy. In addition to geography or strategy there existed, too, a patronizing attitude, expressed by Henry Stimson, who said that he could not work up much sympathy for elections in Poland, since there were few nations in the world, except for the United States and Britain, "which have a real idea of what an independent free ballot is." Yet, as Churchill put it: "In Washington especially longer and wider views should have prevailed. It is true that American thought is at least disinterested in matters which seem to relate to terri-

torial acquisitions, but when wolves are about the shepherd must
guard his flock, even if he does not himself care for mutton."[10]
The Russian conquest of the eastern half of Europe was as unprecedented as it was unnatural. It not only altered the European,
indeed the world balance of power—after all, both world wars
of the century had broken out in Eastern Europe—but in the
twentieth century the nations of Eastern Europe had come into
their own. They were no longer Graustarkian or Merry Widow
principalities, or colorific peasant pawns on the edge of the European chessboard. To accept the fact that after the disappearance of German might Russia would be the preponderant power
in Eastern Europe, was one thing. To accept the condition that
Balkan countries along the Black Sea, such as Rumania or Bulgaria, would have to accord their politics with Russia, was tolerable. But to accept the Sovietization of Hungary or Poland or
Czechoslovakia was quite another thing. It would not only go
against all of the high principles in the name of which the United
States and Great Britain fought the Second World War; it would
open up divisions and future troubles of incalculable consequences.*

* Readers will notice that in these discussions of the developing
American-Soviet confrontation in 1945 I have devoted relatively little
attention to Germany. (See, however, a more detailed treatment of the
division of Germany below, pages 219 et seq.) The reason for this is
that in 1945 this confrontation over Germany was not much more than
sparring. Both the American and the Russian regimes wanted to postpone
the issue of the future of Germany. This was what happened at Yalta,
and also at Potsdam. There developed a tacit agreement to the effect that
each occupying power would settle down in its respective zone. Eventually this agreement prevailed, gradually hardening into permanence. Each

It was a situation that American resolution in 1945 could have still corrected, if not rectified, because of the then over-whelming event of American power. This resolution was, how-ever, wanting. In regard to Eastern Europe the minds of the President and of the government were not clear, they were divided. On the one hand, they seemed to believe that they had some leverage left in Eastern Europe, which they indeed had.† On the other hand, neither the President nor the government was willing to make much of an issue of Eastern Europe; they did not include it on their principal agenda. Beneath these con-fused and, in many ways, contradictory attitudes ran certain po-litical currents. One of them was the growing American preoc-cupation with the dangers of international Communism, rather than with the presence of Russian armed force in the center of

---

side would establish its own kind of German state. The problem of the establishment of a central German government was never seriously tackled. The inadequate arrangements for access to West Berlin were one of the consequences of this.

The Truman administration accepted Roosevelt's particularly unhis-torical commitment made at Yalta to hand over Königsberg and a portion of East Prussia to the Soviet Union proper. Urged by Churchill, it tried to protest against the transfer of an unduly large part of eastern Ger-many, up to the Oder and to the western Neisse, to Poland; but it ac-cepted this transfer *de facto*. The Truman administration differed from the previous one in its virtual abandonment of the senseless Morgenthau Plan; yet there is evidence that *de facto* this was already happening even before Roosevelt died, since the "plan" was not only wrong, it was un-workable.

† In the previous chapter we have seen that Stalin made various con-cessions in 1945, responding to American pressures: he would alter the compositions of the Polish and Rumanian governments, he would tell the Bulgarians to postpone their elections, he would allow relatively free elections in Hungary and Austria, etc., etc.

Europe. Allied with this belief was the American inclination to overestimate the influence of economic factors.‡ Trade and commerce with Eastern Europe, it was believed, would keep it from becoming entirely the dominion of the Soviet Union. (This was perhaps the principal reason behind President Truman's startling and sudden proposal at Potsdam about internationalizing the waterways of the world, including the Danube.) As late as in 1947 Washington hoped to use economic aid and trade as a means of political leverage across Europe, and not only in the western portion of it—the *raison d'être* of the Marshall Plan. And, last but not least, there was the still powerful inclination among the President's advisers, including the majority of his cabinet, to reach *some* kind of agreement with the Russians, after which things could settle down. All of this amounted to a kind of policy where interest and disinterest coalesced in a clammy compound.** It was a great contribution to the begin-

‡ On 7 July 1945 the British ambassador wrote to Churchill from Washington: "I judge that American tactics with the Russians will be to display at the outset confidence in Russian willingness to co-operate. I should also expect the Americans in dealing with us to be more responsive to arguments based upon the danger of economic chaos in European countries. . . . At the back of their minds there are still lingering suspicions that we want to back Right Wing Governments or monarchies for their own sake. This does not in the least mean that they will be unwilling to stand up with us against the Russians when necessary. But they are likely to pick their occasions with care, and are half expecting to play, or at any rate to represent themselves as playing, a moderating role between ourselves and the Russians." Winston S. Churchill, *The Second World War*, Vol. VI: *Triumph and Tragedy* (Boston, 1953), pp. 611–12.

** De Gaulle saw this. The rapid Sovietization of Eastern Europe was clearly the result of Yalta, and Potsdam was already too late for the Americans and the British "to recover in application what they had conceded

nings of the cold war, since Stalin himself did not see quite
clearly: on the one hand, he saw much evidence pointing to
American acquiescence in his control over Eastern Europe; on
the other hand, he could not simply dismiss American criticism
of his actions in Eastern Europe as if that were merely political
rhetoric for the sake of American domestic consumption. He was
worried that the all-powerful Americans†† would, after all, challenge his right to his newly acquired domains. In June 1945
Maxim Litvinov, the advocate of Soviet cooperation with the
Western democracies, lonely and anxious in Moscow, told the
American left-wing journalist Edgar Snow: "Why did you
Americans wait till right now to begin opposing us in the Balkans and Eastern Europe? You should have done this three years
ago. Now it's too late and your complaints only arouse suspicions
here."[11] In other words, much trouble could have been avoided if
the United States and the Soviet Union had made their respective spheres of interest clear earlier, something that would have
kept Stalin from snapping up entire states that seemed to have
been left to him because of American procrastination and American ambiguity.

Procrastination and ambiguity? These inclinations were alien

in principle." *The War Memoirs of Charles de Gaulle* (New York, 1960),
Vol. III, p. 229.

†† Contrast this with the reminiscences of the last free Polish ambassador to Washington. In June 1945 Elbridge Durbrow, "by that time the
highest Department of State official whom I was still admitted to see,"
said to him: "Mr. Ambassador, you appear to have an exaggerated opinion of the power of the United States. You are wrong. America is not
sufficiently powerful to impose her will on Soviet Russia." Jan Ciechanowski, *Defeat in Victory* (New York, 1947), p. 384.

to all that we know of Harry Truman's character. His personality may be summed up—indeed, it was so summed up—in two
words, *brisk* and *precise*, words which memoirists and writers,
ranging from Churchill to some of Truman's brummagem biographers, have repeated over and over again. But in spite of his
energy and his convictions that left a mark not only on American but also on world history, Harry Truman was neither omnipotent nor omniscient. He stood in the center of events—and
also in that of his circle.

We have seen, in a previous chapter, that procrastination was
one of the main elements in Roosevelt's failing to come to grips
with the Russians. Procrastination was—and remains—an endemic characteristic of democratic diplomacy. There are many
reasons for this, the principal among them being the deadweight
of the image of public opinion, and the consequent unwillingness of political figures, as well as of high officials, to be
preoccupied with unpublicized, and therefore seemingly unpopular, problems. The result of this is a long time lag in the
course of the ship of state. Necessary changes in the course are,
more than often, not adopted and announced and put into practice until it is late, and sometimes too late. There are many examples of this, especially in the continuing pattern of American-
Soviet relations after 1941.‡‡ The change that crystallized in

‡‡ As we have seen, opposition to some of Stalin's purposes should
have become American policy two to four years before this actually happened in 1947–48. After Stalin's death there was a possibility of winding
down the cold war in Europe, including a renegotiation of the division
of the continent. Such a policy, which may have yielded certain results

1947 in Washington's policy toward Russia would have been immensely more propitious if it had been adopted two or even three years earlier. Churchill and Stalin were aware of this American procrastination, the first painfully, the second hopefully so. Throughout 1944 and 1945 Stalin kept postponing serious negotiations and confrontations with Roosevelt and Truman on certain issues, very much including Eastern Europe and Germany, since he believed—and with reason—that time was working for him, and that in the end Americans would be faced with a *de facto* situation, in which they would tend to accept the *status quo.**

The hesitation to face some of the problems with the Russians was the result of ambiguity as well as of procrastination. We ought to have some sympathy with those Americans who in 1945 would go far in trying to assure the Russians of American goodwill; who loathed the idea of a bitter political quarrel among the great wartime allies, and the prospect of another global war—were it not that so many of the influential per-

---

from about 1953 to 1957, was reluctantly adopted by Eisenhower and Kennedy around 1960, by which time many of its opportunities had vanished. The United States finally, and formally, accepted the division of Europe and of Germany in the early 1970's; she could have done so, eliciting certain Russian concessions in exchange, ten years earlier. This indicates that the time lag is growing. The so-called détente with the Soviet Union, announced by Presidents Nixon and Ford during the 1970's, has been in reality the basic fact in American-Russian relations for more than a decade.

* This was Stalin's policy both in the long and in the short run—as, for example, when he succeeded in putting off the summit meeting at Potsdam until mid-July, against the wishes of Churchill, who wanted to confront him *before* the final retreat of the British and American troops into their occupation zones was completed.

sonages who cherished these ideas in 1945 were soon to become vocal proponents of an American policy of global anti-Communism. In any event, it behooves the historian to discern some of the elements in Washington, including some of the President's advisers, who were more or less responsible in 1945 for the kind of continued ambiguity in the American policy that worked, at worst, to the advantage of Stalin and, at best, to a belated realization that a definite change in policy could no longer be avoided.

First in order, though not in importance, was the continued influence of certain Communist and pro-Communist people in Washington and in New York. This influence ranged from actual spying to the influencing of public opinion in a pro-Soviet direction. It was not a decisive influence, probably not even in the case of such people as the Rosenbergs, who were instrumental in passing technical secrets about the American atomic bomb to the Soviets; there are reasons to believe that the Russians would have completed their first atomic bomb in 1949 even without this kind of assistance. The case of people such as Alger Hiss, whom this author believes, on the basis of evidence, to have been a Communist at some time, was not very decisive either. Whatever Hiss may have done earlier, there is no evidence that Hiss was an active Soviet agent in 1945 in Washington. He was an ambitious young man who had risen high in the hierarchy of the American foreign policy establishment. Naive as well as ambitious—again we encounter this peculiar American combination—he may have enjoyed, first, his self-importance in being active in a higher cause that was both exciting and intel-

lectually fashionable, and later the self-importance of his high
governmental position.† People with similar inclinations
(though sometimes different personal characteristics), were pul-
lulating in the Treasury Department, an example of them being
Harry Dexter White, an important official. The origins of their
pro-Communist inclinations and activities reached back to the
thirties, to the often heady atmosphere of the New Deal. The
consequences of their earlier affiliations were probably more baneful than were their activities in 1945. The revelations of their
former Communist activities—no matter how inconsequential
these may have been—eventually led to an extreme preoccu-
pation with domestic Communism. The result was a political atmosphere in which ideological anti-Communism became an

---

† This was how I, a refugee from Communist Hungary, saw Hiss when
the scandal about him broke in 1948, having encountered certain people
of his type during my first two years in the United States. I feel compelled to record here a personal reminiscence of an intellectual nature.
Many years later I happened to read Edmund Wilson's foreword (written
in 1953) to a paperback edition of his 1929 novel, *I Thought of Daisy*,
in which he wrote, among other things: "Some time in the late thirties,
at the time when [the Soviets were] . . . coming to seem respectable and
Communism a passport to power in an impending international bureaucracy, I thought of doing a brief sequel to *Daisy*, in which . . . some
Washington official . . . would be giving himself a sense of importance
and enjoying a good deal of excitement through an underground connection with the Communists . . . [their] set would go on drinking, playing
bridge and making passes at one another's girls with the conviction that
these activities had been given a new dignity by being used to cover up
operations which would eventually prove world-shaking and land them
somehow at the top of the heap . . . [but] everybody has now heard
enough about the people I was meaning to satirize." I considered then, as
I consider now, this passage to be the best, and the most concise, description of a certain kind of American Communist.

even greater obstacle to the conduct of an intelligent foreign policy than the influences of pro-Communism in 1945 had been.

What counted was the atmosphere. Creatures such as Hiss
flourished in the atmosphere of 1945, when for so many people
distrust of Russia, and rhetorical anti-Communism, evoked
something that was parochial, isolationist, narrow-minded. In
Washington and in New York, as well as in many other places
in the United States, it was *bon ton* to be *bien-pensant,* to have
the right opinions instead of the wrong ones—an inclination to
which I shall return. Men and women who held these attitudes
were far more influential than were outright Communists. They
continued to believe that American opposition to Russia meant
not only a betrayal of the principles of Franklin Roosevelt, but a
preference for ideas which, instead of progressive, were reactionary ones—this, in modern America, being the worst kind of
intellectual (and social) sin. This belief was shared, at least par-
tially, by many of President Truman's cabinet officers and advisers. Some of these were holdovers from the Roosevelt administration: Henry Morgenthau, Francis Biddle, David Lilienthal,
Henry Wallace. They either resigned during the first months of
the Truman administration or, as in the case of Wallace, were
asked by the President to resign later. Others, such as Dean
Acheson, adjusted themselves to the emerging realities gradually.

Here is an example of the influence of certain people who
were flourishing in this climate. Dr. Ludwig Rajchman was a
cosmopolitan intriguer of Polish origin. He lived in Paris and
Geneva during the interwar years. After the fall of Paris he took
refuge in the United States with the help of the then exiled Polish government, whom he convinced of the importance of his in-

ternational connections. He secured a fraudulent diplomatic passport, causing him some trouble, which then passed. Among progressive-minded circles in New York and Washington he was soon a success. "Rajchman's connections extended into the intimate circle of the White House; among his personal friends were such men as Harry Hopkins, Henry Morgenthau, Samuel Rosenman, Archibald MacLeish, Lauchlin Currie, and Felix Frankfurter"[12]—Franklin's Court. By 1945 he had transferred his loyalties to the pro-Communist government in Warsaw; indeed, he offered his services to them. He got himself invited to Potsdam. The Warsaw people appointed him their chief financial representative in Washington. They wanted credits from the United States; and, more important, the political prestige that would accrue to them by such an American offer. The American ambassador to Poland, Arthur Bliss Lane (who was not included in the American delegation to Potsdam), was bitterly opposed to this course. Acheson and Byrnes overruled him. As late as in December 1945 (the date is significant) Lane's personal friend and chief of the State Department's Division of Eastern European Affairs, Elbridge Durbrow, informed him personally that while Rajchman was making little progress, "I frankly do not feel that we can guarantee that things will remain this way since Dr. Rajchman has many friends, some of whom may be able to swing this away from the firm position we have all taken."‡ The

‡ Vladimir Petrov, *A Study in Diplomacy: The Story of Arthur Bliss Lane* (Chicago, 1971), p. 254. "A few months later, his mission completed, Rajchman got himself appointed Polish delegate to UNICEF. Elected chairman of this international agency, he lived mostly in Paris. In 1957, when he came to New York on a visit, the Senate Internal

ultimate result of this diplomatic tug-of-war was ambiguous. On the one hand, when Rajchman tried to force a wedge between Lane and the Department of State, Acheson manfully and energetically refuted Rajchman's intrigues against Lane, making it a strong statement to the effect that Lane enjoyed the full support of the government in Washington. On the other hand, the Polish government got the credits it wanted—a fact that increased its prestige at home and abroad while it diminished the remaining prestige and influence of Lane in Warsaw. This was in 1946. By 1947 Acheson had become a determined anti-Communist. In early 1949 Truman made him his Secretary of State.**

Security Sub-committee, curious to find out more about his relations with Alger Hiss and Harry Dexter White, subpoenaed him to testify at its hearings. Rajchman chose not to appear, was cited for contempt of Congress, and quickly left the country. He died on the French Riviera a few years later." Ibid., p. 249, note 28.

** In his confidential talk to influential members of the Congress on 27 February 1947 Acheson said that "it was clear that the Soviet Union, employing the instruments of Communist infiltration and subversion, was trying to complete the encirclement of Germany. In France . . . the Russians could pull the plug any time they chose. In Italy a similar if less immediately dangerous situation existed, but it was growing worse. In Hungary and Austria the Communists were tightening the noose on democratic governments." Joseph M. Jones, *The Fifteen Weeks* (New York, 1964), p. 140. This amounted to a vast misreading not only of Stalin's intentions but of the political situation in Europe; but it was useful for domestic political purposes.

One of the people consistently critical of Acheson was Adolf A. Berle. As early as on 24 October 1941 he wrote in his diary: Frankfurter's "candidate to succeed Hull was Acheson . . . Frankfurter remarked that when he had accomplished this he would then be in substantial control . . ." On 10 March 1942: "Frankfurter is continuing his intrigue to throw out Mr. Hull, who continues ill in Miami, though he is getting

Harry Truman, in spite of his midwestern origins, did not share that suspicious kind of Anglophobia that was often current in the Midwest. Still, suspicion of Churchill and of British policies was an important element in Washington in 1945. It was cultivated not only by isolationists and Republicans such as the influential Taft in the Senate and the influential Joseph Martin in the House; the left-leaning Joseph Davies came back from London in May, telling everyone that when Churchill talked about the Russians he spoke like Hitler and Goebbels had used to speak. The briefing paper of the State Department before Potsdam criticized not only the Eastern European but the Western European policy of London. The British, it said, want to build up a Western bloc, "as a 'hedge' against the possible failure of Big Three collaboration in the post-war world."[13] The Republican John Foster Dulles said the same thing: he came out against British attempts to build "a Western bloc"—a statement that Stalin carefully noted.

Convinced opponents of Stalin, such as Lane, took some comfort from the fact that "President Truman seemed capable of making up his own mind; the old White House crowd was on

---

better. His candidate to replace Mr. Hull is Acheson. It has now got into the columns and I suppose we may see developments . . ." On 21 January 1953, writing in retrospect on the Truman administration: "In the hour of victory, it wholly misconceived the Russian position, and ceded mid-Europe to the Communist power up to 1947 . . . Acheson . . . coming into office in 1949 . . . reversed all previous positions, which was the right thing to do—and bases his claim to fame really on hard work, endeavoring to put into practice the principles he fought when they might have done the most good. Well, such is fame, and such is life . . ." *Navigating the Rapids 1918–1971: From the Papers of Adolf A. Berle* (New York, 1973), pp. 377, 405, 614.

its way out."[14] The first half of this sentence was true, the second was only true in part. The influences of the "old White House crowd" lingered on for some time. Other people on whom Harry Truman came to depend were ambivalent in their own minds about the relationship with Russia, especially concerning Eastern Europe. They didn't want to eat that cake; and yet they didn't want Stalin to have it all. An example of this ambiguity appears from the reminiscences of Averell Harriman, one of the best American diplomatists during that difficult period. He found himself in Budapest in early October, on the day after the city election in which the joint Communist-Socialist slate was defeated. Before the building of the American military mission there was "an enormous crowd celebrating the victory under the American flag. It made me feel very humble to recognize how much these people looked to the United States as the protector of their freedom. They expected so much of us—and there was so little that we could do. That scene in front of the American mission had its influence, I am sure, in persuading me that we ought to go on pressing the Russians to live up to their commitments. I simply could not accept the view that we ought to walk away and let the Russians have their sphere of influence in Europe, to do with as they chose."[15] At least Harriman recognized the dilemma: by October 1945 there was little that the United States could do; and yet the situation was unacceptable. Other officials who were less interested gave the entire Eastern European situation a low priority, indeed often no priority at all. Thus, for example, when in March the American ambassador to Poland talked with Stettinius, what impressed him was not only the evident superficiality of Stettinius' thinking but the fact that the Secretary of State was not particularly interested in the Polish question. Four months later Stettinius was out. Truman replaced him with Byrnes. Lane desperately tried to talk to Byrnes. He followed him to Paris when the latter was en route to Potsdam. He finally caught up with him when Byrnes was on his way to a waiting limousine. "Slamming the door, Byrnes said, impatiently, 'Listen, Arthur, these things simply don't interest me; I don't want to be bothered with them.' "[16] This kind of breezy sloppiness was typical of Byrnes. In August, and again in December, he went to the Foreign Ministers' Conferences with the Russians unprepared. Byrnes, who put so much stock in the global leverage that the United States would have because of its possession of the atomic bomb, was inclined to reach all kinds of agreements with Stalin and Molotov on general principles, without going into details.†† He was essentially interested in public relations. Again Stalin, who may have expected a horse trader, found that he had to deal with an American politician.

†† From George Kennan's diary, Moscow, 19 December 1945: Byrnes "plays his negotiations by ear, going into them with no clear or fixed plan, with no definite set objectives or limitations. He relies entirely on his own ability and presence of mind and hopes to take advantage of tactical openings. In the present conference his weakness in dealing with the Russians is that his main purpose is to achieve some sort of an agreement, he doesn't much care what. The realities behind this agreement, since they concern only such people as Koreans, Rumanians, and Iranians, about whom he knows nothing, do not concern him. He wants an agreement for its political effect at home. The Russians know this. They will see that for this superficial success he pays a heavy price in the things that are real." George F. Kennan, *Memoirs 1925–1950* (Boston, 1967), p. 300.

This happened at the end of the year. Truman had had enough of Byrnes. He would eventually replace him with General Marshall. He called Byrnes down for having acted on his own, without keeping the President posted; and, in order to make things clear, Truman wrote out a longhand letter which he read to Byrnes personally as the latter sat facing the President's desk. He told Byrnes in no uncertain terms that he, the President, wanted to be informed and consulted on anything that was taking place. Among other things Truman mentioned Rumania and Bulgaria. They were "two police states. I am not going to agree to the recognition of those governments unless they are radically changed." Yet these were only brave words. The American government not only recognized these Balkan police states but eventually acquiesced in the establishment of police states in Hungary, Czechoslovakia, Poland, East Germany. In the same letter to Byrnes, Truman said: "Unless Russia is faced with an iron fist and strong language another war is in the making." "I'm tired of babying the Soviets." In one sense this was an incorrect image. By January 1946 there were few people in the government who wanted to baby the Soviets; there were more who were willing to stand up to them; there had been, however, certain opportunities to redefine the limits of the Soviet conquest of Central Europe and these opportunities had been missed. In another sense Truman meant what he said. He was taking the first steps that eventually led to the Truman Doctrine, the Marshall Plan, NATO, and the establishment of American alliances and bases all around the world. He moved the hesitant mastodon of the Washington bureaucracy from dead center. Year Zero was over. The undeclared cold war began.

We must pay our respects not only to Truman's courage but also to his realism. How different this was from what that other reputed midwestern horse trader, Harry Hopkins, had said after Yalta: "We really believed in our hearts that this was the dawn of the new day we had all been praying for and talking about for so many years." Slowly, gradually, many Americans began to sense that Harry Truman was no fool; indeed, that he was a worthy successor of Franklin Roosevelt. The progress of this esteem may be glimpsed from the evolution of the often self-consciously sophisticated contents of the *New Yorker* magazine. In a silly column, "Of All Things," the writer Howard Brubaker, both mawkish and arch, wrote in April 1945: "Harry S. Truman begins his job with the profound good wishes of the American people. He should make an excellent President as soon as he, and all the rest of us, get used to the idea." Two weeks later the editorial writer of "The Talk of the Town" wrote: "There is one thing about President Truman—he is made in the image of the people. You go to a men's shop to buy a pair of pajamas, President Truman waits on you. You go to have a tooth X-rayed, Truman takes the picture. You board a downtown bus, Truman is at the wheel. Probably it's those glasses he wears, but whatever it is, we rather like having a President who always seems to be around. President Roosevelt was for the people, but Harry Truman *is* the people." At the end of the year the *New Yorker* ran a cartoon: a boy stands surly before a piano; his mother, an upper-class matron, says: "I bet President Truman never acted like that."

Eventually he became one of the bravest and one of the best of American Presidents: but the fatal circle around him remained, fatal not so much because of divided counsels as because the minds and the purposes of the counselors themselves were divided. They listened to what they wanted to listen to. They heard what they wanted to hear. Few people wrote about this as well as George Kennan. In February 1946 he sent a long telegram to Washington about what could be expected from the Soviet Union. "The effect produced in Washington by this elaborate pedagogical effort was nothing less than sensational. . . . Washington . . . was ready to receive a given message. . . . My reputation was made. My voice now carried."

> Six months earlier this message would probably have been received in the Department of State with raised eyebrows and lips pursed in disapproval. Six months later, it would probably have sounded redundant, a sort of preaching to the convinced. This was true despite the fact that the realities which it described were ones that had existed, substantially unchanged, for about a decade, and would continue to exist for more than a half-decade later. All this only goes to show that more important than the observable nature of external reality, when it comes to the determination of Washington's view of the world, is the subjective state of readiness on the part of Washington officialdom to recognize this or that feature of it . . .[17]

Only this was not merely a Washington predicament. It was an American predicament; and to illustrations thereof in 1945 I must now turn.

VII. A SKETCH OF THE NATIONAL MIND: AMERICAN PUBLIC OPINION (AND POPULAR SENTIMENT) IN 1945

> We cannot understand the meaning of what a man says, unless we know *when* he said it and *when* he lived. Until quite recently, one could read a book or contemplate a painting without knowing the exact period during which it was brought into being. Many such works were held up as "timeless" models beyond all chronological servitude. Today, however, all undated reality seems vague and invalid, having the insubstantial forms of a ghost . . .
>
> —Julian Marias, *Generations: A Historical Method*[1]

What Americans were thinking in 1945 was probably the most important, because the most consequential, matter in the world. Few Americans were wholly aware of this. They were (and still are) trained to think that the basic realities in this world are material conditions, that what people think are the rationalizations of their material situations, the superstructures of their material "realities." Yet what people think and what they believe *are* the real substance of their lives; and the material institutions of their societies, indeed the material organizations of the world are but the superstructures of *that*—a condition perhaps even more real in democratic than in aristocratic ages, and more evident among Americans than among other great peoples of the world.

What were the American people thinking in 1945, when they were the masters of the world? Their easy world war victory seemed to confirm what they believed all along, through generations: *"Perhaps it is only wishful thinking,* but my belief is that as America goes so will go the world." The italics are mine, to emphasize that these were not the words of a radical internationalist; they were written by a conservative isolationist, the Philadelphia lawyer George Wharton Pepper, in the foreword to his autobiography in 1944.

What was good for America was good for the world: in this belief elements of generosity (rather than of magnanimity), of broad-mindedness and of narrow-mindedness, of idealism and materialism, of a national willingness to communicate and of a reluctance to contemplate, existed together. In 1945 Americans were still a young people: but their minds were complicated, as indeed the minds of young people are, all superficial impressions to the contrary notwithstanding. There was an American unwillingness to think beyond certain accepted ideas, together with the unwillingness to admit certain unpleasant realities; there was an American compulsion to rationalize certain choices. The first of these habits was rather Anglo-Saxon; the second was not. For here was another problem. In 1945 American thinking seemed to be extraordinarily homogeneous. The ways of American lives, American opinions, American ideas were standardized, to a very large extent. But this impression could be misleading. Americans were less united than it seemed. Most of them were no longer descendants of originally English-speaking peoples. The era of mass immigration that ceased but twenty years before 1945 delayed the crystallization of the American national character. Mass Americanization, mass education, mass publicity, mass production produced certain extraordinary conditions of American thinking.* Like most young people, Americans had a compulsive need to represent (indeed, on occasion, to wear) certain opinions, sometimes despite their own selves. What was extraordinary was not *what* Americans were thinking; what was extraordinary was *how* most of them were thinking; what was extraordinary was not the content of their ideas but their gestation, their adoption, their public movement.

In 1945 the public, as distinct from the private, impact of ideas in America was extraordinarily large. (There was another distinction, too: that between public opinions and popular sentiments, to which I shall return.) This was especially true of the kind of international affairs about which many Americans per-

* Few people saw that these conditions were extraordinary. An exception in this, as in many other instances in 1945, was *Commonweal*. In an editorial of 5 January 1945, commenting on the Pope's Christmas message, in which the Pope had drawn a distinction between "a real people" and "the masses": "How in the United States are we to develop a people capable of playing their due role in the operation of our American democracy? We have here the most highly developed techniques for the regimentation of mass opinion. Our country is largely and increasingly urban. So many things are standardized. Consider our newspaper chains, mass circulation metropolitan dailies and popular magazines, syndicated columns, nationwide broadcasting chains, nationally patronized movies, the influence of Columbia Teachers College in our vast public school system, our books of the month, our standardized clothes, cars, furniture, food, etc. etc. The pressure is tremendous . . ."

sonally knew little. Their history, and their geographical situation, had been fortunate: they had little direct experience with foreign nations. But in 1945 American isolationism—another phenomenon that was much more complicated than its critics were accustomed to think—reached its last public phase. Soon it was to be transmuted into American nationalism (which had been its basic substance all along). By 1945 the number, as well as the influence, of public spokesmen for American isolationism had dwindled. The internationalists were in the lead. They had acquired a near-monopoly in the representation and propaganda of certain ideas about the world. The public thinkers and the public writers were turning certain ideas into public commodities.† They were not the only Americans who had ideas; they were not the only Americans who possessed or advanced independent thoughts; many Americans were thinking and, on occasion, uttering thoughts and ideas that were different from those entertained by the public thinkers and writers; but these ideas seldom received publicity; and publicity was what mattered. This is what public opinion was all about: publicness, rather than opinion, even when it was being measured, through artificially anonymous techniques, by the organizations of Messrs. Gallup and Roper, forcing it within standardized categories that allowed

† This function encompassed, of course, public entertainment, including the theater, and especially the movies. While public entertainment did not really create ideas, it contributed massively to the already existing categories of public thinking. Thus the pro-Soviet propaganda in some of the Hollywood productions was even more blatant than what was printed in the mass circulation press. (Example: The Soviet pilot in Samuel Goldwyn's *North Star,* made in 1944, who, plummeting to his death, proclaims: "Tell the American people what the Russians are fighting for.")

the persons "sampled" to check off a predetermined opinion—in sum, to select rather than to express; to choose rather than to think.

What this means, for our purposes, is this: it is possible to reconstruct much of American public thinking in 1945 from the press; in particular, from the opinion-making magazines, even more than from public opinion polls or from the newspapers. These magazines were both causes and consequences of the public supply as well as of the public demand for opinions—especially since opinions were often disguised as if they were information, which often they were not. In this respect the period 1938 to 1948 was a transitional decade in the United States. Public opinion was dominated by the magazines. The golden age of the daily newspaper had begun to fade, the era of television had not yet begun, during this decade when many Americans thought that they ought to have opinions about a wide variety of subjects, including world affairs, including matters of which they had few experiences or private impressions or even personal prejudices. In this national mass production—and, more important, in this mass distribution—of opinions the news magazines, the pictorial magazines, the weeklies, and the monthlies, together with the network radio commentators (whose efflorescence, too, was transitory, lasting from about 1935 to 1955), played a role that was even more important (it was certainly often more influential) than that of the newspapers.

In 1945 this kind of publicity exaggerated (and, therefore, distorted) the essence of the existing American goodwill toward Russia (and also toward various kinds of Communism abroad).

These exaggerations had baneful consequences. They impeded the movements of American statecraft. On the highest levels the government was beginning to consider the prospect that in the absence of countervailing power the Soviets and Communism might dominate much of Europe and certain portions of Asia. At the same time the continuous flooding of American opinion with arguments and rationalizations about the behavior of Russians and of Communists was an immense obstacle before the eyes of those (and they were, as yet, few) who were beginning to consider the need for a change in the course of the American ship of state. During the second half of 1945 this flood tide began to abate, here and there: but its momentum was still strong enough to dominate respectable American thinking for many months; indeed, in many ways, for years. In a trenchant passage, written in the 1830's, Tocqueville described this phenomenon of the momentum of public opinion in a democracy such as the American one. It is not true that public opinion in a democracy changes with mercurial swiftness, he wrote. To the contrary, it changes with excruciating slowness; and the danger is not the chaotic quickness of the movement of minds but a kind of momentous mental stagnation.

There were ample reasons for American goodwill toward Russia in 1945. To recognize a certain indebtedness to the massive Russian contribution to the victory over Hitler; to believe that broad-mindedness, rather than suspicion, should govern American attitudes toward Russia was only proper and just. Many Americans shared such thoughts. Yet these inclinations were coarsened and exaggerated by publicity into simplistic and categorical ideas, such as that the Russians could, or would, do little that was wrong, that throughout the world Soviet interests and American interests were, or at least they ought to be, fully compatible; and qualifications of such ideas were ignored or treated with suspicion. These public ideas may have been simplistic—but their purposes were complex. It was not only that the existing American goodwill toward Russia was exaggerated. Its nature, too, was compromised—because its composition had its share of baser materials. In many instances it was the result not so much of naive generosity as of rationalization. In 1945 most American public speakers and writers refused to admit much that was ugly in the behavior of Russians and of Communists in Europe and in Asia. This was less the result of naive illusions than of an increasingly strained unwillingness to admit certain unpleasant realities; and the purposes of this unwillingness were selfish rather than unselfish. They principally involved not the objects of the opinion (Russia; Communists) but the opinion-holders themselves. Often the very same people who would, on occasion, admit that the Russians could be wrong refused to admit that they themselves may have been wrong. They were, after all, liberal-minded, educated Americans, accustomed to taking satisfaction from the condition that they, by and large, were the possessors of opinions of a higher order than those entertained by the commoner mass of men.

The result was the prevalence of rationalizations and of attitudes—including self-chosen blindness, and self-deception—among some of the best Americans, who were often also the most respectable ones. Respectability has a far greater influence in a democracy than elsewhere; and in the United States public opinion was greatly dependent on—indeed, it was often hardly distinguishable from—respectable opinion. Here is one example. Among all American opinion magazines in 1945 *The Atlantic Monthly* was the most dishearteningly dishonest. Dishearteningly: because its readership consisted, after all, of American *bien-pensants,* from Harvard professors to liberal Republicans, and the cultured ladies and the educated Americans in provincial cities across the Republic. *The Atlantic* was not an outright political magazine; it was not outright liberal or radical; with *Harper's* and the *New Yorker,* it was one of the three principal literary and opinion magazines perused by the upper classes of the American democracy. Yet its monthly political reports, printed in the first pages of the magazine, often employed a political language that was indistinguishable from that of *Pravda* or *Izvestia.* The very first sentences in the first issue of January 1945 read:

> When Allied guns pound at the borders of the Third Reich, the revolutionary implications of the war are becoming more sharply defined all over Europe. . . . In nation after nation a bitter struggle is developing between the representatives of the system which produced this war, and the multitudes, backed by patriot groups, who insist that this struggle must transcend mere military victory and achieve deep, democratic revision of governmental systems. . . . Nor are these troubles explained by emphasizing the "perils of communism" . . . in Belgium, as in Italy and in Greece, the forces of reaction emerge more and more confidently into the open. Pre-war appeasers, fascist collaborators, and not a few notorious traitors enjoy strange

immunity from prosecution and are even having their
authority restored. In the liberated countries almost
without exception the purge is lagging . . .

This set the tone for the rest of the year. "The Atlantic Report," in the front of the magazine, spoke of the "fascist aristocracy of Poland" in May; of Greece, "the scene of a white terror"
in July. It was suspicious of English intentions: "Russia
identifies fascism as her mortal enemy—and means it. The
official British policy . . . displays far more tolerance of the reactionary elements" (May 1945). It spoke about "Mr. Churchill's
obsession for restoring kings in Europe" (July 1945). "Russian
policy, however abrupt and rigorous toward Great Britain, appears disposed to favor every possible step helpful to Russo-
American relations," "The Atlantic Report" said as late as in October; "Russia is anxious to hold Germany down, Britain to
bolster her up," in December 1945. As late as November *The Atlantic* chose to publish articles on Poland by the veteran Stalinist
Anna Louise Strong. Throughout the year its favored pundit on
the Far East was Professor Owen Lattimore, then a Communist
sympathizer, favorite target of rabid anti-Communists a few
years later—a regrettable practice, no doubt, but, then, the target
was too obvious to be missed.‡ At times this New England be-

‡ Lattimore: "There is increasing evidence that the Chinese Communists are . . . [seeking] an outlet in democratic activity, and that they
are accommodating themselves to this existing and strong demand instead
of trying to force on the people theories, ideas, and forms of organization
which they do not want" (*The Atlantic*, March 1945). "We shall never
be able to draw up a rational policy toward Japan until we recognize
that only revolution can solve the problem of the imperial institution in

nevolence for Stalin could be bland to the point of idiocy.** At
other times the anonymous author of the "factual" "Atlantic Report" on Europe did not merely misinterpret matters; he simply
(or, rather, complicatedly) invented them.††

Japan . . . [After all] the English people [once] cut off the head of an
English king. Until the Japanese people have done something equally
progressive . . . everybody will be uncomfortable and no palliative reform will be adequate" (January 1945). About Lattimore's *Solution in
Asia* (an Atlantic Monthly Press Book) William L. Shirer said: "if you
want a short cut to basic knowledge of the Far East, read it."

** "During the feverish days when appeasement ruled the roost at
London and Paris a noted Russian diplomat delivered himself an aphorism.
'Peace,' he announced, 'is indivisible.' Stalin, speaking on the Dumbarton
Oaks program, reaffirms the same thesis: 'Can we expect the activities to
this world organization to be sufficiently effective? They will be effective
only if the great powers which have borne the brunt of the war continue
to act in a spirit of unanimity and accord. They will not be effective if
this essential condition is violated.' Stalin's comment is important. It
provides a key with which the enigma of Russia's present policy may be
unlocked. Also it explains the diplomatic high jinks attending Britain's
present policy to build a bloc of four empires, with herself as senior partner" (January 1945). "The purpose behind Russian tactics is neither
sinister nor mysterious. Russia simply intends to see to it that the Germans do the work and run the country for her" (April 1945). Stalin will
"cooperate in a common occupation policy in Germany . . . [His] policy
is to convince the beaten foe that he will be treated as a human being
and given rights if he proves that he is capable of using them acceptably"
(August 1945). "Acceptably" was good.

†† Two examples: In the April 1945 "Atlantic Report": "In Budapest
the Russians discovered a sample of Germany's underground system which
suggests what the Allied armies may expect . . . With an unobtrusive
lamp-works as a blind an enormous subterranean system was found almost accidentally. Carefully camouflaged ferro-concrete hoods, slitted for
observation purposes, led to the uncovering of concealed doorways pro-
tected by gates of steel. Blasting these open, the Russians found wide
ramps leading into the depths of the earth, where they connected with
tunnels built in a network extending several miles. Huge workshops

"If we in the United States base our thinking, our behavior, and our policy toward the Soviet Union on the assumption that the Soviet Union is going imperialist, we shall be preparing for World War III." This was the principal sentence from the Newton D. Baker Memorial Lecture at the Council of World Affairs in Cleveland, delivered by Raymond Gram Swing, the most influential American radio commentator in 1945—a prototypical expression of enlightened internationalist opinion at the time. (Underneath it ran the fear of the unreconstructed suspicions of American isolationism.) The trouble with this kind of thinking was its fatal inclination to deceiving oneself. In the September 1945 *Harper's*, Henry Varnum Poor, an American painter of old stock, published an article about his wartime experiences when living next to some Russians at the air transfer base in Alaska. "The Russians at Fairbanks" was illustrated with two large pencil drawings of Russian types whom Poor had met. The drawings are excellent, down to the peculiar pushed-back angle at which Soviet pilots wear their caps. In the same article this competent American artist described a Soviet government party en route from Russia to Mexico. Every face had "intelligence,

---

equipped with an elaborate array of machine tools were turning out Messerschmitts. Barracks, stores, laboratories, and other structures filled several subterranean floors." A complete fantasy. But where did the author get it from? The previous month he reported that the Rumanian Prime Minister had been "overthrown by public demonstrations," having "thwarted the demands of landless peasants for agrarian reforms," whereafter Vyshinsky, "the Kremlin's trouble-shooter" arrived in Bucharest. The very opposite was true: the government had been popular, and Vyshinsky forced its dismissal, a sequence of events which had been, for once, correctly reported in most American newspapers and news magazines. The author of "The Atlantic Report" turned it upside down.

alertness, and the great gift of complete and serious purpose." So much about a grim bunch of Russian secret policemen and Stalinist bureaucrats. Henry Varnum Poor knew how to draw; he also knew how to write. He drew honestly; but he did not write honestly. He saw what he wanted to see, as did the editorialists of *Fortune*, the prestigious magazine of American corporate capitalism, who reported in January 1945 that the typical Russian factory manager "looks like a midwestern earth mover."

There was a dark underside to this kind of self-deception. One element therein was the youth syndrome of American thinking: the obsession with youthfulness which is often the mark of a preternatural fear of aging. Americans kept telling themselves that they, the Russians, and the Chinese‡‡ were *young* peoples; therefore some of their faults were excusable; therefore they were much preferable to the *old* peoples of

‡‡ The nonsense about the "young" Chinese topped the nonsense about the Russians. In the *American Scholar*, Summer 1945, Professor Meribeth E. Cameron: The Chinese Communists "grant that China is a long way from the dictatorship of the proletariat. Their practical program combines agricultural reform with political democracy." In the Autumn 1945 issue of this scholarly journal, Nym Wales (Mrs. Edgar Snow) thought that Professor Cameron had been unduly critical of the Chinese Communists, who "have had no difficulty in instituting democracy in their areas under wartime conditions—in fact it is this new stake in victory which stimulated the people to resistance. Tung Pi-wu told me there are 707 popularly elected country governments, grouped under 19 administrative areas . . . 'Our governments depend entirely on the goodwill and support of the people,' Tung Pi-wu told me emphatically. 'These are real people's democratic governments.' He also explained that 'The basic character of the economy in our areas is capitalism of a new democratic type.' "

Europe. Indeed, some Americans were worried that, compared to the Russians and to the Chinese, they were not sufficiently young.* "How can we create a spirited industrial society in

---

* The reverse consequence of the American youth syndrome was, of course, the premature treatment of the American young as if they were adults. This national habit, manifest in all kinds of ways, from dressing up little boys in business suits and bow ties to broadcasts of mock United Nations Forums constituted by twelve-year-old delegates, included the belief that the topics of interest for American grown-ups and for American adolescents were (or, rather, ought to be) the same. The result was the unique American practice of commissioning books on serious topics but written for adolescents. Two examples of the 1944–45 Christmas season: *Peoples of the USSR,* again by the veteran Stalinist Anna Louise Strong, published by Macmillan (1945 must have been her financial *annus mirabilis*), and *The Land of the Russian People,* by Alexander Nazaroff (photographs from Sovfoto and the National Council of American-Soviet Friendship, published by the venerable conservative, Republican-Quaker house of Lippincott, in Philadelphia). Excerpts from a review of the former: "Here are the people of the sixteen Soviet Republics, some with the fair, frank faces of the Slav, some with the high cheek-bones and long eyes of the East. But whatever the marks of race, they are all tremendously *alive*. The vitality that speaks from these photographs is an amazing thing. It is equalled by the vitality, the unflagging interest of Mrs. Strong's text . . . an epic tale . . . in words that in some places positively sing with enthusiasm . . . one cannot put the book down. It is a book that will have a very wide appeal just now. There has always [?] been a keen interest in the people of Russia among the young people of America . . . It tells a thrilling story of history made and in the making." The review is by M.G.D. in the *Saturday Review of Literature,* 13 January 1945. From a review of the latter: "Children and young people as well as their elders want to know more about Soviet Russia . . . A manly, creative, and healthy atmosphere pervades the country. The Russian people believe in themselves . . ." The review is by Blanche Weber Shaffer, same issue. What takes the cake is the reviewer's statement about Anna Louise Strong: "She knows what the people of the Baltic States said when they were incorporated into the Soviet Union." Oh yes.

America—one able to compete after the war, in material production and in dynamic ideology, with the world's other great young societies in Russia and in China?"[2]

Let me repeat: this kind of ideology, and this kind of reporting was not a monopoly of the Left. It was typical of the most respectable, most prestigious, most massive instruments of the American opinion-making industry. That the managers of this industry thought of themselves as true opinion-manufacturers, and of their ideas as instruments of American war production, appears clearly from an advertisement of the Columbia Broadcasting System in January 1945: During the last three years of war "CBS used a total of 8,686 hours . . . to tell the American people how the war was being won, how to help win it . . . 46,062 separate CBS broadcasts offered 56,667 distinct ideas forwarding the march to victory."

In the spring of 1945 the massive iceberg of public Russophilia was beginning to show a few small cracks, here and there. The readers of *Time* and *Life* could find a few sentences critical, or at least ambiguous, of Soviet intentions. In March there was a small literary ruckus: Two leading publishers brought out simultaneously books on Russia by American correspondents who had recently returned therefrom. *These Are the Russians*, by Richard Lauterbach, was uncritical and enthusiastic, full of the usual pasteboard figures and clichés; but *Report on the Russians*, by William S. White, was critical of certain Russian attitudes, even as he, too, favored the continuation of the American policy of goodwill toward the Soviets. The liberal and the leftist magazines pounced on White; still, his was the better book; and it slightly outsold the other one. An exception

among the major book reviewers was John Chamberlain of
Harper's; in spite of considerable pressure brought against
Chamberlain, the editors kept his column. *Harper's* was less uniform and less predictable than *The Atlantic.*† The *New Yorker,*
forever fashionable, showed more independence of taste than of
judgment. One exception was its then star reviewer, Edmund
Wilson, the Grand Sachem of American letters. His own experiences with Communism inspired him to write favorable reviews
of certain anti-Soviet books or memoirs, such as Alexandre Barmine's *One Who Survived,* a memoir largely ignored elsewhere.
And, for a breath of fresh air after the prose of malevolent political ladies of the Anna Louise Strong type (or, at that, of benevolent ladies of the Eleanor Roosevelt type), allow me to salute,
with a smile, the indomitable common sense of the American fe-
male, as suggested in the amusing cartoon by Helen Hokinson
in the *New Yorker* in May 1945 (the date is significant). It

† *Harper's* turned more independent after the middle of the year. In
the August 1945 number John Fisher published a very realistic article
("Odds Against Another War"); in the September issue Eugene V. Rostow
sharply attacked the Roosevelt administration's cruel policy of interning
Japanese-Americans ("Our Worst Wartime Mistake"). In October 1945
Temple Fielding (the later famous author of travel books) wrote a sharp
little piece against the cult of Tito, whom he had known in Yugoslavia
during the war. "Anna Held relaxed in tubs of vintage champagne. Father Divine is the Great God Jehovah. Huey P. Long is the martyred
George Washington. Tito is the guerrilla with the ragged pants and the
dagger in his teeth who swooped down from the mountains to save Yugoslavia. There has been more drivel, more sheer nonsense written about
Tito than about Frank Sinatra." He quotes part of this drivel: Tito
"learning Shakespeare and Clausewitz by heart"; Tito overawed by the
genius of Stonewall Jackson and "ready to put an Oak Leaf Cluster on
Stonewall's Tomb."

shows a bright room, a ladies' club: the hefty, well-dressed ma-
trons listening with great seriousness as their lady chairman
addresses them: "The chair will now entertain suggestions as to
what one should do with the Emperor of Japan." Professor Lattimore, move over for Miss Helen Hokinson.

Still what Péguy had written in 1910 was true of the great
majority of American opinion makers and opinion wearers: "It
will never be known what acts of cowardice have been moti-
vated by the fear of not looking sufficiently progressive." This
fear was sufficient to produce universal euphoria about such
events as the Yalta and San Francisco conferences. A typical example, not merely of the reaction to Yalta, but of the propaganda to substitute all private thinking with public categories of
thinking, was that of the liberal columnist Samuel Grafton in
the 23 February 1945 New York *Post*:

> Yalta changes the world, and those who are left out by
> Yalta (or those who choose to stay out) will find them-
> selves members of a cheerless little society, indeed,
> something like the brotherhood of the vanishing buf-
> falo, or the grand lodge of the great auk. This truth
> applies to individuals, no less than to nations, and not
> to be a part of Yalta, at least in spirit, is to be self-
> condemned to a lonely and irrelevant future. He who
> does not think at least approximately along the lines
> of the Yalta Declaration will find himself doing a
> strange sort of thinking indeed . . .‡

‡ Cited in *Politics*, April 1945. Here is another example of the wish
to suppress nonconformist thinking: Raymond Gram Swing about Wil-

Think right, or perish.

The reporting on the San Francisco Conference of the United Nations reached heights of self-conscious seriousness. The *New Yorker* sent out E. B. White, its house stylist and sourpuss author of children's best sellers, who wrote from San Francisco: "The quality of the reporting here is high, and the questioning is done by men who know what they are talking about"—not much of a sentence by a stylist but, in any event, wrong. "The accusing eye of millions of homesick young soldiers," E. B. White went on in another column, "the hungry gaze of millions of famished children, are trained on this hill tonight"[3]—a kind of presbyotic idiocy, alas, not very different from the imbecile rhetoric of *The Atlantic Monthly*'s reporter in San Francisco: "The mood of the conference has never wavered from its basic hopefulness despite its birthpangs. This is different from Versailles. The people know what they want this time. They want peace and security and in their bones there is now a realization that peace and security can be gained by cooperation among nations." This transatlantic reading of people's bones was complemented by *The Atlantic*'s reading of certain facial structures, as for instance that of the wooden dolt Molotov:

> V. M. Molotov, the Soviet Union's formidable Commissar of Foreign Affairs, easily dominated the entire assemblage during its first day. Short, compact,

liam Henry Chamberlin (who was critical of Soviet intentions) in *Harper's,* August 1945: "To have Mr. Chamberlin argue the right of his fears may be touching, but it is of no service to his fellow men."

massive-browed, as trim and collected as a tailor's model, he radiates force . . . He moves easily on his feet; yet one feels, watching him, that some strange force anchors him to earth.**

Before the press, Molotov is completely at ease. Standing at the rostrum in the Opera House to preside over the crowded sessions of the plenary meetings, silhouetted against the brilliant background of lights and the ranked flags of the forty-six nations, he becomes an epitome of efficiency and assurance.††

"In a nearby corridor," wrote E. B. White, "sits the editor of *Harper's* with a gold watch chain, beaming at the scene and taking small, legible notes." This editor was Frederick Lewis Allen. His notes may have been small but his rhetoric was surely big. "Out from an interior parlor," he wrote, "strode Secretary Stettinius, strong, athletic, pink-skinned, half-smiling, at the head of a flying wedge of delegates, advisers, and (for all I know) guards. The loiterers in the lobby caught their breath; this was what they had been waiting for. Here was the white-haired local star of the international game—Ed Stettinius, captain of the home team." The Captain of the Home Team spoke of "the sacred task for which we have met." This religious invocation of

---

** Gravity, no doubt.

†† *The Atlantic,* June 1945. This was the same Molotov about whom the British ambassador to the Soviet Union wrote: "it is my fate to deal with a man totally ignorant of foreign affairs . . ." and the Polish ambassador: "Molotov was the most important authority in the Soviet foreign ministry, yet he was the least interesting. Wooden and unctuous, constantly repeating the same phrases . . . he was the incarnation of banality."

heaven for earth, this universalist sentiment was standard American rhetoric in 1945. In the Autumn 1945 issue the *American Scholar* printed a lead article by Paul Robeson, the spiritual singer and Communist: "And what a vista lies before us! This can be the final war. It is possible to solve once and for all the problem of human poverty, to attain a speedy freedom and equality for all peoples." Once and for all! This kind of wish was not merely the father of the thought: the wish *was* the thought, impure and complex.

The wish was the thought: impure and simple. Impure: because this kind of thinking had the support of respectability.‡‡ Let me say again that I am taking my illustrations not from American left-liberal weeklies such as *The Nation* or *The New Republic*, or from the conventicles of American Communists or Communisants.* In 1945 it was the Harvard professoriate whose imbecility could be intellectually depressing. A kind of preternat-

‡‡ The respectable New York *Times* was not unqualifiedly Russophile in 1945; an assiduous reader could find news items in its daily editions indicating that not all was well with the alliance with Stalin; yet its editors were painstakingly careful in adjusting the articles from its foreign correspondents to the evolving necessities of foreign policy as attributed to Washington. For example, in the first two months of 1945 references to the non-Communist legal Polish government in London in the daily New York *Times* diminished apace with the increase of more or less favorable references to the pro-Communist government in Warsaw, eventually to be recognized by the United States. A crude chart of this kind of "content analysis" may be found in Diana Shaver Clemens, *Yalta* (New York, 1970).

* The attitudes of the latter circa 1945 are reconstructed, in retrospect, in E. L. Doctorow's *The Book of Daniel* (New York, 1970), a "novel" about the Rosenbergs, who, according to this popular author, were of course innocent.

ural senility suffused the discourses of these dominies, with a frozen idiot smile draped over the gray ice on their faces. I am speaking of the most prestigious of the professors, of James Conant the president, or Harlow Shapley the chief astronomer,† not of the itchy-bushy radical assistant professoriate of the 1960's.

† This director of the Harvard Observatory was a prominent public figure in 1945. In October 1945 he wrote in the *American Scholar*: "Science is a basic way of life, more inclusive of all the arts of living and knowing than the schoolbooks have told us. It is therefore high time that Congress should look into this business. For among the voters it is becoming widely known that the basing of conclusions on observations, on testing and logical reasoning, with a minimum of emotional grasping and evading, is the scientific method. It is also the intelligent method. It works." (I Have Seen Science and It Works . . .) "It gets places in a world that competes for knowledge, comfort, safety, and experience.

"Science is a central business of government in the Soviet Republics. . . . Science is basic in the philosophy of Lenin. . . . It has definitely made it possible to win the hardest war in the history of the world and save the nation from slavery. It has provided Russia with the best child-welfare system and the healthiest youngsters to be found in any of the major nations. And science is destined to transform the necessarily stern wartime living standards of the Russians into the richer and more exciting 'life of conveniences' enjoyed by the average Americans. No wonder, then, that in their political system, where the government guides all, we find that the advance and use of science is a major governmental concern.

"But does art suffer in consequence of this recognition and subsidy of science? Most clearly it does not. Painting, sculpture, the theater, belles-lettres, music . . . these arts and crafts are healthy and aggressive in modern Russia. No one questions the leadership of Russian musicians in composition and performance. Paintings are found in the modern art museums which the experts tell us are masterpieces. They are not escapist canvases like those which we so often paint, exhibit, and buy, not experiments in decadence, but interpretations of the grimness, humor, and serious thoughtfulness of life in a society that was reborn in heavy weather only a brief generation ago."

Few people remarked this at the time. One of them was Jacques Barzun, who wrote about the famous 1945 Harvard report, *General Education in a Free Society*, the creation of President Conant: "In the loose modern style, by which everybody is John and Henry, the goal seems to be not so much to transact business as to stagnate in friendly feelings." This is reminiscent of what Maurice Bowra from Oxford, on a visit to the United States before the war, wrote about conversation among rich Californians: "The only ideas which interested them were those which they had in common and repeated like incantations to one another in the hope that this would make them feel good." What Bowra wrote about Republican bankers in the thirties was true, depressingly true, of liberal intellectuals in 1945 and after. This kind of cant was something more (and less) than that of the Puritans. Sinclair Lewis was not a New England intellectual; the poor man was deep in his cups and declining badly in 1945; but he was a public writer and a public figure, and he would still rouse himself to provide a miserable incantation in 1945 about the function of "The Artist, the Scientist, and the Peace."[4] "All along, people like Bernard Shaw and Professor Einstein and Carl Sandburg have seen that their little desks were nothing unless they were joined to all the other little desks in the world and that not least, but most of all men, the artist, the scientist must know and somewhat loudly state whether he is for tyranny and cruelty and machine discipline, or for the people, all the people." (What a choice!) Lewis was not a Communist; but there was a depressing, and alarming, similarity in this kind of rhetoric to the primitive incantations that were standard for intellectuals in Moscow.

At this point the development of American internationalism and the development of an American intelligentsia overlap and meet. In one way or another the public thinkers and the public writers belonged to the intelligentsia. It was, and it remains, difficult to define "intelligentsia" or even "an intellectual" with anything resembling exactitude; as indeed in the case of many obvious phenomena, no definition will really do. The very word "intelligentsia" (as well as the usage of "intellectual" as a noun, designating a certain kind of person), originally quite un-English, had come to England and to America from Russia, only about two generations before 1945. But in the United States in 1945 the phenomenon of an intelligentsia,‡ of a class of sorts, a class not of birth or of wealth or even of education, but a class of opinion, a class with a recognizable function, already existed, and its influence was spreading. This influence had not yet reached its extent of twenty years later: but it was already there, a factor to be recognized and considered by anyone who wishes to sketch the profile of American public thinking at the time. The intelligentsia was liberal or radical, determinist when not altogether Marxist, and internationalist, generally speaking; among its members and adherents isolationists were few, and conservatives almost nonexistent.

The intelligentsia was not, of course, entirely uniform. The phenomenon of an intellectual avant-garde that was to become

‡ Intelligentsia: a word that the Concise Oxford Dictionary "with a touch of possibly unconscious irony" (Richard Hare) defines as "that part of a nation (especially Russian) which aspires to independent thinking."

(regrettably) influential two decades later, and the phenomenon of liberal and radical chic, existed, too, in 1945,** with their strange—or perhaps not so strange—compound of intellectual as well as social snobbery (which was real) with a kind of leftist rhetorical populism (which was fake).†† The articles of the otherwise steadfastly anti-Stalinist *Partisan Review,* too, reflected a kind of aesthetic neo-Marxist coterie thinking that could be as removed from the realities of the world as was the thinking of the Russian intelligentsia under the Tsars—another depressing similarity between America and Russia. The cult of Henry James during and after 1945 (the time had come to show Europe that America had produced a novelist who could be as thin-skinned and sophisticated and snobbish and convoluted as, say, a Proust) would, on occasion, coexist with an idealistic cult of Communism even in some of the better minds.‡‡

** A forerunner of this phenomenon was Mabel Dodge Luhan, the founder of what was perhaps the first American salon around 1912. Later she was living in Taos, New Mexico. She paid a visit to New York in April 1945. Her companion was a Pueblo Indian. " 'He's probably at the movies or taking a Turkish bath or racing around with some of his boy friends,' she said." (The *New Yorker,* 5 May 1945.) A vignette from the 1960's.

†† In November 1945 the then proto-Stalinist *Nation* sponsored a dinner on "The Challenge of the Atomic Bomb," with an array of left-wing speakers, in the grand ballroom of a New York hotel, at $7.50 per person (the equivalent of about $30.00 in 1976).

‡‡ As in the case of the Harvard scholar and critic F. O. Matthiessen. Later he was to commit suicide during the first years of the cold war. Perhaps he could not survive the collapse of his pro-Communist illusions. His tragedy had been typical of an entire generation of finespun American pro-Communists with aesthetic sensibilities, many of whom deserved a better fate. But this fatal inclination of certain New England

But, again: there is sufficient evidence that the pro-
nouncements of the American intelligentsia were not entirely
the products of naiveté. There was another segment of the intelligentsia who were very vocal in 1945: the anti-Hitler Central
European refugees who could not be accused of naiveté; they
were—at least superficially—sophisticated types. Culture-starved
American ladies in provincial cities as well as the New York intelligentsia welcomed these people—their accents, their vocabulary, their acquaintance with a few things in Paris (a way sta-
tion for many of them en route to New York). Most of these
refugee intellectuals took to public speaking and writing in
America like ducks to water. Many of them were serious
scholars who thickened and enriched American learning. Others
had been inhabitants of the Central European world of coffeehouse journalism, including publicity* and movie men, some of
them moving into the fringes, and eventually to the centers, of
American academia. They rapidly conformed to the ideological
and cultural desiderata of the American intelligentsia.† In plain

---

minds for Communism had been described by Santayana in *The Last
Puritan* (in 1937), which few people read in 1945.

* Some of them sported pen names: Louis Dolivet (born in Czechoslovakia) was the influential editor of a fancy left-wing news (meaning
opinion) magazine; Emery Reves (a publicity manager born in Hungary)
wrote *The Anatomy of Peace,* a best seller in 1945, a farrago of third-rate
ideas and clichés. Mrs. Roosevelt had an especial fancy for the older pro-
Communist refugees, such as Louis Adamic (murdered by another Communist a few years later), or Stoyan Christowe, whose autobiography
(*This Is My Country*) "was uppermost on the President's desk at the
time of his death" (*The Atlantic,* July 1945).

† In March 1945 Dorothy Thompson and Erwin Lessner, a German
refugee, were featured in a Town Hall debate. One man from the audience: "Would not the punishment of all Germans inflict needless hard-

English, they were good at telling the latter what they wanted to hear‡ (not always in plain English, but that was beside the point).**

In the case of most native American writers and thinkers the

---

ship on millions of German children who can in no way be held responsible for the crimes of their elders?" Lessner: "Of course it would. These innocent German children are the potential soldiers of World War III, just as the innocent German children who had been fed after 1918 later served in Hitler's army . . ." Within two years Lessner was putting out anti-Soviet stuff.

‡ Example: G. A. Borgese in the February 1945 *Atlantic*: "A Roman anti-Fascist was asked by an American correspondent . . . 'What do these people want from us, now that we are here?' 'Give us,' the Roman unreliantly replied, 'something in which we can believe.'" ("What do Americans want most from us?" Borgese may have asked himself. "To say something they like to believe.")

The exceptions had a hard row to hoe. Example: a thoughtful and honest book by a German refugee, Heinrich Hauser, *The German Talks Back*, was published, as John Chamberlain put it, "with a 'protective' introduction and footnotes by Hans Morgenthau of the University of Chicago. Some of Professor Morgenthau's points may be well taken, but the idea that American readers can't be trusted to read a book for themselves without the watchful admonitions of a papacicerone is just a little bit revolting. I wish the publishers had permitted Hauser to speak for himself. The American people aren't children or rabbits—or if they are, it is time they took their bumps for themselves."

** Many Americans were not aware of the vested interests—or disinterests—in the minds of some of these refugee intellectuals. Here is an example: In May 1945 Leo Szilard, a Hungarian-Jewish scientist, was sent to James Byrnes by President Truman. Szilard was (rightly) against the dropping of the atomic bomb on Japan. He also believed (wrongly) that an agreement to share atomic secrets with the Soviet Union would prevent the principal troubles of the world after the war. Byrnes (who at the time was not yet the Secretary of State) said to Szilard that Russia might be more manageable when the United States had a monopoly of the atomic bomb. Byrnes: "Well, you come from Hungary—you would not want Russia to stay in Hungary indefinitely." Szilard: "I was *not* broad-mindedness of the internationalist and the narrow-mindedness of the isolationist were but two sides of the same coin: the not ungenerous (but, alas, unquestioned) belief that what was good for America was good for the world. In the autumn of 1945 Nora Waln, a Philadelphia Quaker internationalist writer, returned to Germany. She would invent a German conversation:

> "Eisenhower," Gisela kept repeating. "That's a German name. Probably the descendant of someone who went from here to seek liberty in the New World. But it isn't just the German names I think about. Those Americans are the sons of all Europe returned to put down evil. And what a price they have paid for us in their dead and wounded. We must be worthy of it."
>
> "We must be worthy of it," affirmed Karl, "and we must not trust in outward appearances or rest in the belief that Nazism is easily got rid of. There is only one sure way. That is to strike at its root with education—adult education and an education for every child."††

disposed at this point to worry about what would happen to Hungary." [His italics.] What Byrnes either did not know or did not comprehend was that in 1945 Professor Szilard was not particularly opposed to the Russian occupation of his native country, where his relatives had been killed or mistreated by the Germans with relatively little Hungarian resistance.

†† *The Atlantic,* October 1945. Or see a correspondent (Major William Moseley Brown) to the editor of the *American Scholar,* Summer 1945, from "Somewhere in Belgium." "I hope I shall not miss future issues. When we get into Germany, I wish I could give the Germans a big dose of this kind of medicine as a purgative for their vile Nazi doctrines." This purgative function of the *American Scholar,* while perhaps desirable, was yet to be demonstrated.

This author's purposes were generous. What were wrong were the categories of her belief—not about Germany but about America. For the principal problem was not the equation (what is good for America is good for the world) but the value of the first sum itself: what was (and what is) good for America? What did America need most? Adult education, and an education for every child. Miss Waln, meet President Conant.

Such were the principal categories of American public thinking in 1945. There were the bland essences on the bland pages of *The Atlantic*.‡‡ There were the fluorescences on the shiny sheets of *Life*: photographers, originally from North Dakota, who would take such names as Ivan Dmitri, others with names such as Gjon Mili, strange Oceanian names that foreshadowed the names of the shadowless, dead-white coral isles of the atomic age. In 1945 in the pages of magazines such as *The Atlantic* (as in the cushy coves of certain New York hotels, half Chicago, half Fabergé) a kind of phony homespun Americanism existed

‡‡ There was this curious correspondence of cognomenology not only with physiognomy but also with rhetoric, of the names of people with what they represent, of outward form with inner content. Paul G. Hoffman (then president of Studebaker and chairman for the Committee of Economic Development) in the July *Atlantic*: "The more planning we do now, the more jobs we shall have later. It is as simple—and vital—as that." Alvin H. Hansen, Littauer Professor of Political Economy at Harvard: "And business in all the democracies, I feel certain, will more and more join with labor, agriculture, and government to guide and mold the planning so that it will be sound and constructive and will promote a better-functioning market economy." Lieutenant Commander C. Leslie Glenn in the September *Atlantic*: "Why I Read the Bible." "A good rule to follow is that suggested by a great Indian Christian, Sadhue Sundar Singh. He read rapidly, skipping here and there, until he came to a passage that held him."

side by side with the Russo-English verbosity of a Nabokov.*
The Century of the Common Man (Henry Wallace); but also
the American Century (Henry Luce). And, indeed, the glue
that held the bland essences and shiny fluorescences together
was inherent in the pages of *Life,* shiny and tacky at the same
time. At least *the image* of international America in 1945 was
reflected by Time-Life: America a supermodern, superdynamic
glass-and-steel skyscraper, pulsating with light and heat over the
cold and battered, dark and inky world. No one talked about
multinational corporations in 1945; and yet it was then that the
international influence of the images of *Life* and TWA and
PAA was a reality, it was enormous. Soon European and Latin
American and Asian magazines were to be modeled on *Time,*
modern time, time that was money, twentieth-century TIME,
an American Invention. LIFE, shiny, public pictorial life, life
absorbed, indeed consisting of the image of life, quick, large,
shiny, rich, was an American invention, too. One American airline simply named itself Trans World. The name and the form
of the other was perhaps even more telling: Pan American, with
its China Clipper image shown by the suggestively China Sea
serif at the broad base of the PAN AM lettering: Pan Am the

* Example of the former: First sentence of a short story by Ben Hur
Lampman, one of the *Atlantic*'s favorite storytellers: "Forty years ago or
such a matter, Old Bill Smith taken a notion for to get him a deer, because Marthy was down to the bottom of the salt pork bar'l." Example of
the latter: "I was born in Paris. My mother died when I was still an infant, so that I can only recall her as a vague patch of delicious lacrimal
warmth just beyond the limit of iconographic memory . . ." (Nabokov's
story is about Richard Sinatra, "an anonymous ranger dreaming under a
Telluride pine.")

mot juste, suggesting both the American Century and the pan-Americanization of the world.

All of this happened before television was to make Americans a more self-absorbed people (contrary to what the media experts have been telling us to think). In 1945 many Americans were still book readers; and the list of their intellectual best sellers was a good reflection of the new internationalism, with its twin ingredients of the American Century and the Century of the Common Man. A prototypical example of the new American internationalism was the 1945 volume in the Lanny Budd series, entitled *Dragon Harvest,* a new kind of American-internationalist politico-historical novel constructed by Upton Sinclair, a California sage, with Lanny Budd a combination of Alger Hiss and Andy Hardy, a young American international genius, adviser to FDR, talking with Churchill and Stalin throughout the book, and occasionally putting them (especially the former) in their places. Hamilton Basso wrote in the *New Yorker* (10 June 1945): "The Lanny Budd books have been praised so highly by Thomas Mann, H. G. Wells, Albert Einstein, and Bernard Shaw that I feel some hesitancy about entering a dissenting opinion, for, to come right out with it, they struck me as being just about the weirdest books I have ever read."†

Here are some of the typical best sellers in the year 1945: *Stuart Little,* by E. B. White; *The Age of Jackson,* by Arthur Schlesinger, Jr.; *Days and Nights,* by the Russian Stalinist writer Konstantine Simonov, which had surprisingly good sales,

---

† It is pleasant to record that the American reading public did not altogether share the enthusiasm of Mann and Wells and Einstein and Shaw: the sales of the Lanny Budd books were less than sensational.

as had *Forever Amber,* the popular success of the year (less sur-
prising were the sales of *Some of These Days,* by Sophie
Tucker, and *Doctors at War,* edited by Morris Fishbein, M.D.).
Conservatives, no matter how high their previous reputation, did
not get much of a good press. About Santayana's *Persons and
Places* (a gem) Edward Weeks wrote that it was "written with
the self-satisfaction of egotism and the cool breeze of serenity."‡
Edmund Wilson's reverse puritanism exploded against Evelyn
Waugh's romantic *Brideshead Revisited:* he called it "shameless
. . . the novel is a Catholic tract."[5]

So much for American public opinion in 1945. And that was
what it was: American *public* opinion. But, then, public opinion
is often something quite different from popular sentiment. So it
was in 1945. Twenty-five years before a gag writer for a corrupt
Vice-President would invent the phrase "silent [that is, inartic-
ulate] majority," there were all kinds of evidence that public
opinions and popular sentiments in the United States were not
necessarily the same. There were millions of Americans whose
ideas—and, perhaps more significantly, whose reactions—were
very different from, and in many ways quite opposed to, those of
the public elite. For example: we have seen that in 1945 the massive waves of pro-Soviet public opinion in America were still running at their flood tide, barely beginning to ebb here and there;
yet there is evidence suggesting that in 1945, indeed as early as

‡ "'Why do you bother with that old buzzard?' asked my friend, a
liberal, who saw that I was reading Santayana" (*The Atlantic,* May 1945).

1944, surprisingly many Americans were worried about Communism, while they felt surprisingly sympathetic toward Germany. This is the kind of low-level evidence of popular sentiment that is difficult to detect and reconstruct in a democratic society where the surfaces are dense and thick; but it does nonetheless exist, and its expressions may be found in all kinds of fragments,** suggesting that the public opinions purported by the elites of a democracy may be in disaccord with the sentiments current among large masses of people.

This potential appeal of anti-Communism was more widespread than superficial evidences would indicate. Most of the elements of the kind of thinking that equated anti-Communism

---

** Examples: in certain letters to the editors of small-town newspapers (where such letters on world affairs, because of their relative infrequency, are less likely to be ignored by the editor); more significantly, in random books by foreign observers, to wit: J. Dutheil, *The Great American Parade* (New York, 1949), passim; in the memoirs of Jan Ciechanowski, *Defeat in Victory* (New York, 1947), significant because the purpose of this author, the Polish ambassador in exile, was to illustrate undue American forbearance for Russia, not for Germany. Cf. his conversation with Justice Frankfurter, pp. 266, 285: "the sudden appearance in political circles and in some sections of public opinion of a movement of sympathy for the Germans . . ." "In some American circles, *especially outside Washington* [my italics], pro-German sympathy was growing because of increasing fear of Russia and of communism . . ." H. Montgomery Hyde, *Room 3603: The Story of the British Intelligence Center in New York during World War II* (New York, 1962), p. 203: in December 1944 sentiment in America "was beginning to favour a lenient peace with Germany . . ." A short story by Vladimir Nabokov, "Conversation Piece, 1945," is significant, too: the villain, "Dr. Shoe," is a German, with barely disguised Nazi sympathies, and he has a surprising impact on the credulous American women with whom he is talking.

with American patriotism††—a dogmatic, stultifying, and eventually disastrous kind of public thinking that became dominant after 1947, reaching its flood tide in the early fifties, with regrettable consequences—were already there in 1945. To put this in other terms: in spite of the continued influence of leftist thinking among the public opinion makers in 1945, there were millions of Americans whose sentiments rather resembled those of a radical Right, though they would not categorize themselves in that way. In 1945 it seemed that isolationism in America was dying: but perhaps this semblance was wrong. Its principal ingredient, American nationalism, was as strong as ever: indeed, it was getting a new lease on life.

This requires a little explanation. In 1932 even Franklin Roosevelt ran on an isolationist platform. By the time he departed from it, in the late thirties, he had lost many of the convinced isolationists who had once voted for him; and he remained acutely conscious of the extent of American isolationist sentiment throughout his presidency. Contrary to the accustomed belief, the Second World War against Germany had not been uniformly popular among the American people. Very few Americans were pro-German, let alone pro-Hitler; yet Roosevelt's principal allies, Russia and Britain, were unpopular among many. The unpopularity of the latter was largely due to cultural and national prejudices. The main ingredient in the minds of those whose thinking diverged sharply from that of the public elite

†† More precisely: the kind of public thinking that elevated ideological anti-Communism as if it were not only an ingredient but *the* principal measure of American patriotism.

was a kind of populist Anglophobia, rather than isolationism pure and simple. For isolationism, like American internationalism, was not a pure and simple, but an impure and complex phenomenon. Consistent isolationists were few. What determined isolationist or interventionist attitudes was the particular enemy or the particular ally, at a particular time. Many of the same people who in 1940 had been vocal, or sullen, opponents of American intervention on the side of Britain, in 1945 were on their way to becoming supporters of American intervention against Russia anywhere in the world. While on the one hand many of the Scandinavian-Americans in the Midwest who had been mainstays of isolationism during World War I were no longer isolationists in 1945, on the other hand one of the mainstays of the Democratic Party, the Catholic vote, was beginning to erode. While on the one hand the so-called conservative Republicans, supporters of Hoover or Taft, were declining in influence,‡‡ on the other hand a national groundswell of uneasiness about the Rooseveltian heritage began to rise soon after Roosevelt's death.* In 1945 this transformation was not yet

‡‡ Typical expressions of their attitudes were composed by editors with owlish faces and names such as Ben Hibbs, the editor of the then still popular *Saturday Evening Post,* reflecting a kind of cramped economic determinism that smelled of another era, in spite of the folksiness of the style. Titles of its editorials: "Your Uncle Sam Only Has Two Hands," etc.

* "Had Enough?" was a clever slogan, sufficient to carry the Republicans to their congressional victory in 1946, eventually leading to the Twenty-second Amendment to the Constitution (February 26, 1951), limiting future Presidents to two terms—a reaction against the Roosevelt memory. In 1945 direct attacks on the latter were expressed in public only by certain extreme (and often vulgar) commentators such as Fulton Lewis, Jr., or Upton Close. Their hatreds were strong even as their ideas

completed, but its crystallization had begun. Anglophobia was still strong, indeed in many quarters even stronger than Russophobia; but soon it would be transmuted into anti-Communism, the principal public *and* popular philosophy of an upcoming political generation, for fifteen years at least.

The most evident expression of a kind of popular sentiment which was very different from the categories propagated by public opinions, which was both radically nationalist and isolationist in a primitive way, and which was not the particular patrimony either of Irish Catholics† or of midwestern isolationists, was the behavior and the attitudes of many American soldiers in Europe. It was disturbing enough to deeply vex certain thoughtful Americans, and to appear consequently in print, here and there. In a profound and moving article C. G. Paulding ("The Returning Soldiers") said about the American GI's who talk too much:

> They talk so much the ones that talk; they never want
> to see England again or France or Italy; they do not

---

were confused, which was evident in their rhetoric. For example, Close's mixed-metaphorizing, 1 July 1945: "The nation is baffled by the cloying sweetness of honeyed idealism which more and more fails to dovetail with reality."

† Certain Protestants in 1945 thought that Catholics were natural Rightists (wherefore it behooved the former to be allies of the Left—as indeed during the Spanish Civil War, in which otherwise fundamentalist and domestically right-wing Protestant churches and organizations supported the fight against Franco). This odd American combination of Protestantism and Stalinism would vanish circa 1950; but in August 1945 the editor (Kenneth Leslie) of *The Protestant* would still write: "The Russians have a very simple and forthright way of looking at international affairs. They are in favor of those who are against Hitler's Germany. This is what Catholics can't understand."

like the French or the Italians or the Russians or the British; the ones that talk, the ones that get themselves interviewed; the ones that come back and tell you about France and all there is to say is that you get gypped in France and tell you about England and all there is to say is that they do not like England, and tell you about Italy and all there is to say is how the bootblacks sell their sisters. . . .

Those of the returning soldiers who talk too much are bringing us false generalizations about various peoples of Europe . . . and we have American soldiers hating all Europeans—except perhaps the Germans . . .‡

As Paulding wrote: the testimony of the soldiers returning from Europe was, really, "testimony concerning themselves." Plainly, the thinking and the sentiments of many American soldiers in Europe were not admirable. Plainly, American popular sentiment was not much preferable to American public opinion. It had ugly manifestations, including racism on all kinds of levels.** Let me repeat: In 1945 America was less united than it seemed. It was divided: and often the division resided in the

‡ *Commonweal*, 28 September 1945; Genêt in the *New Yorker*, 15 August 1945: "It is time to state that on the whole our Army here has decided it likes the Germans best."

** In 1945 a film produced by the War Department bore the title: "Have You Killed a Jap?" The subhead in *Time* about the Battle of Iwo Jima read: "Rodent Exterminators." In most far western states the marriage laws in 1945 still forbade marriage "between Mongolians and white girls"; in four states this prohibition included Filipinos and Malays together with other "Mongolians." From the *Congressional Record*, 24 July 1945, a letter from Senator Theodore Bilbo, of Mississippi, to a critic: "Dear 'Dago': So will you please keep your dirty proboscis out of the other 47 States, especially the dear old State of Mississippi? It is to this same mind, in the mind of the so-called common man, whose mind was (and still is) a much more complicated phenomenon than we have been told to think.

The few people who understood these divisions knew how a broad and democratic and popular sentimentalism could coexist in the minds of millions with a kind of suspicious and radical nationalism; that the strong underground resentment against Roosevelt's alliances and his philosophy of the war was not confined to conservatives or Republicans but that it was widespread among German-Americans, Irish-Americans, Slovak-Americans, Democratic voters, and that this resentment might surface again in the form of a crude and radical and populist Americanism. This was a phenomenon that liberals would continue to misinterpret and misread because of their own accustomed categories of thought†† or, what was perhaps more regrettable, out of their

State that I am directing my efforts and I have no one to account to except the people of Mississippi." Another letter, same author, same source: "Dear Congressman Marcantonio: You are a notorious political mongrel and how dare such a creature have the nerve and audacity to pass upon the ethics and the judgment of a United States Senator whose very heartbeat synchronized with the ideals and principles of the founding fathers . . . I do not believe you really know what the word 'Dago' means . . . a perfectly good English word . . . it is an old southern custom to use the word in referring to members of the darker-skinned races from southern Europe and it is generally used without any suggestion of contempt . . ." To Dr. Gilbert, a pastor in Savannah, Georgia: "I think I am safe in saying that 9 out of 10 of the members of your race that have shown any real progress and abilities are mongrels or half breeds . . ."

†† To their peril: as in the case of the rise of Senator Joseph McCarthy (the son of an Irish-American father and a German-American mother, straight from the Wisconsin populist tradition, or at least from one dominant strain of it), whom Edward R. Murrow in a famous broadcast in 1954 (!) referred to as "someone to the right of Louis XIV."

inadequate comprehension of human nature. The young Arthur Schlesinger, Jr., wrote in his best seller, *The Age of Jackson*, published in 1945: "Man is neither beast nor angel": a safe, liberal, gray, centrist view of human nature. To the contrary: as Pascal (not a Harvard favorite) wrote three hundred years before, man (including the common man) is both beast and angel —a lesson that succeeding generations of Americans were yet to learn.

One thing most Americans had in common: their belief in science and in progress. This was the cement that bonded together their otherwise disparate sentiments of willing generosity with their sometimes unwitting parochialness. As the "Washington Report" of *The Atlantic* said in May 1945: the United States "is committed to political universalism. That is to say, it wants to see the nations of this earth banded together according to one set of international rules."‡‡ (An American set, that was.) The most prominent scientists were saying that the United States should share her knowledge of the atomic bomb with the rest of the world; yet their view of human nature could be astonishingly narrow. (Vannevar Bush in July 1945: the writer in the future will be dictating into something like a computer: "All he needs to do is to take advantage of existing mechanisms and change his language." Of course.) Americans had an unques-

‡‡ In the 1970's, when all kinds of people are concerned with the fantastic extent of governmental bureaucracy, it is important to remember that in 1945 it was liberal public opinion that regarded "the State Department . . . still tied to a dead-and-gone world in which . . . the submission of its too small budget . . . is slightly humiliating" (*The Atlantic,* "Washington Report," August 1945).

tioning belief in men's mastery over things,* and yet they were
not really materialists: they taught themselves to think in terms
of materialist categories, and yet they believed that all of this
existed for the ultimate service of an idealistic humanitarianism.
The Catholic writer Michael Williams made a searching examination of this duality in an editorial article in *Commonweal*.
The aviation editor of the New York *Herald Tribune*, Gill
Robb Wilson, had written an article with the title "The American Potential for Peace on Earth." This potential was American
air power. The white five-pointed star painted on every American war plane "now flying in their thousands in all the skies and
over all the seas of this war-tortured world," was, for Wilson,
more "luminous with hope and joy and peace and good will for
man than was the star which heralded the birth of Jesus Christ
in Bethlehem." Americans "are the one nation whose men and
women have naught but peace and good will in their hearts."
Both politics and religion have "failed." The star which is
"painted on the ever-increasing swarm of planes now flashing
everywhere above the broad earth . . . American power quest-
ing for the liberty of humanity . . . is a new star in a new
world." The white star of the United States Air Force is "the
symbol of undefeated idealism to isolated millions . . . who will

* Example: a DuMont advertisement for television in April 1945:
"When Lincoln heard of a book, he walked miles to borrow it; read it
by a flickering log fire. Tomorrow's children, through the great new me-
dium of Television, will be enrolled in a world university before they
leave their cradles. They will enjoy magic carpet lessons in never-ending
variety, will have a 'widely traveled' familiarity with public men and affairs, will appreciate complex scientific projects and industrial processes
—and almost before they have laid aside their dolls and toys. Think what
this means. How splendidly equipped they will be while young and filled
with fresh imagination, with driving spirit and health to carry the torch
of civilization forward into undreamed of fields."

find God in the throb of an engine, the controls of an airplane or the operation of a radar system." It will lead to "security, which means world peace, because the United States is strong enough to determine the result of any issue which arises among nations . . ." Fortunately, "such power will be in the hands of a people which has naught but peace on earth and good will toward men in its heart." All over the world there are "millions of upturned faces which . . . look up expectant on the white star from the west." "To sustain the brotherhood of man!" The pride, Michael Williams wrote, "which this lucid and stirring writer himself feels and which he, in common with so many other apostles of Aviation,† seeks so ardently to spread among the rest of us, is the sort of pride—it seems to me—which if allowed entrance into our souls will obsess us as a nation, even perhaps utterly possess us, with the demons of vainglory and evil pride."[6]

Commonweal was, in retrospect, one of the best American magazines in 1945: it represented a kind of Catholic humanism that was very different from most of the publications of other Catholic Americans‡ as well as from the thinking of the progres-

† The apostles of aviation were among the biggest bores of the forties, a vintage decade for bores. One of them was Alexander de Seversky, the author of *Victory through Air Power,* about whom the New York *Times* reported on 3 November 1945: "Fresh from an audience with Emperor Hirohito, Major de Seversky said the Emperor believed that aviation would play a major role in cementing friendship among the nations of the world." Cited in *Politics,* March 1946.

‡ An example of their cheery vulgarity: the eight-column banner headline of the Christmas number of the *Catholic Universe Bulletin,* Cleveland's official Catholic diocesan newspaper:

IT'S A BOY IN BETHLEHEM
CONGRATULATIONS GOD—CONGRATULATIONS MARY—
CONGRATULATIONS JOSEPH

(*Time,* 31 December 1945.)

sive science enthusiasts. In their unending struggle against Catholic parochialism and isolationism its editors often tried too hard to argue in favor of liberal internationalism; they were only too willing to accept some of its illusions in 1945; but their insistence on a view of man that was more profound than almost anything else found in print in the United States does them honor. Their editorial in the 3 August 1945 issue, reaching people but a few days before the atomic bomb was cast on Hiroshima:

> In trying to save the old nationalism by a new internationalism, we are on the threshold of a house not remarkably dissimilar from one the Europeans have seen destroyed over their heads. We are about to go through what they have already gone through. Although the materialism of our magnificent machine civilization is ultra-modern, everything non-material about us, our hopes and our ideals, our dreams and our ambitions, our political thinking and feeling, is of the past. . . . Even from the point of view of modern science, the American myth with its corollary of infinite human perfectibility and limitless material progress is old-fashioned. The philosophical journalists and religious writers of western Europe whose political orientations would be considered reactionary by most American liberals and progressives are actually more advanced than the writers and journalists of America. For they have noted that the probings of science downward into the microscope and upward into the cosmological have reached a floor and a ceiling: there are limits to man's freedom, imposed not by religion but by the nature of man himself.

It was in 1945 that Bernanos said something to the effect that not to believe in original sin may have even worse consequences than not to believe in God; and that "between those who think that civilization is a victory for man in the struggle against the determinism of things . . . and those who want to make of man a thing among things, there is no possible scheme of reconciliation."

How true! And yet: America was still the place, the vast place, where resided the willingness of the heart. The rest of the world did not really understand this. They thought that the power and the success of America was the result of the American willingness of the mind. In 1945 a few lights in the blackened and half-destroyed cities of Eurasia were beginning to come alive again; but their pale flickering was nothing compared to the shining towers of America that blazed during the day and glittered during the night. Had the United States offered free immigration to the masses of Europe in 1945, many European peoples would have been decimated.** In 1945 all over Europe large numbers of undernourished men and women stood in line before certain movie theaters, ready to spend their thin money to see the wonders of America in American films. The prestige of the United States was enormous, unquestioned, accompanied only by a kind of sad solicitous envy. At night across the Atlantic the great cities of America blazed like modern cathedrals of Providence, warm with human kindness and golden optimistic light, full of a dynamic and strong people who were untouched

** A political party in Sicily in 1945 campaigned for the admission of Sicily as one of the states of the American Union.

by despair. This is how most Europeans thought: Providence, indeed, because Americans were the chosen people, because they had chosen for themselves the kind of life they were to lead. A kind and generous people, the inheritors of all that had been best in Europe: the democratic liberties, the symphony orchestras, the great paintings, the universities, the leading artists, the leading scientists of the world were in America, Americans now (soon, for the first time in history, American university professors were to come to Europe, to teach Europeans science, democracy, social wisdom). The news of the atomic bomb had surprisingly little reaction in Europe: it was, after all, so American, so typical of the awesome but expectable wonders of a new world, of a new age. The fact that the United Nations was to be set up in New York seemed only logical; for wasn't it an American idea, after all? Wasn't the American nation destined to lead the world to the future?

This was the European image of America. The American reality was less simple than that. In some ways America was still a nineteenth-century country in 1945. One of the *New Yorker*'s covers (that ironic record of the ephemeral realities of America) in the spring showed an elegant young couple in church, the wife surreptitiously looking for something in her purse under the prayer book; young marrieds of the Protestant upper classes were still Sunday churchgoers, even in New York. (Between 1926 and 1945 church membership increased 35 percent; the population increased 18 percent.) More important: there was a decency, a coziness in the towns (and in 1945, even in the suburbs) across America that was not merely the veneer but the fiber of American sentiment itself. Yellow lights, enclosed porches, fam-

ily Thanksgivings, the very forms and scenes of American sentimentality were (and still are) superior to English or German
sentimentality. In 1845 German and English sentimentality
were probably preferable to its American forms and essences; by
1945 much of the iron and Victorian-Gothic American harsh-
ness had melted away. That nostalgia for a simpler and better
past that became a national trait of mind twenty or thirty years
later, had not yet existed in 1945, when the national optimism
about a progressive future was still a universal instrument of belief. In 1945 the brittle black humor of adolescent cynicism
that was to become the stock in trade of American literature *and*
of popular entertainment, was still confined to certain quarters
of New York and to the minds of certain professional writers. In
1945 one could find moving, and decent, expressions of American sentimental generosity on all kinds of levels. On the day
after the final defeat and surrender of the Third Reich, Chancellor Hutchins of the University of Chicago arranged for a
religious service. He led the assembly in singing the German
hymn "Ein fester Burg ist unser Gott." He spoke about for-
giveness and human respect for a defeated people. American
humanists such as the old Norman Thomas spoke out against
the mass propaganda stirring up American hate: "In fact it is
the effect of this war of annihilation upon our sons who must
wage it and our own civilians who applaud it which most con-
cerns me. Cruelty is cruelty whatever its excuse and I tremble
for the effect upon Americans . . ." Less than a month after the
Japanese surrender the *New Yorker* printed a cartoon of a modest Japanese couple, who were holding a baby: "We've decided
to name him Douglas."

The American people, full of goodwill, longing to be left to themselves and yet afraid of loneliness—a split-minded condition full of perils; and a condition from which many people in the world, including this writer, would subsequently profit.

VIII. YEAR ZERO

In 1945 the Presidents of the United States often talked like prophets. Roosevelt pronounced in his State of the Union address, on 6 January: "This new year of 1945 can be the greatest year of achievement in human history." We heard Truman proclaim upon the news of the atomic bomb: "This is the greatest thing in history." A decade later Harry Truman reminisced in his *Memoirs:* "Peace and happiness for all countries were the goals toward which we would work and for which we had fought. No nation in the history of the world had taken such a position in complete victory. No nation with the military power of the United States of America had been so generous to its enemies and so helpful to its friends. Maybe the teaching of the Sermon on the Mount could be put into effect."

Did they believe what they were saying? I think they did:

For we know in part, and we prophesy in part.

I Corinthians 13:2

Yet, as Horace Walpole wrote to his son two centuries ago: "Prognostics do not always prove prophecies,—at least the wisest prophets make sure of the event first." The event—the American vision of history, of universal justice, of world government, of revolutionary progress, of unmitigated change—did not come about. And this brings us to an astonishing constatation: 1945 was followed by a period of extraordinary stagnation, in more than one way.

In 1945 there were only two superpowers left in the world: the United States and the Soviet Union, the first richer and more powerful than the second. So it is today. In 1945 the United States and the Soviet Union, for all practical purposes, divided Europe, and Germany, and the city of Berlin, and portions of the Far East between themselves. The lines of these divisions were often unnatural, corresponding to few sensible conditions of land or of population. They seemed to have been written into sand. Yet for more than thirty years they have remained the same. Europe divided, Germany divided, Berlin divided in two; the European states without real power, Britain declining, the Soviet Union governed by tyranny, the United States by an ever more centralized bureaucracy—the state of affairs in 1945, the state of affairs in 1977, no essential change during the last thirty-two years.

Thirty-two years after the end of Napoleon's wars much of the world had drastically changed. Thirty-two years after the end of the First World War the world had utterly changed: Lenin, Hitler, Mussolini, Roosevelt, and the entire Second World War had come and gone. During the thirty-two years that followed 1945 it changed not much at all. "Prognostics do not always prove prophecies." Our public thinkers keep telling us that we live in an era of unprecedented change, at a revolutionary pace that is so fast and breathtaking that the minds of most people find it difficult to cope with it. In reality the opposite is true. Most people, at least in the Western world, are bored, since there has been surprisingly little real change in their lives and in their minds, all superficial impressions notwithstanding.

In April 1945 the meeting of American and Soviet troops in Central Europe was a great event. They had come from the far ends of the world to the middle of Germany. Among the soldiers who were slapping each other on the back and taking swigs from the same bottles that day there may have been some who had come from California and from Siberia, all the way from the shores of the Pacific Ocean to the center of Europe. Their rowdy fraternization did not last. But the underlying realities remained. What some people had predicted in 1945 happened: the Anglo-American-Soviet alliance broke up soon after the last shot had been fired in Germany. The cold war that followed was neither war nor peace, and utterly unrevolutionary, at least in Europe. After the First World War revolution followed revolution, in Central, Eastern, Southern Europe. After the Second World War nothing like this happened. After the Russian army had come into a country, it installed Communists in power, usually against the wishes of the vast majority of inhabitants. Subsequently Stalin did not raise a finger to help Communists west of the iron curtain. When east of the iron curtain the Hungarians, for a few days, rose gloriously against the Soviets, Eisenhower and Dulles did not raise much either. In Asia and the Near East there have been wars of a limited character, in Korea, Indochina, between Israelis and Arabs.

No great wars, no great revolutions: the dominant reality of the last thirty years.* This postwar era of more than three decades of no great wars and no great revolutions may be now approaching its end. Fortunately this writer is a historian, not a prophet.

Nineteen forty-five was both Year Zero and Year One. Year Zero, *Jahr Null*—this is what a generation of Germans called the year 1945. Year One, Year I of the Atomic Age, this is how certain intellectuals, editorialists, scientists kept referring to that year, at least for a while. These terms eventually faded, because of the gradual weakening of memories and the passing of a generation. In retrospect Year Zero, rather than Year One of the Atomic Age, fits 1945 better.

The main event of 1945 was not the atomic bomb but the end of a united Germany, the end of the era of two world wars and of many other things besides. The twenty-fifth of April in 1945 was a Wednesday. That day Germany was broken in two. Himmler offered her surrender that day. It was the day when in the middle of Germany Americans and Russians met, clasped hands, broke out the vodka and whiskey, and to the strains of wild and awful accordion music celebrated into the night. Rather than V-E Day or V-J Day, this was the true end of the

* The other great reality was the dissolution, instead of the consolidation, of empires. The architects of this development were Wilson rather than Lenin, and Roosevelt rather than Stalin. The principal slogan behind it was national self-determination, not the class struggle. I shall not expatiate upon it here, since it was something that had begun long before 1945, and it shows all the signs of continuing for another hundred years at least.

Second World War. The formal capitulation of the German armed forces was still a few days away, Hitler was still alive in his Berlin cellar, but these things no longer made much difference. Hitler's last hope was smashed. He had hoped that the unnatural alliance between the Anglo-Saxons and the Russians, between Capitalists and Communists, would break up before the end of the war. Now their soldiers were shaking hands over the broken body of his Reich.

April 1945 marked more than the end of the Second World War in Europe. It was the month during which Franklin Roosevelt and Adolf Hitler died. It was the end of a twelve-year era in the history of the United States and in the history of Germany. It was also the end of a chapter in the history of the world that had lasted for seventy-five years. The era of German domination had begun seventy-five years before 1945, with the German triumph over France and with the union of the Germanys into one Reich. After 1870 Germany became the most important nation in Europe, in some ways of the world. Unlike most other European nations, she had not been united before 1871. She was not to be united after 1945—surely a monumental milestone in the history of Europe and of the world.

In 1945 most people believed that the demarcation lines running across Germany were temporary, that the division of Germany into military and occupational zones was unnatural, it would not last. They were wrong.

What would happen to Germany after the war? She would be devastated, and she must be wholly defeated: on this all of the Allies agreed. What happened after the First World War must not be repeated. This time *all* of Germany must be occupied, at least for some time. The British and the American and the Russian governments began to make provisions for this during the war. They were unwilling to enter into much planning beyond this condition. Beyond it, Churchill wanted to see the political geography of Central Europe remade along more or less traditional lines: the drastic reduction of Prussia; a southern, peaceful, "cow-like" German state separate from the North, a Catholic confederation with Vienna at its capital center, including perhaps Hungary: a reconstituted important element in a new European balance of power. Stalin seemed to agree with this, at least for a while;† he had no objection when, at the Teheran Conference, the Allies pronounced their intention to re-create an independent Austria after the war. Roosevelt talked vaguely about the necessary dismemberment of Germany; the State Department seems to have been in favor of a disarmed and democratized but essentially unitary German state. The French wanted to break off a goodly portion of southwestern Germany for the purposes of their own aggrandizement and security: their age-old ambition, at that. None of this was to matter much in the long run.

What mattered were the arrangements for the occupation zones. Like France and Paris after the final defeat of Napoleon, Germany and Berlin were to be occupied after the final defeat of Hitler, to be administered entirely by the victorious Allies. For

---

† In 1944 he began to oppose such plans. He wanted to be sure that Hungary would be no part of such a construction. He saw his opportunities, and his appetite had begun to increase.

this purpose demarcation zones had to be defined. They were drawn in during protracted negotiations between second-rank American, Russian, and British delegates. What is interesting in the record of these secret negotiations is that they are not very interesting at all. There was relatively little disagreement and difficulty in arriving at mutually acceptable lines. They were, except for certain minor details, limned out and agreed upon a long time before the war ended. The final protocols were not signed until late in 1944, and even in 1945 there were a few emendations here and there, but the essential lines of the zoning of Germany had emerged and had been accepted by all sides as early as January 1944, perhaps even earlier. The most detailed and painstaking research into the confidential development of these negotiations reveals little that is worth revealing. The British military were the first who addressed themselves to this task. The first "blue pencil lines were . . . faintly sketched in" as early as April 1943.[1] Their purpose was to avoid trouble later, and to make sure that the British and the Americans would have some legal ground to assert their presence in Germany in the then not unlikely event that the Russian armies overran the Germans and met their Western allies somewhere along the Rhine at the end of the war. Stalin, who was less confident of such a prospect, readily agreed. Often it was the Americans, rather than the Russians, who held up the final signing of the zoning agreement. Roosevelt, on the way to Teheran, in November 1943 drew a line on a sketch map that came to a peak at Berlin, including it in the American zone—the kind of straight and abstract line so dear to American politicians and surveyors ever since Jefferson or Mason and Dixon. Later he relented and said

that he had not meant that line very seriously. He was more ada-
mant in arguing against an American occupation zone in the
South of Germany, instead of one in the North; he was also
against giving the French a zone. In the end much of the original British plan remained. It allotted about 54 percent of the
prewar Reich to the Western Allies, 46 percent to the Russians.
A much larger proportion of the German population, and of
German industry, was in the Western zones. It was not altogether unreasonable (considering that its main lines had been
agreed upon before the Anglo-Americans set foot in Western
Europe); it was not wholly unhistorical (the lines, in most cases,
conformed to certain provincial boundaries in Germany); but it
was not very foresighted either. As I said before, Stalin did not
object to it—because as late as 1944 he was not yet sure of how
much he could get away with in Europe.

In any event, it was not Stalin's resolution, it was the general
irresolution—Roosevelt's, Churchill's, and to some extent even
Stalin's—that eventually led to the division of Germany. The
demarcation lines were, as we have seen, mainly the result of
British initiative; there *was* some speculation among the British
and the Americans about what these demarcation lines would
lead to, but not much. In early 1945, however, this would
change. A nervous sense of urgency was rising on all sides, as
the end of the war drew near. Each side was now worried that
the other might get to Berlin, or beyond the occupation zones
previously agreed upon. In this respect the fatal difference between British and American purposes was perhaps even more
decisive than the fatal chasm opening up between the Soviets
and the West, something that was almost certain to happen after

the disappearance of Hitler anyhow. Churchill wanted to race ahead and occupy as much of Germany as was possible, including Berlin, meeting the Russians well to the east of the demarcation lines;‡ Roosevelt and Eisenhower and Truman did not. After the German surrender the British wanted to employ the presence of the American and British armies within the Russian zone as a trump card, in exchange for certain Soviet concessions; the Americans did not.** Still there was a trade-off, of sorts: the Russians allowed the entry of American, British, and French occupation troops into their respective zones in Berlin and Vienna

‡ We have seen, in Chapter II, that this was made possible through the partial acquiescence of the Germans themselves; their military resistance melted away faster before the advancing Americans and British than before the Russians.

** There was a subtle change in the attitudes of Washington; but it came too late. At the end of May, Halifax reported from Washington that the Americans "were determined to abide by German agreements and implement them on Soviets' request whatever the behavior of the Soviet government. They were unprepared . . . to use the tactical advantages of their occupation of the Soviet Zone 'to manoeuvre against the Soviet Union' . . . Responsible officials in Washington saw the position of American forces 'not as a bargaining counter in negotiations with the Russians but as a potential cause of a head-on collision with them.'" 4103, 4128/20/70, cited in Tony Sharp, *The Wartime Alliance and the Zonal Division of Germany* (Oxford, 1975), p. 153. Ten days later Halifax, having talked with certain Washington officials, noted that the latter were beginning to recognize the "'valuable leverage' of the occupation of the Soviet zone and assured him that the American government 'would weigh our representations with the greatest care.' But Truman was hearing more weighty recommendations from elsewhere." U 4488, 4519/20/70, ibid., p. 158. About "elsewhere," see above, Chapter VI, "Truman and His Circle." Another six weeks later Halifax reported that the Americans were more willing to stand up against the Soviets; see above, p. 150.

as the American and British forces withdrew from the Soviet zone during the first days of July.††

The final zonal protocol, including Berlin, was signed on 26 July 1945, while the conference at Potsdam was in session. There were few people, even at that time, who foresaw what was about to happen—or, rather, what was not about to happen. What everyone thought of as a temporary arrangement became a permanent condition. Germany would remain divided. The former Allies could not agree on the conditions of a united Germany because they did not really want to. There would be no central German government, not even a German administration covering the city of Berlin. That much was becoming evident a year or so later. Less than three years later two German governments had come into being, a western and an eastern one, the former largely democratic, the latter determinedly Communist. For a while the Russians were impressed with the success of West Germany, and they were worried about the prospects of

†† There was another issue, a momentous one. The 46 percent of prewar Germany allotted to the Russian occupation zone included (a) the slice of East Prussia, with the city of Königsberg, that was to be incorporated into the Soviet Union, and (b) the large portion of East Prussia and of eastern Germany up to the Oder and western Neisse rivers that were given to Poland. The idea of compensating Poland for the loss of her eastern portion to the Soviet Union with territories taken from the eastern portion of Germany was, again, British in origin; but by 1945 Churchill realized not only that the Poles were receiving too much (in Potsdam he argued, in vain, against accepting the western Neisse line *de facto*) but that this very large territory taken from Germany would make any Polish government fatally dependent on Russia, at least in the foreseeable future. He did not have his way. The Western Allies acquiesced in the Oder-Neisse line for all practical purposes, at first *de facto,* and twenty-five years later *de jure.*

their old bugaboo, an American-German alliance. West Germany, with a population more than three times that of East Germany, was strong and prosperous, East Germany was not. The West Germans, with every reason, would speak contemptuously of the East German state as "the Soviet Zone"; they would also refer to it as "Middle Germany," in order to distinguish it from the territories further to the east, acquired by Poland, that comprised "Eastern Germany" for them. This may have been geographically correct, but politically it led nowhere. At times the Russians pondered the advisability of leaving East Germany if the Americans would move out of West Germany in turn, but they were not very serious about it. During the fifties the Americans would make occasional statements in favor of a united and democratic Germany, but they were not very serious either. The Russians and their East German satraps were more worried about the magnetic presence of West Berlin in the middle of Communist territory; after much talking and threatening they solved this problem by running up a wall across Berlin in 1961, whereupon the division of Germany was completed. Another ten years passed: and this division was not merely accomplished *de facto*, it was recognized as more or less permanent, not only by Americans, Russians, British, French, and Poles, but by the Germans themselves.

In 1945, Year Zero, there were still millions of Germans who could remember the time of Bismarck; many of them were born before 1871, when Germany had not yet been united. Thirty-two years after 1945 only one out of every two Germans could remember the time of Hitler; most of them had grown up in West or

East Germany, at a time when a united Germany existed no longer.

The history of the German people was, however, a matter different from the unity of the German state. In that sense Year Zero marked a momentous lurch forward. During the last winter of the war a mass exodus of Germans from Eastern Europe began. By the end of Year Zero most of it was completed. The result was a situation without precedent. For the first time in eight hundred, perhaps one thousand years, there were hardly any Germans left east of the Germanys. Before Year Zero, the German minorities amidst half a dozen Eastern European nations constituted a problematic and often formidable presence, since they could be influential well beyond their numbers. Now they were being herded together in the occupied zones of a devastated Germany. Many people, including this writer, believed that this crowding of millions of dispossessed and expelled Germans into an already overcrowded and destroyed country would surely lead to the gravest economic catastrophes and political explosions. They were wrong. The very opposite happened. Instead of a burden, these refugees became an asset to the West German economy; because of their *embourgeoisement* in that prosperous state, their original political resentments melted away. The result of the war and of Year Zero was that the German people became more homogeneous than ever before during their long history—an event which, in the long run, may have been the most important outcome of the Second World War, in Europe at least.

For seventy years before 1945 Germany, with few inter-
ruptions, was the leading power in Europe. Her leadership was
not only military or political; she was a leader economically, culturally, educationally, intellectually, in more places than people
cared to admit. For one thing, the principal movement of the
twentieth century, the conjunction of nationalism and socialism,
was of German origin. Nineteen forty-five, then, marked the
end, not only of the domination of German power but also of
that of the German spirit and, perhaps, of the German mind.‡‡

In 1945 the defeat of Germany meant more than the defeat
of Hitler. It marked the end of two world wars, indeed of
a period of great wars. One hundred years before 1945 most
thinkers and prophets, including Marx, foresaw an era of great
revolutions. What followed after 1848 was an era of wars, not
revolutions. The Germans, at any rate, were better at the former
than at the latter. It took the other powers two world wars to
beat them down. The other European powers, including Great
Britain, could not do it without the Americans in the First
World War, nor without the Americans and the Russians during the Second. There are many reasons to believe that twenty

‡‡ Perhaps: because even while Nazism—that most extreme and Ger-
manic version of the combinations of nationalism and socialism—disappeared with Hitler, various other manifestations and forms of this
combination lived on, with socialist nationalism or nationalist socialism
remaining the principal political reality during the twentieth century
throughout the world. (One example: during the same year that Hitler
died Perón came to power in Argentina. With all of its cheapness and
vulgarity, "Perónism," too, was a combination of a grandiloquent nationalism and socialism, with potent appeal to the masses.)

years after the First World War the Germans would have been on their way to becoming again the greatest power in Europe, even without Hitler. Their rise would have been slower, more difficult, less dynamic. They would have risen nonetheless. That frightening phenomenon, Hitler, was an exception during the history of the twentieth century: one of the few men who really accelerated the movement of events. Surely he was very different from what the Kaiser had been. Still the thirty years from 1914 to 1945 belong together in the history of the world. The entire physiognomy of the twentieth century was formed by the two world wars. They were the principal events of this century, far more important than the Russian Revolution or the atomic bomb or the end of the colonial empires, all of which were the consequences of the two wars, and not the other way around.

Year Zero was the end of many things, among them that of the European state system. For at least three hundred years the destiny of Europe depended principally on the continuous relationship of its states, on the balance of power within that seamed web. In 1945 the fate of Europe depended largely on the United States and on the Soviet Union, all of the subsequent efforts of a few men such as De Gaulle notwithstanding. Already during the First World War (which had begun as an all-European war) the two most important events involved America and Russia in 1917, when the first had chosen to enter the war, and the second to withdraw from it. This withdrawal of Russia from Europe, together with the subsequent defeat of the Germans, resulted in an unprecedented condition: the existence of more than a dozen independent national states in Eastern Europe, between Germany and Russia, new elements in the European state system. Once Germany and Russia began rising again, their independence crumbled away. This happened even before the Second World War, at the end of which it was evident that not only the independence of Eastern Europe but the independence of the entire European state system was no longer a reality: the real centers of power were in Washington and in Moscow. This was the end of the European Age, which was also the so-called Modern Age, in the history of the white race at least—probably the richest and the most expansive period in the history of mankind.

The Modern Age and the European state system had crystallized together largely during the seventeenth century. The establishment of the latter was confirmed by some of the arrangements set up by the Congress of Westphalia in 1648. Its characteristic principle, without which the arrangements made in Westphalia would have been inconceivable, was that of the sovereignty of the state, covering everything, including religion. In 1555 the princes of the Germanys, their domains having been racked by religious civil wars, hesitantly subscribed to this principle: each ruler determined the ruling religion of his state, *cuius regio eius religio*.* In 1945, nearly four hundred years later, this principle returned to Europe with a vengeance. The ruler determined the political religion of his domains. In the

* It contributed to the protracted disunity of the Germans. Thus their most powerful prophets of national unity, Luther and Hitler, achieved the very opposite of what they had intended: the division of the Germanys was the end result of their lifework.

countries that the Russian armies occupied, the ruling order was to be Communism, preferably of the Muscovite rite. In the countries that the Americans and the British had occupied or liberated, the ruling order was parliamentary democracy, preferably of the American rite. *Cuius regio eius religio.* This was exactly what Stalin wanted. His predecessor Ivan the Terrible, a contemporary of the Treaty of Augsburg, would have understood, as indeed would another contemporary, Elizabeth of England. *Their* main concern, too, was that of absolute sovereignty over their domains, of which the state religions of Russian Orthodoxy and of English Protestantism were but the instruments, not the other way around.

In the year Elizabeth became Queen, less than three years after the Treaty of Augsburg, a long chapter in the history of England had come to an end. During the last months of the reign of her predecessor, Mary Tudor, the English had lost the city of Calais,† their last possession on the Continent. This loss of the last English royal lands in France turned out to be a blessing in disguise. It helped to direct the energies of the island people westward, away from Europe, across the oceans. This happened at a time when seaborne movement had become faster than movement on land. Sea power was becoming even more profitable than land power, and the monopoly of trade even more than the possession of gold. The result was the piecemeal establishment of the British Empire, emulated by many people

† It is interesting to note that in December 1941 Stalin suggested to the visiting Anthony Eden that the English should reward themselves and augment their security by acquiring Calais and Boulogne after the war.

and admired by others, including Adolf Hitler, who wanted to rule most of Europe while the British Empire could maintain its rule over much of the world. The greatest figure in modern English history, Winston Churchill, would have none of this. He was right. During the Second World War Churchill also proclaimed that he had not become Prime Minister in order to preside over the liquidation of the British Empire. He was wrong. By 1945, for all practical purposes, the United States was inheriting the British Empire, and much else besides.

In 1945 it seemed that the world would be ruled for the foreseeable future by the three victorious Great Powers: the United States, Britain, and the Soviet Union. This was one of the few basic assumptions that Stalin and Roosevelt and Churchill shared, even at Yalta. Because of the imprecise wording and because of the fudging of certain issues at Yalta they were soon pretending to disagree about what exactly the division of Europe and of some other portions of the world among them was to mean. Yet Stalin, for one, never doubted that the Great Powers were to rule most of the world, indeed, that they would extend their domains so far as this was practicable. He, too, had a considerable respect for the British Empire. During the remaining seven years of his life Stalin was amazed to see how rapidly that empire was dissolving. He thought that the Americans were devilishly clever in picking up the remnants of their ally's empire; indeed, on one occasion Stalin even permitted himself to speculate aloud whether at a certain point the British would not revolt against the encroaching American domination, an event which would then find the Soviet Union in an advantageous position. He was wrong.

In some ways 1945 was reminiscent of 1815, as the end of the
Second World War resembled in some ways the end of the
Napoleonic Wars. In 1945 as well as in 1815 a great maritime
power turned out to be the principal architect of victory. In
1945 as well as in 1815 this great maritime power provided a balance against the land power of the Russians stretching across two
continents, even though it could or would do little to force the
triumphant Russians to disgorge what they had gobbled up. In
1945 as well as in 1815 the great maritime power was the richest
country in the world, with entire governments depending on its
financial assistance. In 1815 the great maritime power was England; in 1945 it was the United States. The years 1815 in
England and 1945 in the United States were followed by a domestic conservative reaction. Eventually the English would
make their most famous general, Wellington, Prime Minister,
and the Americans would make their most famous general, Eisenhower, President.

There, however, the parallel ends. The Pax Britannica of the
nineteenth century was one thing: the Pax Americana of the
twentieth century quite another. The latter spread wider than
the former: it has also been more popular with the peoples of
the world, no matter what they have been pretending to think.
The British empire grew up without much of a plan and without an ideology. The American empire grew up without much
of a plan but with an ideology. To make the world safe for
democracy: let me repeat, for the last time, that this Wilsonian
slogan is, after all, not very different from the belief that what is
good for America is good for the world. For a half-century, from
Wilson to Nixon, the evolution of the world consisted largely of

its Americanization. This had not much to do with the power of Wall Street or of the Pentagon. Long before 1945 there were millions of people in dozens of countries who knew the names of American film stars while they knew not the name of their own prime minister. Neither the allies nor the opponents of the United States were impervious to this kind of Americanization. Hitler and Goebbels were admirers of American films, of American football rallies, of American picture magazines; one of their few enduring achievements was the building of superhighways. Of all foreign peoples Americans were most popular with the peoples of the Soviet Union in 1945, indeed throughout the twentieth century. In this respect 1945 was neither Year Zero nor Year One, only another milestone along this pan-American evolution that has been transforming much of the world.

But evolution is one thing; history is another. The first is largely predictable; the second is hardly predictable at all. There is no place for humor in evolution. History, on the other hand, is full of irony. The greatest hope of well-meaning Americans at Year Zero, the United Nations, turned out to be the greatest failure and the greatest bore. Of all empires in the world the Soviet Union turned out to possess the greatest degree of stability until now. No capital city, except for Warsaw, had been destroyed in 1945 like Tokyo; eventually Tokyo became the largest city in the world. One of the key obstacles that had led to the collapse of American negotiations with the Japanese before Pearl Harbor was the Japanese presence in Indochina. Less than a generation later the American people would have been only too glad to finance the Japanese to replace their sons and husbands in Indochina. The favorite honeymoon place for masses of Japanese newlyweds in the 1970's has been Hawaii, including a tour of Pearl Harbor.

There were, and there still are, many more such examples of ironical twists of history. They are not merely the results of unpredictability. They were the consequences—largely unforeseen at the time, more and more recognizable in retrospect—of certain ideas and events, of the thoughts and the acts of men in 1945. Roosevelt, Stalin, Truman, Churchill: their decisions in 1945 made the world in which we still live now.

This includes Asia. There the defeat of Japan in 1945 was almost as great a milestone as the defeat of Germany in Europe—almost, but not quite. In many ways the rise of the modern Japanese empire and the rise of the modern German empire had been astonishingly similar. But Germany was a greater power than Japan, and a greater threat to the rest of the world. The secret decision of the American government and military, taken months before Pearl Harbor, to the effect that defeating Germany must take precedence over defeating Japan, was the right one. In 1945 Germany's defeat meant Japan's defeat, too, even though these two allies had been living and fighting apart. Another sensible American decision was to maintain the monarchy in Japan. Had Wilson chosen to keep the monarchy in Germany in 1918, possibly by way of the Kaiser's constitutional abdication in favor of the Crown Prince, there would have been no Second World War, surely not in 1939, and Adolf Hitler might be still living today, say, a retired draftsman somewhere in Bavaria.

In a typically American fashion, the Second World War ended with a bang and a prayer. The bang was the atomic bomb; the prayer was that American ideas would prevail in the world. The latter was a more promising prospect than the putting of the Sermon of the Mount into effect. The dropping of the bomb was of course a monstrous event. Oddly enough, the Japanese did not particularly resent the Americans for it (or indeed for anything). Americans feared that on landing in Japan they would be confronted by a grim and hostile people, reduced to daggers. Instead, the Japanese, deeply impressed with American power, smiled and bowed. Years later Japanese were perplexed, rather than impressed, with the American and European breast-beating over the atomic bomb. *Hiroshima Mon Amour* was a French film, not a Japanese one.

The American occupation of Japan was a success, in more than one way. General MacArthur's image fitted the psychic vacuum perfectly: a square peg in a square hole. Americans, as Truman rightly said, are not ungenerous to their former enemies. In the Far East, as also in Europe, many of the wartime enemies of the United States fared better than some of her allies. This proved to be all right in the case of Germany, for, unlike after the First World War, after the Second World War the Germans were not able to play one of the victors against the other. Many people in 1945 believed and feared that Germany would rise again. No one believed that Japan would again become a great power. She was physically devastated, deprived of her outer possessions, with nearly one hundred million people crammed together on four small islands. What followed went not only against the political projections of 1945; it went against the projections of the demographers and the population experts, without the slightest effect on their reputations of course. Fif-

teen years after the war Japan was the most powerful Far Eastern nation—which is where the United States had come in.
What the Japanese (and also many other people) learned after
the Second World War was that mass prosperity was preferable
to national self-assertion, indeed that it was a form of national
self-assertion—the political philosophy that had made the
United States an economic and a political giant among the peoples of the world. Less than twenty years after the war a thus
Americanized Japan became an economic giant while remaining
a political pygmy. By and large so she is today. Will this satisfy
the spirit of her people for long? We may doubt it; but, then, we
do not know.

In 1945 the dissolution of China that had begun one hundred
years before was nearing its end. The Japanese cleared out of
China; within a few years the Americans and the Russians also
left. In 1945 China had two chieftains, Chiang and Mao;
within a few years she had but one, the latter, who proclaimed
China a united and Communist state. Perhaps that, too, makes
less difference than one may think. In 1945 Roosevelt proposed
that China was a Great Power, and that this was good for the
United States; thirty years later Richard Nixon proposed the
same thing. The demise of both Presidents would presently follow. Neither Stalin nor Churchill believed that China was a
Great Power; they were right. Despite her enormous mass of
land and of people, China has remained far less prosperous than
Japan;‡ her influence in the lands bordering her—Korea, In-

‡ In this respect Communism in China after the Second World War
may have been a blessing in disguise for the rest of the world, just as

dochina, Mongolia, India—has remained less than that of other, faraway powers, notably Russia; all in all, a situation not wholly different from that of the old Chinese Empire, centuries ago. In 1945 both Chiang and Mao were worried by the Russians—or, rather, they tried to make use of them for their own political purposes, with varying degrees of success. In turn, the Russians could not make use of the Chinese much, if at all. Stalin saw this coming. None of this was very new. In 1945 most people thought that there were but two great political forces left in the world: Communism and Capitalism, the first embodied by the Soviet Union, the second by the United States. Instead the principal political force in the world after 1945 turned out to be what it was before: nationalism, with ever newer variants.**

Communism in Russia after the First World War had been. Had Lenin not come to power in Russia, the latter would have been one of the victors of the First World War; as things turned out, she was compelled to return into isolation, and gave up all influence over Eastern Europe for twenty years. Had Mao not come to power in China, the latter might have become the largest industrial power in the Far East, to the immediate detriment of Japan, and to the eventual detriment of the United States —a speculation that is sustained by the very example of Taiwan, industrious and prosperous beyond belief.

** It is an odd paradox that Churchill, who had to witness, though he had refused to foresee, the dissolution of the British Empire, foresaw the eventual dissolution of the Soviet Empire. In a very private remark to De Gaulle before the end of the war he said that the Russians would not be able to digest their conquests. He was entirely right. Half a dozen countries (Yugoslavia, Finland, Manchuria, eastern Austria, northwestern Iran, North Korea) that in 1945 lay under the Russian thumb eventually escaped Russian rule, even though some of them continue to live under the shadow of aforesaid digit. Other nations, such as Hungary, Poland, Rumania, though their governments are officially Communist, have been evolving ways of life that are quite different from the monotonous primitiveness of the Soviet Union. The fact that their governments are (or,

It was a hot night in Washington when President Truman announced the surrender of Japan. There remains, of that night, the kaleidoscopic picture of a great democracy celebrating yet another of its great triumphs—the enormous crowd in Times Square; the pretty girls in the backs of convertibles, careening around the streets of small towns—a picture which by now is a period piece, from the first and confident half of the twentieth century, an American period piece, from the American Century. There was nothing like that in Europe, where, after the end of the war against Germany, the end of the war against Japan was an anticlimax. There was a brief disorderly outburst of popular joy in the ruined squares and parks of London, not much in Paris or even in Moscow, among peoples for whom the Second World War was mainly a European war, from beginning to end. But in America, too, many people who remembered the end of the First World War (in 1945 they were still the majority of the population) felt, and on occasion said, that, compared with V-J Day, Armistice Day in November 1918 had been more exuberant, more joyful.

In the wake of the two atomic bombs came a wave of mental shock. The public thinkers spoke up. From now on there were only two alternatives, they said: the United Nations or the Third World War, world government or the end of the world. They were wrong. In 1945 the dropping of the two atomic

---

rather, that they call themselves) Communist makes less and less difference in the long run, while within the Soviet Union itself the Georgian, the Ukrainian, the Armenian, the Uzbekh, and other peoples, including their Communists, are beginning to show signs of appetite for some kind of independence.

bombs on two cities in Japan was a great and monstrous event. Yet its consequences were overrated, both in the short and in the long run. In the short run, as we have seen, the atomic bomb was not the cause of Japan's surrender, since the Japanese government had been willing to negotiate some kind of an honorable capitulation months before the event of Hiroshima. In the long run the existence of atomic weapons changed the consequent world order (or disorder) surprisingly little. The possession of atomic and hydrogen bombs made the great states of the world less powerful, not more. For the first four years of the so-called Atomic Age the United States had a monopoly of the atomic bomb. This did not change the course of events a whit, since the United States had not the slightest inclination to use the atomic bomb in order to rectify the division of Europe or to rescue China from Communism. Fifteen years after 1945 the United States had enough atomic and hydrogen bombs to blow up most of the world; yet its government felt compelled to tolerate the establishment of a self-styled Communist dictatorship in Cuba, of all places. Ten years after 1945 Britain, fifteen years after 1945 France had their atomic and hydrogen bombs. The decline of their power was even more precipitous than before. Of course we do not know what might happen if Levantine terrorists or petty tyrants get hold of atomic bombs. But in this book we deal not with the future but with the past, which, indeed, is the only thing about which we know something. What we know—or, rather, what we ought to know—is that the atomic bomb, as Bernanos put it instantly in 1945, was "a triumph of technique over reason." And when technique triumphs over reason, human progress slows down instead of accelerating, and the result is a long and protracted kind of stagnation.

In 1945 the Prime Minister of Great Britain was a man born and brought up under the reign of Queen Victoria. In 1945, as we have seen, there were still millions of Germans who had been born and brought up during the age of Bismarck; there were at least one million Frenchmen who had been born under the reign of Napoleon III, and at least three million Americans, including President Truman's mother, who had been born when Lincoln was still alive. At the time of this writing less than half of the people in the world were born before the Second World War. This generation gap—or, more exactly, this memory gap—ought not to mislead us. No matter when or where they were born, people still live in a world that was fashioned by the decisions that had been made in 1945. This kind of relative stagnation, obscured as it is by the frenzies of publicity, has been rare in modern history. It has had certain positive consequences. The memory of Hitler and of the Second World War had a monumental influence. Few people, except perhaps for successful journalists or writers such as Hemingway, had pleasant memories of the Second World War. The greatest deterrent of war has always been that of the memory of war in the minds of a generation. This explains the prosperity, the pacific temper, and the rejection of political extremism by entire generations, especially in Western Europe, including Germany, who after 1945 set themselves to restore the prosperity of their countries and the comforts of their private lives. It even explains the relatively peaceful evolution of an ardent people such as the Spanish, among whom the memory of their 1936–39 civil war has been the most decisive obstacle against radical revolutionary experiments.

For about twenty years after 1945 much of the world was still governed by these generations. Then there came a change. Their sons and daughters and their nephews and nieces found this kind of material prosperity boring. For a while it seemed that the relative stagnation that prevailed since 1945 was coming to an end. This impression, too, was misleading. These new generations were playing at revolution, not making it. Eventually they grew tired of this kind of game. By the 1970's the revolutionary temper subsided, because it was not genuine. All superficial manifestations to the contrary notwithstanding, the so-called revolutionary ideas and the radical practices of the new generations were not that different from those that had been current in Year Zero. In the United States, for example, the notion that the children of the 1960's or 1970's—many of them the grandchildren of a generation of flappers—were revolting against a parental generation of strict, narrow, and Victorian or authoritarian manners and standards is not even worthy of the name of legend: it is a tale profitably told by public idiots, signifying nothing.

After 1945 intellectual progress ground to a standstill, all of its publicitarian frenzies notwithstanding. In 1945 the predominant intellectual categories in the West were Darwinism, Marxism, Freudianism; so they are at this time of writing. By comparison with any other thirty-year span during the last two hundred years, there has been little significant progress in medicine, infant mortality, the life span, or in art or architecture, at that. The glass slab of the United Nations could have been built in 1974 as well as in 1947, it matters not when. More and more it looks as if the twenties had been the only really modern period in this century, the only truly revolutionary decade in arts, manners, fashion, music. The world in 1925 was very different from the world in 1895, it *looked* entirely different, and this included the ways in which most people dressed, undressed, danced, moved, listened, read, thought. Compared with these changes in manners and modes of art after the First World War, the highly publicized changes after the Second World War amounted to little or nothing.††

One of the reasons for the political stagnation after 1945 may have been the atomic bomb, which, instead of inaugurating a new age, rigidified the already existing division of the world. But it was not the only reason. The democratic phenomenon of inflation was pervasive. Beyond and beneath the inflation of money and of materials there exists an inflation of communication and of words: in sum, more and more of everything, meaning less and less. As Tocqueville wrote, contrary to the acknowledged fears and accepted opinions of his day, in the democratic age great changes in accepted ideas will be rare, because of the slowness of the movement of minds at a time when intellectual life becomes more and more dependent on standardized

†† In the United States the new novelist who came out of the Second World War was Norman Mailer, the newest social thinker was B. F. Skinner, the newest thing (and best seller) was the sex research published by Dr. Kinsey. Thirty years later Mailer was still the principal literary figure, Skinner the principal behaviorist, and sex researchers went on being best sellers.

and massive practices of publicity. Instead of radical change, therefore, protracted continuity, the continuation of whatever seems to be going on, with the publicity given to the interpretation of events affecting the very structure and the nature of the events themselves—in sum, an intellectual degradation of the democratic process. In 1945, too, the triumph of the United States and of the Soviet Union revived the intellectual prestige of materialist public philosophies. In this respect 1945 was not the beginning of a new world: even though the new era was represented mainly by young peoples, it led to the last phase of the old one. The result of all of this was obvious: the movements of intellectual life, the public philosophies, the fashionable forms of art, the practices of public education, the publication as well as the very conception of books, the interpretation not only of recent but of past events became more and more predictable—a condition that the incessant agitation of the surface would obscure, though not for long.

Yet history, which means the history of the human mind, still remains unpredictable. For example, something happened in 1945, in a most unlikely place: in the pine forests of East Prussia, forsaken by God, surrounded by the debris of war, under the cap of a Soviet captain, into the gray fur of which the metallic red star was deeply impressed. Something had crystallized in his head. A cold and crystalline thought which, through the mysterious alchemy of the human mind, was produced by the passionate heat of intensity. It eventually led this man far, far enough to reject the entire mental system of the world in which he was born and in which he lived, to the point where the very rulers of that enormous empire began to worry about him and to fear him, while to millions of other people he became that new thing, a Light from the East. Truly a single event in a single mind may change the world. It may even bring about—and not merely hasten—the collapse of the Communist system, which is inevitable, though only in the long run. If so, the most important event in 1945 may not have been the division of Europe, and not the dawn of the Atomic Age, but the sudden opening and the sudden dawning of something in the mind of a ragged Soviet officer, Alexander Solzhenitsyn, in the East Prussian marshes and woods, an event compared to which the two flashes of the two atomic bombs were but ephemeral feats of technology.

The great, the profound Bernanos wrote, also in 1945: "What if life really were the free thought of this world, this world which appears to be controlled and determined? Life, that is to say that mysterious and immaterial energy to which modern physics reduces matter itself." In the United States, too, there were isolated thinkers who saw far ahead. There was, for example, the lonely and misanthropic Robinson Jeffers, probably a greater seer even than poet, who wrote to a friend during the war: "Hitler and Germany may be smashed of course, after years; but I wonder whether anyone realizes what the state of Europe and the world will be by that time? Even if those 'four freedoms' were to be honestly established at a peace conference, nobody but the United States could enforce them; and we shall never be Roman or German enough to police the world for a long time. And if we did—could this be called freedom?" "One thing seems even more clear . . . that it is up to each person to keep his own integrity . . . It is going to be a very difficult job."‡‡

‡‡ *The Selected Letters of Robinson Jeffers,* Ann N. Ridgeway, ed. (Baltimore, 1968), p. 226, note 29.

"As to a stable world-civilization in the future," Jeffers wrote near the end of the war, "I don't believe in it—any more than in a world-state. People don't unite effectively except against enemies. They may live together in a heap, amorphous and passive, as China used to do; but if there is the energy to organize there is the energy to divide . . . But there is that famous law of diminishing returns, and it seems to me that a few years from now, when Anglo-America and Russia will stand looking at each other, we shall have become about as 'global' as Providence will permit. The images will split and fall apart, the kaleidoscope will turn and make new patterns . . ." Ibid., pp. 295–96.

PART II

RECALLING ZERO

A global milestone — Auto-history — Zero Minute — The flood — The continuity of life — Expecting the Russians — Wishful thinking — Varieties of memory — The wave of the future — Débrouilleurs and opportunists — Intellectuals — Americans — The British — Russians — Communists — A conversation — Expectations and disappointments — Fleeing to the West

Nineteen forty-five was a global milestone, perhaps for the first time in the modern history of the world. Hundreds of millions knew and felt this, on at least four continents, including peoples to whom 1914 or 1917 or even 1939 had meant little or nothing. Still 1945 meant different things to different people. For peoples of the Western Hemisphere, for most of the peoples of Western Europe, for some people even in Japan, it meant the end of the war and the reappearance of certain things and institutions and conditions of life to which they had been accustomed once, or to which they were to be accustomed anew: in sum, a revolutionary year but also one of restoration, a year when continuity would appear again. For other peoples, especially the defeated nations of Central and Eastern Europe, 1945 marked a change so profound and drastic that the Germans would invent the term of *Jahr Null*, Year Zero, as if that year had been the dead center, the dead end of almost all of the continuities that they had known. So it was for my native country Hungary, where I was living then, a turning point even more than a milestone; and while the witnesses of great events, of historical milestones, are observers at best, anyone who passes through a turning point is not merely an onlooker but a personal participant, whence the auto-history that follows.

Auto-history. I am now compelled—compelled, rather than eager—to write about myself. I have written different books but I learned one thing from the beginning. For all kinds of people the author counts more than the book. At their best, they will judge the author *by* his book. At their worst, they will make judgments about the book *because* of the author. Fair enough. In my native country, where everybody knew everybody, the question that governed one's reading of something new in a paper or a journal or a book was this: "What is he up to now?" The American question is somewhat different: "Who is this guy?" This is as true about the authors of serious scientific works as it is about a letter to the editor in a college newspaper. I have thought about this condition and I think I know a good deal about it. All knowledge, including historical knowledge, is personal; and all knowledge, including personal knowledge, is historical.*

Personal, however, does not mean *subjective*. In an unjustly

* The reason thereof: whatever we know, comes from the past; and all of the past that we know is, at least to some extent, our own.

celebrated little book (*What Is History?*) that is very English in being disarmingly well written and alarmingly poorly thought out, E. H. Carr proclaimed the principle: "If you want to study the history, study the historian." Unfair enough. This is nothing else but subjective determinism, something that the Germans had discovered, with a vengeance, fifty or sixty years before Carr, with all kinds of disastrous consequences. It says that before reading my history of Burgundy or of Hungary or of Philadelphia the critical scholar should know some things about me—not only where I was born, but from what social class I issued (the decisive fact for the Marx-oriented Carr, who was once called, exaggeratedly, the Red Professor of Printing House Square). An émigré in America, according to Carr, of middle- or upper-class background, born in Hungary in the early 1920's, can and will write but one version of history, because he can and will see the world but in one particular way. What nonsense! People from my background have turned out to be positivists and idealists; Conservatives, Marxists, Fascists, and Liberals; coffeehouse journalists, research historians, psychiatrists, and politologues; painters and fakers; sellers and buyers. Carr cannot distinguish the motive from the purpose of the historian. (The proper question, I once wrote, should be: "What is Carr driving at?" and not "What make is this Carr?")

Of course Carr is not entirely wrong. It *is* senseless to separate the historian from his history. We participate in everything that we know. The realization of this common-sense principle marks, incidentally, the end of the Modern Age, the basis of the science of which was Descartes' separation of the universe into objects and subjects, of the observer from the thing observed. But history is a kind of participant knowledge par excellence. The past is past but it is not dead: it lives on in myriads of ways, of which some are mysterious, and all are real. When we think or write about Julius Caesar we are, in some sense, participants: our imagination, together with our associations, vitalizes the past. This is obvious about times and scenes and people that we have witnessed; yet the difference between this kind of participant knowledge and that of our knowledge of Julius Caesar is, at the most, one of degree: it is not one of kind. Eyewitness history and remote history are not two separate categories, because the second, while remote in time, is not necessarily remote in our minds. The conception of the eyewitness may be as right or wrong as that of the remote antiquary. There have been many historians whose reconstructions of ancient or medieval matters were more reliable than their understanding of what was going on, and what things really meant, in their own times.

I do not know what my motives are in writing this book—any book—but I shall say something about my purposes. This chapter is principally addressed to Americans. It is not an indulgence in autobiography. It attempts something else: an auto-history. Auto-history: something that, in my opinion, may become a new narrative genre someday, when a superbly gifted, superbly imaginative, and historically conscious writer will, for the first time, bring about a perfect work superseding—and not merely combining—categories such as the novel and history and perhaps even autobiography.† This chapter is only a fleeting sketch, a series

---

† Readers interested in this argument may wish to look at some of my speculations about this matter in *Historical Consciousness,* Chapter III, and in my article in *Salmagundi,* No. 31–32 (Fall 1975–Winter 1976).

of vignettes. My purpose is to describe some of the things I saw in 1945—or, rather, some of the things I now see that I saw. It is not about myself; the subject is not "I"; it does not say: "This is who I was in 1945." It attempts to say: "I want to tell you things that I remember having seen in 1945: things that you can see and understand as well as I." My attempt is that of reminding, the evocation of something in the minds of readers that they, in some way or another, already know. I lived in Hungary in 1945; yet somehow I am convinced that I know nothing that American readers do not, to some extent at least, also know, the purpose of our interests being common: human conditions, nothing more, nothing less.

Zero Minute. I am expecting the Russians. I am a deserter (so are about forty thousand others) from the Hungarian army, hiding in the city of Budapest, living in a cellar. I have false military identity papers. If I were to be found out by the National Socialists or by the field gendarmerie I could be shot on the spot. I fled my unit in November. We were about to be shipped westward, eventually to Germany, together with the retreating National Socialist government and the army, or what was left of it. The Russians were less than forty miles away. We thought that they would march into the city in a few days. Together with my mother and a dozen friends we moved into a subterranean office and warehouse managed by my stepfather. But the Russians were very cautious then. They did not besiege the city until they had entirely surrounded it, after Christmas. Thereafter they progressed very slowly.

Each day they advance through fifty, perhaps a hundred,

blocks. Each day the Germans pull or drag back their remaining tanks and trucks, trying to stable them in the narrow streets of the inner city where we are. They have no antiaircraft guns left. The Russian planes start circling over the broken rooftops as the pale morning arrives, and drop bundles of small bombs on anything that moves, and on any kind of vehicle, including complete wrecks that are burnt out. The scene is a Last Encampment of the Third Reich, an Augean stable of what was once militant metal. We shiver in the cellar. We are very hungry. Frozen grim days and nights. We hear the Russian loudspeakers at night: songs, proclamations, inviting the Hungarian soldiery to surrender. I am game to surrender, I wanted to be liberated from the Germans for a long time, preferably by the British or by the Americans, or now by the Russians, it matters not which. Now they are only half a mile away. It is still dark. Three big rumbling thuds. The Germans may be blowing up the bridges across the Danube. I climb up to the street level, impetuous rather than brave, in my dirty half-uniform, wearing my sheepskin first-rank cadet's coat, with the fake orders in my pocket (". . . assigned to the remaining garrison of Budapest for unspecified duties"), worth nothing. I glimpse a patrol of the feared and hated field gendarmerie, moving self-consciously amidst the rubble in the street, fifty yards away. I slink back in an instant. It is a dark morning, the Russian planes vroom overhead, but their bombs sound farther away. The crack and rattle of small arms goes on, but now there is the sense of a strange sea-like quiet underneath. Now we hear voices from the street. We hush ourselves. Loud sounds of a strange language. Is it Russian? It sounds Russian. Now the sounds multiply. Two of us go up to the ground floor of the house. It is risky, but we no longer care. And as we stand in the doorway, peering out, the Russian soldiers come by, one by one. It is nine forty-five in the morning of 18 January 1945. Zero Minute, Zero Year.

The flood. The first ones came in single file, close to the peeling, bulging, crumbling, shot-pitted walls of the dark gray apartment buildings. The first Russian was the first Russian I ever met, and the nicest Russian I was to meet for a long time. He was some kind of officer, wearing a tightly padded uniform, a fur hat, with large binoculars hung around his neck. He had horn-rimmed glasses and a large mouth. He looked like a Weimar Berlin film image of a Red Army officer, the kind of Russian who speaks German, likes chess and children and Beethoven. As matters turned out to be, a rare kind.

An hour or so after the first Russians had arrived we packed together bits of our belongings and bundled up for a trek across the city, to the house, about two miles away, where my mother's parents lived, coincidentally very close to my father; from there it was only a short distance to our own apartment house. As we came out into the narrow street we saw that the city was destroyed. The two-story building opposite that I had seen bomb-damaged but two or three days before was now a complete ruin. Smoke rose from the rubble into the morning. There were fires here and there and much noise, shouting, in Russian. When, after five minutes of slow trekking, we turned into one of the big boulevards, I saw a scene that I shall not forget. There were a million Russians around. Of course there were not that many: but this is what it seemed. The boulevard was littered and empty. A few burned-out automobiles lay crumpled along the curbs here and there. The torn overhead wires drooped down in angry loops. Many houses were burning. But the dominant impression was that of an ocean of green-gray Russians, all coming in from the east, a few among them cantering around on horseback, some of them zigzagging fast in open jeeps (the first American jeeps I saw) with their caps pushed back from their low foreheads, in characteristic Soviet fashion. The mass of the milling soldiery was on foot, many of them dark, round, Mongol faces, with narrow eyes, incurious and hostile.

The German occupiers had come from the west. These occupiers came from the east. The Germans were close, they had come from close by. But now something elemental had happened: a green-gray flood had reached us from the great Hungarian plains, coming from the east, a great oceanic tide which had risen somewhere near Asia.

(Nearly thirty years later I leaned out, a visitor, on the white stone parapets of Buda, contemplating my native town, looking over Pest. Behind the sea of houses there was nothing but the heavy, empty horizon: the great, flat Hungarian plains, stretching to the east. From there my father's ancestors had come to live in this city, more than one hundred and fifty years ago, I thought; and I had another thought, a less agreeable one. It was 1972; the Russian flood had thinned out; Budapest was reborn; but I had an uneasy sense of the emptiness of that Hungarian plain, fraught with unseen danger, a sense that sooner or later another flood of people would come from Asia, an ocean of round-headed Mongols, whereof the Russians were but the forerunners, in 1945 . . .)

By noon the news about their looting and raping reached us through the whispers of acquaintances whom we brushed against during our trek across the city, sometimes through whispers of other trekkers on the street. But this was not even necessary: one could see the Russians robbing and destroying and rounding up people; one could see a kind of naked emptiness in the faces of some of them, and a low kind of twisted ugliness in the faces of some others, besides the narrow-eyed Mongols.

We trudge past the house where my mother was born: it is burning. She cries. Twenty minutes later someone asks her: "What are we going to *do* tonight?" "We'll play bridge," she says.

The continuity of life, even amidst the most extreme circumstances. Here are three examples:

On the night before Christmas the Russians moved in around the western end of the city, in the hills of Buda. All day we heard the dull thudding of guns from that unaccustomed direction. The city was covered with snow, the Danube carried many dead, mostly Jews, who had been shot that night or the night before, and yet on that Christmas Eve one could still see many people carrying small Christmas trees and packages. My Italian teacher lived in the Buda suburbs. When he got to the circular trolley terminus where he had to change to another line the conductor announced to the passengers that he did not know how far his car would go. The trolley screeched along in the dark. My Italian teacher got out before his stop. He had heard the cracking of machine pistols from somewhere. He decided to take a shortcut through the woods to the hilly street where he lived.

Suddenly a Russian soldier moved out from the trees in the dark. He grabbed my Italian teacher. The Russian put his finger to his mouth. "Pssst!" he said to his captive, and let him go.

That day, 24 December 1944, a friend and I had lunch at the Ritz. One of the reasons for this choice was that we were hungry, and there were few places open; the other was a kind of dare. The Ritz was full of all kinds of people, most of them refugees and fugitives, with papers as false as ours. We had a large dish of dried split-pea soup, served in the china plate of the Ritz, I can see the blue crest on it now. Some of the big plate windows were broken. There was no heat and no electricity; it was a gray and cold high noon. There was the continuous muffled thudding of the guns. It was a mere accompaniment to the feverish subdued talk at the tables. The dining room still had the atmosphere and the noise of the dining room of any European grand hotel at Sunday midday, aquarium-like; more surprisingly, it still had some of that lingering bouillon scent of a first-class restaurant during the midday meal. Some of the waiters still wore white cotton gloves. We got home—home, to that cellar—having escaped a police razzia in the nick of time.

Next night it snowed again. All electricity was gone and, what was worse, the water, too. We now knew that the Russians had encircled Buda—from the battery radio on which we could still tune in to the BBC for another two or three days. I was in love. My lady love lived in Buda. I tried the telephone—to my surprise and joy it still worked. (For many months now telephoning had been a gamble: more often than not one could not get a dial tone, even more often there was nothing but a faint diabolical hum after the dialing.) I dialed. It rang for a short moment. Then she answered. She said that the Russians had been there since the early morning. How do they *look?* I asked. She started to tell me, then she said that she'd better hang up. The German and the Hungarian military evidently forgot to cut the telephone off. And so for a few hours one could telephone across two worlds, across the front where the two greatest armies of the world were fighting down each street, sometimes shooting it out from building to building, floor to floor. By early afternoon the telephone was dead. Still this was one of my more significant experiences during all that time: the automatic insensitiveness of a few remnant wires transmitting human voices and thoughts, the continuity of life through the dumb impassiveness of technology, cutting two ways.

Expecting the Russians. It was obvious that people whose very life was threatened until the Germans retreated in defeat— fugitive soldiers, Jews, people with Jewish relatives, anti-Germans, democrats, resisters, underground Socialists, Communists, etc.—looked forward to the Russians' arrival. What was less obvious, and more interesting, was that the Russians were only a little less eagerly awaited by the aristocracy, by the better gentry, by high officials of the former semi-feudal state, by landowners, by bishops.‡ The very people whose properties and possessions

‡ Gossip overheard in a Budapest cellar by its intended victim, an independent and elegant woman with a certain presence. A chambermaid: "She says that the Russians will be here soon and it won't be bad at all. Is she a Jewess, perhaps?" Janitor's wife: "Oh, no. She is supposed to be the mistress of the Bishop of Veszprém." (She wasn't.) Maid: "Oh! She must know what she's talking about."

and ways of life were to be liquidated by the Soviets hoped for the Germans' defeat. The very people who would profit from the Communization of Hungary—streetcar conductors, janitors, metalworkers, hired hands—still hoped for a German victory. So much for the Marxist theory of class-consciousness. It was class-consciousness, all right: but in the reverse order. To favor the Germans, to believe in their propaganda of anti-Communism was poor form, it showed a deficiency in taste, in education, in culture, in one's knowledge of the great world. Chances were that a common parish priest was a nationalistic anti-Communist; his bishop was not, he would be more *nuancé*. A few second-rate actresses had thrown in their lot with the pro-German party; a truly first-rate actress would not do so. A low-level bureaucrat would conform to the directives of the pro-German regime and follow its officials, eventually to Germany. A high-level official, more often than not, would stay, frequently in hiding, and wait for the Russians to arrive. To some extent (but only to some extent) this was not unlike the American syndrome of that time: anti-Communism was so vulgar and so primitive, it was represented by such unspeakable people that to be anti-anti-Communist was almost a natural reaction.

Unlike in the United States, in Hungary there were elements of a Greek tragedy in this. The often vulgar and radical pro-Germans during the war bitterly attacked the upper classes for being disloyal to the German ally, for pursuing a mirage, since the defeat of the Third Reich would mean that the Soviets, and not the Anglo-Saxons, would reign over Hungary thereafter. The pro-Germans were, sadly enough, proven right, though for the wrong reasons, while many of the best Hungarians were unwilling to side with the Third Reich for the right reasons, because of some of their traditional and unprogressive and often reactionary convictions of decency.

Wishful thinking. As so often with my native people, the wish was the father of the thought. Only this phrase does not go far enough: like the father who carries within him the seed of his children, the wish is the flesh and blood of the thought, the wish *is* the thought. The arrival of the Russians would mean the end of the war, in Budapest at least. It would mean the end of the German era. For a considerable portion of the people, including most of the remnant aristocracy, almost all of the self-ascribed aristocracy, and the overwhelming majority of snobs, this was decisive. They would welcome the Russians because the latter were the allies of the English. To arrive at London via Moscow, this was what Hitler had wanted in 1941. This is what we wanted in 1945, though for different purposes. Few first-class snobs in Hungary were not pro-English, especially after 1941. There was some opportunism in this, but not much. It was rather romantic. Men and women who should have known better expected that very soon after the Russians occupied Budapest, British and American missions would arrive, replete with smart officers and diplomats from London and Paris and New York, whereafter the new era in our national history would properly begin. There were those who had a lingering anxiety about the Russians but these were suppressed, they were few. There were reports in the newspapers about the Russians raping and pillaging: we stopped for a moment, read them, and said to ourselves: it isn't true. It was in the German, in the National Socialist press: atrocity propaganda. We, on the other hand, were listeners of the British Broadcasting Corporation. *We* knew.

This willingness of people to deceive themselves was not especially new in 1945;** but it was then that I learned how the lives of people, including some of their most essential choices, are often determined by their thoughts and by their wishes even in times when their very lives depend on enormous external events and circumstances which they cannot control.

Varieties of memory. From this feverish period I can recall certain reactions of people to the horrors they had been living through. For months after the siege was over people tried to trump each other with horror stories about the extraordinary perils and sufferings they had experienced. Ten days without food beat five days without food and water, etc. What was curious about this was that often the same people who kept

---

** It was perhaps even more typical of those who believed in a German victory throughout the war. In August 1944 a Hungarian general staff officer, a friend of our family, visited us. He was pro-German. He said that he had just returned from western Hungary, where the Germans had demonstrated one of their new miracle weapons to a Hungarian staff. American bombers flew overhead; the Germans got busy with a box-like device; they aimed a complicated mirror skyward, pushed buttons, and three bombers burst into flames in an instant. It was a Death Ray. For a moment my mother and I, anti-Germans, were startled and frightened. Then we knew: this could not be true, as indeed it was not. Extraordinary about this was the fact that our friend was a decent man. I have been thinking about this episode ever since. He had invented it all. What is that astonishing alchemy of the human mind that produces inventions such as his? He did not only wish to deceive us; he obviously wished to deceive himself—a case in which, for once, the *why* may be more evident, and less complicated, than the *how*.

repeating, and embellishing, the recent bloody tapestry of their own experiences (personal stories of horror become bores through their repetition as does anything else) would also take pride in, and similarly embellish, stories about how exceptionally and how well they managed to live under the worst of conditions. The same man who felt compelled to describe the details of a sewer burst by a bomb that suddenly flooded a cellar, drowning frightened people before the very eyes of the horrified witness, would also narrate how he and his friends, at another time and in another cellar, had a champagne party on New Year's Eve. I understand this dual inclination: remember my vivid memories of that lunch in the Ritz. I have been thinking about this odd conjunction since, and I think I have an explanation for it. We are fascinated by violent changes as well as by the astonishing continuities in this world: we take a masochistic pride (yes, pride) in telling—telling, not merely remembering—what we had been living through, together with a different, perhaps slightly sadistic, kind of pride in telling—again, not merely remembering but telling with flourishes—how well *we* made out, compared to others.

But the converse of this phenomenon existed, too: the suppressing of memories, for all kinds of reasons. For example, the aim of Jews throughout Europe was simple: to survive the war. This naturally intelligent and pessimistic people never doubted the tremendously disastrous possibilities of anti-Semitism, either before or after the war. At the same time they not for a moment doubted that Hitler would lose it, sooner or later. Until that time they had to survive. I am inclined to think that Hitler knew this. The Jews knew that Hitler would lose the war; and Hitler knew that they knew. Perhaps this is why his fanatical hatred from them burned with such fierce force until his end. They were his central and deepest obsession from his early life onward; his hatred for them may have been the outcome of something that he hated in himself. His memory was selective, too: it was phenomenal, but mostly about people and things other than himself: there are evidences suggesting that, on occasion, he lied to others about his past because he may have lied about it to himself. I did not think about this in 1945, though I have been thinking about it lately when I read a lot about Hitler and the last war. Another thing that I did not know until recently was the secret deal between Himmler and American representatives in 1944; it is—inadequately, because of space—summed up in a footnote on page 129. In this way, and also because of the shelter offered to many of them by their Hungarian relatives and friends, about one half of the Jews of Budapest survived the war, while about nine out of ten Jews who lived in the provinces of Hungary had been killed in the gas chambers before Himmler's deal jelled.

In 1945 some Hungarians, among the minority who had assisted Jews when this had been neither politic nor opportune, were bitter because of what they thought was an insufficiency of gratitude on the part of those they had helped to survive. This attitude, involving the occasional exaggeration of one's memories about one's meritorious deeds in the past, was not commendable; but it was at least a natural kind of frailty. What was ugly, and not excusable, was the lack of remorse in the minds of those Hungarians (another minority) who had helped, by deed or word, or who at least passively rejoiced in the delivery of perhaps as many as four hundred thousand Hungarian Jews to the Germans for their gassing camps. There are Hungarians, as there are Germans even now, who simply—or rather, complicatedly—refuse to believe that so many Jews were actually killed in 1944 and 1945. And there was yet another element in this psychic mystery. Unlike other Hungarians, most Jews did not seem to want to talk about their recent sufferings. Were they ashamed of their humiliations? Or did they think that their shattering experiences were too profound, too serious, for the purpose of talking about them? I cannot tell. What I can tell is that in 1945 both the Jews in Hungary and the accomplices of their enemies had this in common: because of different purposes, and perhaps also because of different motives, neither of the two sides wanted to think much about what had just happened.

The wave of the future: anti-Communism. Three or four weeks after the fighting was over, a young boy, a relative of our janitor, helped me load some firewood on a paralytic wheelbarrow of sorts. There was a faint sound of gunnery in the distance. He said: "The Germans are coming back." His face shone with seriousness and anticipation. I don't remember whether I told him that he was wrong, that there was no chance of that. I knew that he only said what many of my countrymen hoped, especially after their experience with the Russians: they hated them and they hated everything that was connected with them, including the prospect of Communism. The Russians and the Communists were cautious, they declared that they had no intention of imposing the dictatorship of the proletariat, that they were the principal proponents of democracy, that they wanted to secure its establishment in Hungary; and indeed, in early 1945 it did not seem that Communism, certainly not the 1919 variety, would be immediately imposed on Hungary. What seemed inevitable was that the country, for the first time since 1919, would be ruled by the Left, by some kind of government from the Left. The fighting was not yet over when the first cabaret opened in Pest, in typically Hungarian (or, rather, Pestish) fashion; the title of the show, one read on freshly printed posters, was "Leftward Ho!" In 1945 people in Budapest, as in New York, believed that this was now the main thrust of history, the wave of the present as well as of the future. I did not. I believed then, as I believe now, that this triumph of the Left was artificial and superficial. I knew that most people disliked the Left, what it stood for, or what it pretended to stand for. The Left did not appeal to them—because of the particular circumstances of Hungary, including the people who were its particular, and vocal, representatives; but also because of something deeper, because of its thoroughly false conception of human nature. I cannot honestly say, because I cannot honestly remember, whether I saw this as clearly then as I came to know it soon thereafter. What I knew was that the Russians had come to stay; but also that, all appearances notwithstanding, the Left was not the wave of the future, certainly not in the long run. The press, and almost all politicians, spoke of "revolutionary" changes in 1945. The changes were indeed revolutionary in the literal sense of that word, the wheel of Hungarian fortune having been forced to undergo an entire revolution: but there was little that was revolutionary in the minds of people. Indeed, the greatest revolution—and by "greatest" I simply mean that more people took part in it than in any other revolution in the history of Hungary, and proportionately perhaps more of them than in any revolution in the entire history of the world—a large order, that—exploded eleven years later, and it was an anti-Communist revolution, *tout court*.

Débrouilleurs and opportunists. A certain existentialist attitude was current across Europe in 1945. In France and in Belgium during the war and especially toward the end of it, the *débrouilleur* was a fashionable figure: the person who made out. Yet he was not the kind of "hard-faced man who did well out of the war"; he was not the kind of person who trafficked with Germans as well as with partisans, he was not a black-market new rich, like the dairyman immortalized by Jean Dutourd in *Au Bon Beurre*. The débrouilleur was rather dashing and knowledgeable and brave: in cutting corners he could also cut a fine figure of sorts. He had a contempt—a healthy contempt—for all bureaucracy, authorities, regulations: a contempt for every kind of man-made system. He skipped over, rather than snaked through, obstacles and labyrinths of regulations, knowing in his bones that they were senseless and stupid, that unlike all definitions, including philosophical ones about essence, existence is all that matters, because it is real—indeed, that the preservation of it means the preservation of God's gift: in sum, the existentialist attitude.

Now the knowledge of what is opportune (materially, rather than intellectually) is essential for the talents of the débrouilleur. Yet opportunists and débrouilleurs are different. The opportunist is deadly serious in his calculations, secreting them within his inner self; the débrouilleur is a brilliant improviser, taking nothing very seriously and, at his best, laughing even at himself. It is like rendering Liszt vs. playing Cole Porter: the first the suitable subject for shameless rendition, the other for sprightly improvisation. Of course there are occasions when débrouilleurs degenerate into mere opportunists, and the reverse. From close up, such developments are not especially attractive to contemplate: but from a certain distance they may be amusing, and perhaps even instructive.

After the Russians arrived, there were all kinds of interesting affiliations. The oddest kinds of people joined the Communist Party. They included a rich stockbroker friend of ours, a tough-minded capitalist if ever there was one. He was one of those hardheaded (rather than hard-faced) men who made out well not only after the war but during it, including the siege. One could always be sure that F. had a car when no one had a car any longer, that he had a black-market supply of gasoline, food, fuel, clothes, napoléons d'or, etc., etc. In short, a merchant-adventurer, a master opportunist, rather than a mere débrouilleur. I always had a certain liking for him, for he was not ungenerous, he had an appreciation for good reading, and a fine cynical sense of humor. I told him that, in my opinion, he was wrong to join the Communist Party and I tried to explain why. That it was morally wrong, and bad form, I did not say, partly because he was an older man, and also because I knew that it would cut no ice with him. I explained my theory of the antiquated nature of Communism, and of its evident failure in the long run. He listened patiently but I saw that he was a bit bored with it: it was too theoretical for him, too idealistic perhaps. Yet he was not as hardheaded as he thought he was. The few advantages of his party membership were not worth the game. He thought that his quick and shameless adjustment to the powers at hand would provide for his independent comforts in years ahead: he convinced himself not only that Communism was in Hungary to stay but that his kind could stay in Hungary under Communism. He was wrong. He mistook the wave of the present for the wave of the future: the occupational hazard of opportunists, including the most talented ones. He eventually progressed from Communism to débrouilleurism: in 1949—after two years of unnecessarily protracted expectations and anxieties—he bought himself a legal passport for a large sum (obtainable for much less to non-Communists two years before), and emigrated to Australia, where he eventually died on a ski slope at the age of sixty.

Intellectuals. They, with some honest exceptions, were the most practiced opportunists of all. This was nothing new—it was all part and parcel of the emergence of the professional intellectual as a recognizable person of a certain class, of a certain self-ascribed social function, something that was less than a century old in 1945, certainly in Hungary; and yet something that has been reminiscent of the functions of theologians five or six centuries before, toward the end of the Middle Ages. The intellectuals, the formulators and representatives of certain ideas, were masters in adjusting their ideas to circumstances, rather than the other way around.

In the dark December month of 1944 I brushed against one of the self-conscious secret resistance conventicles which—alas, too late—were finally sprouting in Budapest and which, for once, were mostly composed of what could be called professional intellectuals: university people, journalists, cultural officials of the former government, young men and women on the fringes of cultural diplomacy. The leading figure of this group, J., was in his thirties, the son of respectable Calvinist gentry, dark, saturnine, and handsome except for his buck teeth, a former *boursier* of the Horthy regime, with the then relatively rare accomplishment of speaking English, having been in the United States on a government study grant in 1940–41.†† Another older friend had brought me to his wife's apartment. J. announced that he was a Communist. This was before the Russians arrived. I was impressed. His announcement instantly suggested a new kind of Hungary, in which *this* kind of man might be an important personage *as* a Communist. I thought that J. was a very knowledgeable Machiavellian, a younger statesman of sorts, who would reach some kind of a high position in the new Hungarian regime, and employ all of his Anglo-Saxon contacts with profit to himself as well as to his country *because* of his Communist affiliation. I was impressed with the cleverness of this kind of calculation which, as I later learned, was not unique. J.'s wife was a former theater critic, a high-strung intellectual, whose brother, a prominent National Socialist journalist, helped to hide a number of Jews during

†† The government of Hungary at the time, like the Vichy regime in France, had cultivated its connections with the United States before Pearl Harbor, proceeding from the partly erroneous assumption that the then still officially neutral United States would be more conservative, less radical, less committed to the support of Soviet Russia than was Britain.

the last months of the National Socialist mob regime—whether out of his truly changed human convictions or out of a judicious and balanced concern for his own skin after the inevitable defeat, I cannot tell. Probably both.

After the Russians had arrived I met J., sporting a proletarian cloth cap, in Lenin's style, which he wore day in and day out, in the streets as well as inside their unheated apartment. Perhaps because he had studied the 1917 strategy of the great Lenin, J. struck out for a great career not so much within the Party (his membership in which he did not cease to flaunt) as within the organization of the trade unions: the Soviet track. He and some of his friends occupied a gray and grimy building, suitably situated in one of the gray and grimy working-class districts of Pest, and established there the Association of Trade Unions. The bureaucratic possibilities of such an organization seemed considerable. In Hungary the trade unions, with their venerable Socialist past, were relatively few, even though they had been allowed to exist under the Horthy regime. The time was ripe, J. and his associates considered, to apply the union principle to all kinds of professions, and especially to government and municipal offices—or, more accurately, the time was ripe to secure new and important positions for themselves through the impeccable instrument of Trade Unionism.

Besides providing leadership for my suddenly diminished family (my stepfather, hit by a shell on the street during the last days of fighting, died after three days of agony) I had relatively little to do. The university had not yet reopened; at any rate, I had few courses to complete. Every day I trudged through the desolate city in ruins, to the headquarters of the Association of Trade

Unions, where one of the attractions was the bean soup, free, distributed to the staff every noon. Very soon I suspected that not much would come out of this unionism. The older unions, of printers or of metalworkers, were already controlled by the Communists or by some of their grimmest fellow travelers, their organizations presided over by a former trolleyman by the name of Kossa whose very countenance—mean, suspicious, and impassive—was sufficient to freeze the voluble J. into silence, which was no mean thing. Having glimpsed the two together on one occasion I sensed what was coming: Kossa had but a slight regard for the Association of Trade Unions, very much including the latter-day Communist J. The order of the day was to let these people exist, as long as they had no real power, which, indeed, was the case, except that J. and his friends did not really know it. They were wholly preoccupied with their activities, having convinced themselves that playing at power was the same thing as the exercise of power—the occupational disease of bureaucrats and, even more, of intellectuals. It was all clearly told by Thomas à Kempis in *The Imitation of Christ:* "They who are learned are desirous to appear, and to be called wise," but, of course, they are not wise at all, since "there are many things the knowledge of which is of little or no profit to the soul"—or to the body, I might add.

Very soon after arriving at the Association of Trade Unions I found that I had really nothing to do. Nor did the others. They, however, concealed this condition with a feverish activity of meetings, conferences, associations, and "workshops" (I have yet to encounter a "workshop" that has anything to do with work), often behind closed doors. It was my first experience with the

kind of intellectual bureaucracy that followed the phase of intellectual bohemianism as surely as other phenomena of the twentieth century followed those of the nineteenth. My colleagues
were making paper work for themselves; and they were taking
their functions, paper functions, very seriously. After the siege
there was in Budapest a shortage of everything, from flour to
matches, even a shortage of water. Of paper, miraculously—or
perhaps not so miraculously—there seemed to have been no
shortage at all. Already on the second day of my appearance at
the Association of Trade Unions I found that the most febrile
kinds of intrigues were being constructed: confidential meetings
within closed doors from which certain people were excluded,
others suddenly admitted; groupuscules with convincing no-
menclatures were being formed and re-formed, all of them instruments thinly concealing the particular and hidden ambitions
of the persons who called them into being. I soon found that the
most secret of ambitions and designs were also the most obvious.
Yet the convention of their confidentiality was kept up, not only
by their perpetrators but by the latter's bitterest and most suspicious rivals. It was an elaborate game of bureaucratic *Kriegs-
spiel*; unlike, however, the war games of military staffs, the sand
tables were not reproductions of the actual terrain, they were
crisscrossed by paths that may have come from somewhere but
that surely led to nowhere. Indeed, within a year the Association
of Trade Unions was gone; within five years J., the Early Communist, found himself in prison; another five years later he was
acquitted, whereafter he was appointed to an important position
within the government export-import organization, having
finally acquired the official limousine and the diplomatic pass-

port—a Communist pilgrim's progress, a not untypical Hungarian career during the middle of the twentieth century.

Americans. Late in March the Americans arrived—an event that I must describe in some detail. According to the arrangements made at Yalta, there was to be an Allied Control Commission in each of the former satellite countries, composed of Soviet, British, and American representatives, a political and a military mission. The Russians, of course, ruled the roost in Budapest, and everywhere else in Eastern Europe (just as the Americans ruled similar commissions, say, in Rome). In retrospect, this American and British presence in Hungary was so ephemeral (the missions left in 1947 after the peace treaty was signed) that in the long and tragic history of my native country it is hardly worth mentioning at all. This remains a fact; and yet, oddly enough, it was not quite that way. Something of that air of American omnipotence in 1945 that I tried to define earlier in this book, the impression that the United States, in an unprecedented way, was the greatest power in the world, transpired throughout the globe, lightening even the gloomy and depressing skies over Budapest. Americans had an influence in Hungary well beyond their numbers, and beyond their political limitations. There were perhaps not more than two hundred Americans, less than one hundred of them in uniform: yet somehow their presence in the capital seemed to be as evident, and sometimes almost as ubiquitous, as that of the Russians, especially in what had remained, and what was beginning to revive, of downtown, very much including places that both seemed and were expensive.

This condition, of course, was inseparable from the sudden and passionate Americanophilia of my countrymen, many of whom translated all of their expectations accordingly, by which I mean patriotic as well as personal expectations. I must say something about the latter. Months, perhaps years before the war ended, hundreds, maybe thousands of people who knew some English daydreamed about getting a job with the British or the American mission. On the morning when the first Americans arrived, a nervous teeming crowd of people was besieging the entrances of the building they were to occupy; I heard that some people had arrived in the freezing dawn hours to get a first glimpse of the promised Americans in order to rush at them from favorable starting posts. As the day advanced, this siege by supplicants turned into a bitter struggle, each man (or woman) on his (or her) own. Three or four days after the Americans had come I entered the American Legation on a self-imposed mission (about which anon). A man was ensconced in a kind of niche behind the reception desk. I recognized him: he was one of my father's acquaintances, a bachelor of middle age, a former agent of the Hamburg-Amerika Line in the dim dear twenties, a kind of floater during the war, regaling his friends with reminiscences of Cuxhaven and Cherbourg, asserting that he was just the kind of person whom the Americans would badly need and profitably employ the moment they arrived at the end of the war—all this despite the fact that, so far as I could ascertain, the little English he spoke was, if not altogether nasty and brutish, certainly poor and short. Now he hardly returned my greeting. His features had frozen into the kind of snarl with which a hungry dog is prone to protect his recently acquired bone; he was pale with the kind of suspicion with which human beings are so prone to protect recent acquisitions to their self-importance. I learned later that not only had he literally forced his way into the American building an hour or so before the first Americans arrived to be *en poste,* but that this man, who had had no particular interest in Communism before, would eventually volunteer his services to the political police in order to ensure that his clerical position at the American Legation would remain fixed and secure at a later time when most of the Hungarian employees of the Western legations and missions were either arrested or forced to relinquish their jobs. To be associated with the Americans meant everything in the world to him; there was nothing he would not sacrifice for it, including old friendships, loyalties, self-esteem. He was not merely an ambitious man who had plenty of gall; he was the kind of man who had courage enough to be a coward.

As I suggested before, he was but an extreme case of a syndrome that was widespread. Presently just about every American, whether high officer or enlisted man, became the acquisition of a Hungarian wife or mistress. The second in command of the military mission was a major general, former governor of Oklahoma, a genial and handsome man who had his son posted to Budapest, where the latter was promptly annexed by a young *bourgeoise,* his father's ambitious secretary, who had fought for her desk on the first day and won it by gleaming tooth and red-lacquered nail. They were subsequently married and left for the United States on a special American military plane. What happened to her in Oklahoma, I now wonder; at the time her story was a miracle tale, one of the *fabliaux* of 1945, Year Zero.

I would have liked very much to be annexed to the Americans

or to the British, but I did not participate in the crush and rush of the first days, not so much because it would have been demeaning but because I had suffered from intellectual ochlophobia, the fear of crowds, since an early age. I thought I'd write my own ticket—a resolution that, again, involved me in an enterprise in which nobler and baser purposes were hopelessly mixed. Having recognized the futility of my association with the Association of Trade Unions, I spent a night at home, literally burning the candle at both ends (candles were rare and electricity still nonexistent), composing a political memorandum in English that I intended to hand over to an American diplomatist of the first rank. The memorandum consisted of a list of items that I thought were unavailable elsewhere, all of them involving misdeeds by the Russians or the Communists. (I recall two principal items: one of them dealt with the murder of Bishop Apor of Györ, an aristocratic prelate who had distinguished himself in protesting against German and National Socialist brutalities as well as in protecting his flock: he was shot down by a Soviet soldier as he attempted to save a woman whom the Russian was about to rape in the cellar of his episcopal house; the other dealt with certain Communists who were camouflaged as members of other political parties and associations.) My idea was very simple: I would inform the Americans about such matters, not only for the benefit of my country but also of myself, since they would soon learn that there were few, if any, persons in Hungary who understood the realities of politics, expressed themselves in English, and, generally speaking, were as knowledgeable as I—a recognition from which all kinds of advantages could ensue.

Somehow I had secured a list of the entire American personnel in Budapest, wherefrom I deduced that the person I ought to contact was the First Secretary of the Legation, a man by the name of Squires, since I was sufficiently aware of diplomatic practices to know that with such matters one should not confront the Minister or the Chief of Mission, at least not in the beginning. Accordingly I presented myself at the Legation about a week or so after it had established itself in Budapest. The line of supplicants and applicants had not much thinned, but the very fact that I asked for Mr. Squires by his name seemed to have made an impression on the Hungarian receptionist lady, who, after a moment of hesitation, took the small envelope containing my visiting card, on which I had written, in impeccable English, something like this: "The bearer of this card would like to have the honour and the pleasure to discuss certain matters of interest with Mr. Squires." I was admitted to Squires's office. He must have thought that I was about to offer him an array of exquisite secondhand jewelry for a song. I did not know this then, but I understand it now. I vaguely remember him: he was a large, affable man, not quite as diffident as a British counterpart of his may have been, but reflecting, rather, the peculiarly American compound of being both perplexed and incurious at the same time. I babbled something in English about how important it was that the American mission be properly informed about certain important matters. I do not remember his saying anything. I put the memorandum upon the table. He said, "What can I do for you?" or words to that effect. On a coffee table I saw copies of *Time* and *Life* magazines. I hadn't seen their likes for long years. I said something to the effect that I would be only too glad to furnish him with the most confidential, and accurate, kind of political information about developments in Hungary if he were only to let me have a small supply of these superb American journals. He told me to help myself. I felt that I had just achieved a great, an unimaginable coup. I clutched several issues of *Life* and *Time* to my chest. I floated homeward in a cloud of triumph. In our unheated dwelling, grimy and redolent with the saddening odor of poverty, I faced the ruined beauty of my Anglomaniac mother. "Guess what I have!" I said. My mother turned radiant. She could not believe my luck.

Squires was one of those rich Americans from a good family who had entered the Foreign Service in the thirties because it was a more interesting career than banking: a type that, I am sorry to say, has disappeared from the ranks of the American Foreign Service by now. This I recognized later, having also learned that his main interests included liquor and polo, a kind of period mix that makes me almost nostalgic. He seemed not very much interested in Hungarian politics, perhaps because he was smart enough to know that there was not much that the United States could, or even should, do. He was also enough of a man of the world to know how to disembarrass himself, in a smooth and professional way, of this young freak who, for all he knew, might be a Soviet or Communist agent. Eventually—and I cannot now remember exactly how—I found a less unwilling recipient of the kind of information that I had to offer. He was Rear Admiral William F. Dietrich, the third in command of the American military mission: an honest and erect navy officer of the old school, a practicing Catholic who abhorred Communism without at first openly saying so, who would not only welcome my confidences in a fatherly manner but who, a year later, would be the main instrument in getting me out of political trouble, would arrange for the transportation of my only suitcase in his personal car across the border to Austria, whereto I escaped, and would furnish me with the kind of character reference that ensured my receiving a priority visa to the United States once I presented myself to an American consulate in the West. In short, he may have saved my life.

By the time Admiral Dietrich and I had become friends, in the summer of 1945, I knew many of the Americans in Budapest, at least by sight. There was not, as far as I can remember or ascertain, a mean one among them. Every one of them was benevolent, including those who, according to later evidence, were more than considerably crooked. There was, as I can now see in retrospect, a paradox in this situation. To us the Americans seemed the brightest, the smartest, and the best among all the human types who were to be found in Hungary in those crucial and tragic times; and, indeed, in many ways so they were. In any event, they were the living sources of untold and unaccountable bounty, material and spiritual: they had plenty of dollars, they were above the law, and free. Eventually it dawned upon me that these Americans in Hungary were even more fortunate than were the recipients of their available benefits. In 1945 an American in Hungary, whether in or out of uniform, found himself to be privileged beyond the dreams of avarice and of glory. American money, because of the poverty and the inflation raging in Hungary, gave him freedom to buy or do everything with ease. He was coveted by every woman because of the single virtue of his Americanship. I can recall only two types of Americans who left unpleasant memories. They were not members of the American mission. Sometime in the late summer of 1945 the news that a visit to destroyed Budapest promised certain paradisiacal prospects for certain American visitors must have begun to circulate in certain circles in New York. Cognoscenti (*Am.*: wise guys) such as the publisher of *Esquire* magazine would arrive on a visit, hugely enjoying the pleasures of the flesh that were easily available to them in this downtrodden and beggar-poor country. There was something obscene in this, especially when they later described their visits in the style that was typical of *Esquire* at the time and that, alas, has become typical of most American magazines since that time: the kind of prose whose principal purpose is to tell what kind of shoes, what kind of cheese, what kind of people, and what kind of sexual compositions are "in," a concept of connoisseurship that is public, not private: for what is the use of the discovery of a superb little wine from an unknown vineyard, or of a superb ruined city where formerly aristocratic privileges and pleasures can be secured for peanuts, unless the fact, even more than the subject, of one's discovery can be displayed in public?

The other kind of unpleasant visitor was the sort of émigré who, having left Hungary before the war, and being well on the way to a lucrative or spectacular career in the United States, usually in the capacity of either a Scientist or a Moviemaker, would arrive in Budapest from a paramount studio or from a rockefeller university, often in the resplendent uniform of the U. S. Army or, more than often, in that of the U. S. Army Air Force, full of a compound of arrogance, unease, and contempt for the miserable and despondent people of the country. I particularly remember one of these tatty birds of passage, already beyond the prime of his life, decked out in the regalia of an American colonel or brigadier, shuffling his flat feet across the lobby of the American mission building, outside of which he kept his waiting relatives, who were speechless—almost, but not quite—in their wondrous contemplation of this apparition from their own flesh. I read about him a few days later: he was professing the right kind of leftward opinions of the time. His sour countenance seemed to reflect his opinions: Hungary got what she had coming to her, that is, the Soviet occupation, the best thing for a people who had been stupid enough to be allied to the Germans. Years later in America he became a scientific adviser of the Eisenhower administration, one of the scientist spokesmen for the production of bigger and better hydrogen bombs. In an interview he gave in the fifties I read: "I know what Communism means: I know what the Soviets did to my unhappy country."

The British were a slightly different story. There were fewer of them; they were more diffident, and also more aloof. Because of geography, because of tradition, and because they were the early standard-bearers of the world war against the Third Reich from the outset, we thought, before Year Zero, that the British, rather than the Americans, would be the chief Western power in our part of Europe after the war—which, of course, did not turn out to be the case. They were far less impressed with the charms of Hungary and of Hungarians than were the Americans; they acted as if they knew that Hungary now belonged to the Soviet sphere of interest, and that there was not much left to do. It seemed to me, at the time, as if they were in command of some kind of superior reserve knowledge about the ultimate fate of Hungary: it rather seems to me now that they had few instructions that were relevant. My first meeting with them was sad. I was plodding home on a late March evening, when the suddenly warm and liquid air and the lightness of the twilight promise the pleasantness of summer for people in more or less normal conditions, while for others this development of implacable warmth and of light only serves to illuminate one's wretchedness and misery—March, and not April, being the cruelest month, at least in my native city. I knew that the arrival of the British and American missions was imminent. Suddenly, rounding a bend on the empty boulevard, I came upon two British officers, with red tabs, one of them carrying his cane, taking a brisk after-dinner walk, no doubt. I stopped. "Are you British?" I asked. "Oh, it is so good to see you"—or words to that effect. We exchanged a few words, and they went on. I was only twenty-two years old, but even then I felt that this encounter had the sad tinge of a long unrequited love. So they had come, after all—even if it was too late, after so many years of disappointments, after so many years of waiting, of hope, of tragedy. I sensed a kind of embarrassment as they went on. We, who loved the British in 1940—memories that even now give me a *frisson*— imagined their future victory: the triumph of a British-led Europe where freedom, decency, and a kind of easy elegance would exist anew. But it was not to be such a world.

At any rate (certainly at any rate of exchange), the British were poorer than the Americans. Their mission and their social life were less opulent. On the day of their arrival they were besieged, just as the Americans, by job seekers, by all kinds of people who wanted to be associated with them. They hired few people: they preferred to hire certain recognizably frayed women of the former aristocracy and the gentry. Perhaps this had something to do with habitual British snobbery. They were poorer than they had ever been, but as snobbish as ever. I thought about this for a long time, coming to the tentative conclusion that, for the British, unlike for other peoples, snobbery is the outcome of diffidence as much as of arrogance, perhaps even more. They were unwilling to get involved with men and women whom they could not place and on whom, on occasion, they might have to depend. It was all restrained, modest, and cold, with a slight touch of being almost shabby. It was all contrary to Hungarian expectations. Our best people still expected the British to be the Great Power in Europe, counterbalancing the Russians, to intervene eventually in Central Europe, including Hungary. In certain circles, including the apartment of the J.'s, people passed around editorials from the London *Times*, taking deep drafts of encouragement from some of them, which in the late spring and early summer of 1945 contained, on occasion, carefully worded criticisms of certain Soviet actions. When on a Sunday afternoon in late July the news came that the English people had repudiated Churchill and elected a Socialist government some of my older friends reeled: it was one of the bitterest of blows.

Still Anglomania lived on. One of my pathetic memories of Year Zero includes a wedding reception in the fall. A Hungarian girl whose family I knew, the only daughter of an impoverished, gray-faced doctor, had fallen in love with a British sergeant—or, perhaps because he was British, she convinced herself that she had fallen in love with him. He was a decent sort, a North Englishman from Newcastle or Sunderland, with the long, knobby face of his class, which, as I instantly recognized even before he spoke, was that of the lower-middle variety—but this his bride, and her family, did not (or perhaps did not want to) know. I can see him still in the living room of the doctor's apartment (the reception was held at home), furnished with the remnant scatteration—German china, Bohemian glass, faded runners, grayed lace, a worn rug—of a destroyed bourgeois past that once had belonged to a world that was civic, fussy, stuffy, but, after all was said, reasonably honorable. For a moment in its long and misery-ridden history, a corner of that room was lighted by the bride's nervous smile. Some of her unsophisticated relatives, too, were smiling. The luck, the fortune, to be married to an English soldier at this time, to be carried off as a bride to England! I, and perhaps some others, knew that there was something very wrong with this: that her progress from this broken-down boulevard apartment with its low-bourgeois bibelots to a gas fire-grate somewhere in the Midlands was not necessarily up. After all, for someone born in Hungary even the ubiquitous cooking smell of paprika and onions frying in cheap lard—especially ubiquitous now when it could no longer be contained to kitchens—was preferable to the coal-smoke and sultana-cake and weak-cocoa odor of mid-England; even in a Sovietized Budapest the sun would shine in June with a laughing fury; and even the broken remnants of a past, that grand piano whose chords had long lost their twang and whose polish had long lost its shine, and the doctor father's Collected Works of Goethe in the glass bookcase, were symbols of certain things that would not exist where this girl was about to go. I confess that I felt, at the time, less compassion for her than for this decent and good Englishman, who stood there uneasily and self-consciously cracking jokes with two of his pals, blokes, who had come to enliven the festivities, representing England. He was getting roped into something that was embarrassing and difficult. I doubted that the marriage would last a year. Perhaps he did, too. The bride, well tutored, articulate, Hungarian, did not know it. So much for the reputedly superb wiles and sophistication of my countrymen and my countrywomen. In a very Hungarian way, the wish *was* the thought, again, and again.

There was also more to this. I have often thought that the personal relations of men and women who belong to different nationalities, rather than to different classes—especially when they try to comprehend each other in a language which for the one is his or her native one, while for the other it is not—is a subject not only for low comedy but a potentially profound subject for drama or even high tragedy which few, if any, writers have yet attempted. It involves conflict that issues not out of differences in class or out of differences in libido (perhaps the least important of all differences), but out of something far more important: it issues out of differences in nationality, residing in deeply rooted matters such as habits of speech and, therefore, of thought. While it is true that the underlying subject matter of the modern novel, of the principal literary creation of the bourgeois age, may have dissolved together with the dissolution of social classes, which is the main reason why a contemporary version of a Jane Austen or a Trollope or a Balzac is no longer possible, a great and profound account of the tides of passion,

of the incomplete understandings—and of the, surprisingly, no
less incomplete misunderstandings—between, say, a Frenchman
and an Englishwoman or between an American man and a
Hungarian woman, remains to be written—and not on the level
of comedy, either: in this respect the readable Pierre Daninos,
the linguistic Fabergé art of the readable but unspeakable Nabokov, and even Nancy Mitford at her best, will not do.‡‡

The English at their best comprehend European peoples; but
they do not really wish to know them. At their best, certain Europeans know the English; but they cannot really comprehend
them. But enough of these paradoxes. A day or so after *ces noces
tristes*—no, that would be too elegant, too romantic for what
had really taken place, which was *noces ternes, en haillons, at-
tristées*—something else happened that remains peculiarly
carved in my memory. The girl who worked with me as a part-
time secretary and who was also a part-time secretary to an English officer, asked me what at the time was certainly an unusual
question. Did I know of a Catholic priest who would be willing

‡‡ The greatest event in the history of the United States has been
mass immigration. There have been, as yet, no historians worthy of the
subject; no novelists, either. At first, this is surprising. So many great
events in the history of the American people have been reflected more
clearly, and better, by its novelists than by its historians—probably because of the peculiar and, until recently, unique structure of the history
of this democratic people. On second thought, there may be a reason for
this absence of immigrant novels. The few that exist were written either
from the knowledge of an Americanized immigrant who knew his people,
including their lives in America, but who did not know Americans
enough; or by an American who knew immigrants but not really where
they came from, remaining unaware of the complex and, in the course
of passage, often twisted roots of their speech and thought.

to baptize an Englishman? The English officer for whom she was working was an odd bird, to start with; he was so quiet as to be a veritable recluse, he did not seem to like parties. Now he told her that he had taken instructions; he wanted to be baptized a Catholic, as soon as possible, preferably tomorrow. She had no Catholic background or interest in religion, she did not understand it at all. I quickly thought of some of my priest acquaintances and religious relatives; for a moment my snob reflex rose to the surface of my mind; I thought of one or two of the Anglophile *abbés*, the habitués of the pseudo-aristocratic and anti-German salons before the collapse; it would take some time to find them but I'll find them all right. She sped off to the British mission, returning in an hour or so; the officer did not wish to wait, the event should take place tomorrow or latest the day after. I went to the Basilica, within walking distance, looking for the cappellan. He asked something about papers about which I knew nothing. Suspicious and not very cooperative at first, he agreed in the end. Tomorrow, before the second Mass in the early morning, he said. Late in the evening the girl sent a message to our apartment (we had no telephone) to the effect that she had to accompany the officer to the Basilica in the morning; that the officer wished to thank me and that he wished to know whether I would come to introduce him to the cappellan. I told her that this was quite unnecessary; the cappellan would be waiting for them; besides, I had no great desire to get up to go to Mass on a weekday morning (my Mass-going, at best, was very irregular in Year Zero); I was irritated at her; then I agreed.

I arrived at the depressing square in front of the Basilica a few minutes late, on a dark and dank and depressing morning.

An English officer was coming down the steps. The girl, tagging behind, caught up with him and said something in his ear. (I had missed the Mass, which must have been speeded up because of the cappellan's convenience.) He looked at me, briefly nodding his head. His face expressed something that I still remember: a kind of infinite seriousness. He went on, leaving the girl behind; he turned left into a desolate street opening up before him; in a minute his figure disappeared in the morning darkness and the ugly fog. "A strange man," the girl said. "*Különös ember!*" I didn't think so. He had given me, us, the whole world, the impression that he wanted to be alone. He was alone. I suddenly felt an elemental surge of compassion, of sympathy for this lonely small thin figure. It was, to begin with, a novel experience. Perhaps for the first time in my life I felt sorry for an Englishman. I was sorry for this lonely officer; but I was not sorry out of condescension; it was the kind of sorrow that, strangely enough, is composed of human admiration together with human love, the kind of sorrow for a lonely follower of Christ. Many years later I came to feel, and I still feel, that English Catholics are a breed apart, perhaps the most serious, because in many ways the loneliest, Catholic Christians in the entire world. Twenty years later I sensed this very strongly, when I had taken it upon myself to fly to London at the time of Churchill's funeral, with my little son. The day after the funeral we went to Mass in a Roman Catholic church in Kensington. "It was not a very attractive church," I wrote in my diary, "set back between the brown brick houses. It was full of people, a few Poles, but the majority of the congregation was English, infinitely serious English men and women with their children.

Living through the last phase of the Protestant episode, of the long unhappy chapter of Roman Catholicism in England, with some of the old suspicions and mistrust melting away, these English Catholics, perhaps better than any other Catholics in the Western world, know what it means to be Christians in a post-Christian land." "In this people" (the English), I went on, "who ushered in the modern age there is still a near-medieval strain, a strain that has been part and parcel of their Protestantism, of their puritanism, of the industrial evangelicalism, of their English socialism. It is there in this living strain of English Catholicism which, in the twentieth century—curious paradox in the spiritual history of England—has become one of the strongest subterranean streams of a particular Englishness. To be hounded by heaven is one way to put it—but it was not only the Francis Thompsons who sensed this . . ." The English officer was going away, alone: a representative of one of the victorious powers of this world, especially enviable in these small and sordid surroundings of defeated Hungary, he for reasons known only to himself and to God had chosen the religion of the defeated of the world, of sinners and sufferers; he had taken the Via Dolorosa, on his own.

Russians. I have now filled page after page about the few hundred Americans and Englishmen who were temporary residents of my native city at the time. But how about the Russians, of whom there were hundreds of thousands around, who ruled my country, and all of the surrounding countries then, and ever since that time? The Russians? Well, there is not much to say about the Russians. They were everywhere; and they were nowhere. I have no inclination to describe them in detail. All kinds of funny, and some not so funny, books have been written about them, about their childishness, their primitiveness, their brutality: about the Russian soldiers who tried to shave out of flush toilets, mistaking them for washbasins, who gulped down entire bottles of eau de cologne, mistaking them for perfumed vodka, the most desirable object of whose robberies was a watch, but not just any kind of a watch: they were entranced with the kind of toy watch that had something like Mickey Mouse on the dial face. During the eighteen months that I spent under Russian occupation I did not meet a single Russian with whom I could talk more or less intelligently, and not one who spoke an intelligible French or English or even German. They all seemed to have been stamped out of a mold: their minds even more than their bodies. Under the Soviet rule the eternally passive masses of the Russias had been activated—up to a certain level, in certain ways. They were taught to read and write; they were taught to think in public categories, for the first time in their history. They had acquired a new skill: they had learned words and phrases that were public answers to public questions. They were more than satisfied with this achievement: a verbal achievement that rendered them civic and "cultured." Yet this was exactly why intelligent conversation with them was impossible. It was exasperating, especially for someone who was impatient by nature. During and before the war I had occasionally talked with Germans who were Nazis. What made me despair then was their arrogance. They had an answer to every question, which went something like this: "Maybe so; but there are certain hard realities in this world which we have come to understand, whereas you are unwilling to admit them." (Examples of these "hard" realities: the "inevitable right" of a land-hungry people to conquer and colonize, the "inevitable fact" that the thinking of a Jewish scientist was necessarily inferior to that of an Aryan one, etc., etc.) When one talked to Russians one found that they had certain answers to certain questions, beyond which they were totally unwilling as well as wholly unable to go. The Germans had prided themselves on having found a satisfactory accord between the public ideology of their folk and their private thinking. The Russians seemed to be quite unaccustomed to private thinking. There was public thinking; and there was private behavior. That there were enormous discrepancies between the two did not bother them, since they did not recognize this at all. I think that the Soviet soldier who had just robbed a passerby of his watch or overcoat would, if asked, wholly agree with, or perhaps even be able to repeat, the slogan that he was a citizen-soldier of the most disciplined, most scientific, and most progressive army of the world: the Red Army of the Soviet Union.

There is but one incident that I have been thinking about often since that time. The apartment house opposite ours had been sequestered by a group of Soviet sailors and their officers. They kept the lights blazing and played the gramophone at full volume day and night: their love for ear-shattering noises was to be matched only by American teen-agers. Down the street a young Jewish man had returned from deportation. He was alone; his family, I understood, had been killed. He decorated the wall underneath his window with slogans in Cyrillic letters welcoming the Soviets and proclaiming their glory. One of the few possessions that had survived his family was his collection of

ship models; he displayed these proudly in his small apartment
and invited the Soviet sailors, especially one of their warrant
officers, a good-looking young Russian, who would come to his
apartment and play with the little ships for hours. He had some
money and food, and entertained these Russians handsomely.
One day we heard a lot of noise, shouting and slamming, at high
noon. I looked out the window at an ugly scene. The young
man was out in the street, shouting desperately, banging at the
door that was slammed shut by the Russians. They had gone
into his apartment, taken his entire collection, thrown some of
his stuff into the street, together with its owner. That was bad
enough; but even worse than their brutality were the broad grins
on their mugs. They thoroughly enjoyed the pitiful pow-
erlessness of their former admirer and friend. They were split-
ting their sides at the sight of his lamentations; his repeated peti-
tionings produced bursts of enormous laughter. They had
nothing but contempt for him, because he was helpless, because
he was weak, because he was a fool, and probably also because
he was a Jew. It was one of the ugliest scenes I witnessed during
that ugly year; I have always found the humiliation of a human
being to be the most shattering of scenes. This contempt for
human weakness was something typically Russian, I had seen
other expressions of it during Year Zero; years later I read in one
of Dostoevsky's novels about a Russian who, having cheated a
fool out of a thousand rubles at the horse fair, said upon his return: "How I despise that man!"; many years later some of
Solzhenitsyn's accounts of social life in the Gulag rang a bell in
my mind, his searingly angry description of how in the Soviet
concentration camps the roost is often ruled by common crimi-

nals who are even worse than the policeman guards and who, because of their brutal contempt for any kind of human decency and of human weakness, are respected and often depended upon by the prison administrators themselves. Which was worse, I thought at the time: the Germans who had arranged for the murder of people such as this young man in obedience of what they thought was a principle; or the Russians who would rob and murder out of impulse, not only for no particular principle but for no purpose except that of enjoying their power over the temporarily powerless? I could not tell, just as I cannot tell which is worse in America: the robber who stabs the store owner after his robbery, or the gang member who stomps his victim for no purpose except that of enjoying his savage power over him.

Unlike the Germans, the Russians seemed to me to be a people utterly without pride. At their worst, the Germans were shameless; among the Russians one could occasionally sense the shamefulness of the brute. They were probably less inhuman than the Germans at their worst; but their humanity was certainly a low and complex one. During Year Zero I lost whatever respect I had for the self-professed Christianity of Tolstoy and Dostoevsky; among Russians I found not only the Catholic convert Chaadayev but agnostics such as Turgenev or Chekhov infinitely more humane and Christian than these great bearded puritans belonging to the Russia that produced Rasputin. What impressed me even at that time was their deep-seated feeling of inferiority. They, the conquerors, seemed thoroughly stiff and uneasy during the receptions at the American mission; in spite of their elephantine and hideous power they would react to the slightest kind of criticism; they insisted that respect be paid

to them on any and every occasion; all in all, they were very
unsure of themselves, perhaps especially in front of Americans, for whom, I am sure, they had an emotional kind of admiration that they tried their best, and also their worst, to suppress. I was not in the least surprised when, a few years later,
Stalin initiated the ridiculous campaign proclaiming to the Soviet peoples and to the world that the inventors of the telephone,
the airplane, etc., etc., had not been Americans or Europeans
but Russians.

It was mainly, though not exclusively, because of the Russians
that the distaste for Communism in Hungary was so extraordinarily widespread. I thought then, and also much later in the
United States, arguing with Americans about this in vain, until
I was blue in the face, that Communism was not much of a danger, that once the Russians would remove themselves from a European country they occupied, Communism and Communists
would vanish therefrom. The very fact that something was propagated by the Russians, the very fact that something looked or
seemed Russian, made it repugnant. Other European peoples
who had lived under Russian rule decades before—Finns, Bal-
tics, Poles—had had this experience. In this respect German
rule, precisely because more civilized on the surface, would have
probably harmed Hungary more in the long run, since in that
event the culture of the country could have become considerably
Germanized. Had Communism come to power in Germany and
not in Russia after the First World War, its attraction within
Europe would have been immeasurably greater.

Communists. This brings me to the deficient appeal of Communism and of Communists. During Year Zero I could see who were the kinds of people who joined their party. The brightest among them were the opportunists such as the abovementioned J., or the capitalist friend of my family who decided to join the winning side because it was the winning side, *pur et simple*. (Among opportunists no less than among revolutionaries there is such a type as *un pur*: the person who will allow no compromise to sully his dedication to the supreme virtue of opportunism.) Oddly—or perhaps not so oddly—the Russians, forever eager to be appreciated, especially by people who were naturally smart, had a considerable regard for such opportunists, far more than they had for the motley variety of convinced Communists. What struck me at the time was how many of the latter were—how should I put it?—inferior types, poor specimens of humanity, men and women whose very faces and whose very bearing showed evident marks of tremendous humiliations in their lives, people with a deeply embedded sense of personal, rather than cultural, inferiority. All of us suffer from the wounds of some kind of humiliation; all of us nurture at least one complex of relative inferiority in our breasts; but there are some people who allow these sentiments to grow to an extent that they become a dominant factor in their personalities and aspirations; and this seemed to be the case with most of the Communists I met in 1945. They were unsure, suspicious, narrow, and bitter: in sum, preternaturally *old*—as was indeed the philosophy of Marxism, that cast-iron piece left over from the junk-heap of nineteenth-century ideas. (Compared to them, the Nazis and Fascists I had known, including Nazi and Fascist intellectuals, seemed young. A Nazi and Fascist intellectual was the kind of person who would rather be vulgar than boring; with the Communists it was the reverse.)

This was true in a physical sense, too: most Communists were physically ugly, some to the point of being repellent. Sometime during the summer of Year Zero I met Georg Lukács,* one of the few famous Communist intellectuals, who had just arrived from Moscow. He, too, had the appearance of a tired survivor from another age: a leftover from the Weimar period. Everything about him was drooping and sliding down: his glasses, his eyelids behind his glasses, his ears, his nose, his large cynical mouth, his coat, his cravat, his tobacco-stained hands. His countenance, curiously like that of so many other Weimar intellectuals whom I would later encounter in America, reminded me of a crumpled ashtray. He knew German better than he knew his native language, which he spoke with a weary coffeehouse accent. His conversation, or what I remember of it, consisted mostly of tired *Kaffeehaus* witticisms with which he tried not only to lighten the customary Marxist platitudes but also to cover up the condition that he knew remarkably ("remarkably" being the *mot juste*) little about what Hungary had lived through and what Hungarians were thinking. His last contact with his native country had occurred more than a quarter of a century before, during Béla Kun's regime, which, for him, were halcyon days. In sum, an intellectual fossil.

Most of these still-believing Communist intellectuals were Trotskyists rather than Stalinists. Of course they would go to

* I am no relative of this man, with whose name mine has been often, and disagreeably, confused. His international fame was resurrected—or, rather, artificially inflated—by Anglo-American intellectuals *circa* 1960. Few people have bothered to read him in his native Hungary.

any lengths to deny this. This is, too, why I was not at all surprised when, on Stalin's orders, a few years later the police government of Hungary began to get rid of some of them in the most cruel and brutal manner imaginable; no matter how cowardly and conformist, they were, after all, international Communists, not dumb Muscovite minions; they were not particularly good at being both brutal and vulgar, unlike their Russian masters. This was also why I was not surprised that most of these surviving Communist intellectuals were in the vanguard of the 1956 Rising, when they had—finally—realized that the rule imposed on them was so stupid and senseless as to be intolerable. They also realized that "intolerable" is what people no longer want to tolerate: in 1956 they took tremendous sustenance, intellectual and spiritual, from finding that, for once, what they said and thought was in harmony with what the vast majority of the downtrodden people of Hungary, whom they had for so long shamefully ignored, were thinking and saying. What they did not realize even then was that this salutary condition was not entirely the result of their own spiritual courage. They could get away with it for a while when the Russian government, too, was beginning to bend, unaware of the condition that revolutions tend to break out not when the terror is harshest but when it has begun appreciably to lessen. But that is another story.

What made me pessimistic for the long run was that their masters were very different from them. The Russians who gave them orders gave a very different impression: they were young, not old. Years later I would run across Soviet men and women who seemed not to doubt, because they were not thinking about,

the superiority of their system. One day, many years after Year
Zero, while waiting for interminable hours at Le Bourget airport, I watched a Russian airline pilot walk and talk:
superficially handsome, with a large, naked face, a believing
Russian and a believing Communist, the prototype of the Soviet
engine man, half mechanic, half Cossack, like the writer Sholo-
khov. Unlike those of European Nazis, unlike those of European
Communists, the bearing and the expressions of this man were
both vulgar and boring, which did not bother him or the surrounding Aeroflot personnel in the least. His was not the last
gospel: but he represented both the power and the glory of the
immense Soviet Union, at least for the time being.

A conversation in 1945 with V.B., a young and not unin-
telligent baroness. "Well, we were at the top long enough. It is
their turn now." She is wrong, for a number of reasons, the principal one being that *they* are not really the lower classes. *They*
are merely another ruling group, essentially lower middle class
in origin, one kind of bureaucracy replacing another. What she
says is not ignoble; but it is a rationalization. It is a rationalization of one's misfortunes, not of one's misdeeds. It is a rationalization of resignation and not of envy. It is the opposite of
sour grapes: sweet wine.† (I like dry wine.)

Expectations and disappointments. During the second half of
Year Zero my position as secretary of the Hungarian-American
Society kept me busy, together with my remaining university

† *Pourriture noble. Edelfäule.*

studies. We had an impressive membership, in quality as well as in quantity: the people who hoped for their salvation from the Americans were numerous beyond belief, and so were some of their expectations. In October the cultural section of the American Legation planned a reception where they would show some war films; they asked me to help prepare a guest list, including some of the professors from the university. The professors, with notably inspiring exceptions, were not the bravest of men. I went to see some of them, including one of mine: an intelligent and saturnine man who had few hopes about the Americans or the British. He told me his doubts. "Why should I go there?" he said. "What for?" I babbled something until suddenly the most obvious matter came to my mind: there would be plenty to eat, lots of hors d'oeuvres, at a time when most people, very much including scholars on a fixed salary, went hungry day after day. I felt I could not say this in so many words to this distinguished scholar. I said simply that there would be "a sumptuous reception." He indeed showed up, together with at least two dozen of his colleagues who previously, for reasons politic, professed to restrain their public admiration for things American, including the Hungarian-American Society. There *were* lots of tea sandwiches; they disappeared fast. I can still see the gray gaunt scholars approaching the buffet first carefully, slowly, and then nervously repeating this progress, faster and faster, until it ran like a film moving jerkily forward: it was comic and tragic at the same time.

More pathetic were the non-material expectations that people nurtured about the Americans. One of the top positions—executive vice-president or chairman of the board, I forget which—of the Hungarian-American Society was occupied by L., a professor of astronomy, whose main claim to this post was a former Rockefeller or Carnegie Fellowship under which he had visited the Harvard Observatory and become friends with its director, Professor Harlow Shapley, about whom he would often talk with joyful expectations. One day I happened to run across the title of an article in an American magazine written by, lo and behold! Harlow Shapley. I got it out of the American Library, thinking how pleased L. would be. Next morning, as I read the article in a crowded trolley car, I was astonished to find that this eminent Harvard astronomer was a fervent admirer of the Soviets and a political imbecile. I said that much when I gave the article to L. I saw that he did not want to believe me; indeed, later in the day I saw that whatever affection he may have had for me (it was not much) had just about vanished. To this day I do not know whether he thought that I wanted to shame him, or whether he did not know enough English to comprehend the idiocies in Shapley's article. I hope the latter.

There was A., an old family friend, a run-down member of the former gentry and a romantic snob, who told me repeatedly that he would like to meet some American diplomats, especially members of their staff of a certain eminence, as he put it. This happened in the spring of 1946, after Year Zero, but the story may be worth retelling. By that time there was enough food around to allow for a kind of tea party. I told my mother, who immediately rose to the occasion, as indeed I knew she would. Neither Admiral Dietrich nor Colonel Townsend was free on the designated afternoon, but I succeeded in corralling T., the cultural attaché of the Legation, a pipe-smoking American liberal with a toothbrush mustache of the kind that I later saw repeated above the lips of Brooks Atkinson and Harrison Salisbury, a liberal mustache of a certain period; he was also the first man I ever saw wearing shirts with button-down collars, the practicality of which has escaped me then and ever since. The conversation around our tea table was a disaster. T. mentioned Count Michael Károlyi, the quondam president of the Hungarian Republic in 1918–19, who had been instrumental in the catastrophes that befell Hungary at that time. T. asked whether Károlyi was an intellectual, as he had read. I said, yes, of sorts. Well, T. said, then it was true: Károlyi must have been a spiritual aristocrat if there ever was one, probably the finest kind of man Hungary could show to the world, and did we agree? A.'s answer was to the point: Károlyi was a traitor to his class, and to his country. He asked me to translate the exact words into English. "A weakling." "A scoundrel." After this the talk degenerated fast. A. produced certain rare and exquisite cases from the repertory of Russian atrocities, whereupon T. said that homesickness among the Russian soldiery ought not be discounted. He quoted the latest issue of *Time* magazine, about American and Canadian soldiers having gone on riotous rampages in Le Havre or Cherbourg before their embarkation homeward. Later I told my mother that I thought A. had been a bit tactless, whereupon my mother remarked that she thought so, too, but then so was our American guest: "if this man had been posted to Dachau he would have probably told the inmates how Americans have been mistreating Indians."

In September, Baron U., a great banker and capitalist, and a very genial man to boot, gave a party in his relatively untouched

mansion in Benczur-utca, where he invited leading members of
the government and of the political parties, including Rákosi,
the potato-headed unscrupulous boss of the Communist Party,
back from Moscow. (I was not among the guests.) I asked F.,
U.'s relative—an older man, another former great industrialist
and an officer of the Hungarian-British Society—why U. would
do such a thing. "You are too young to understand, my boy," F.
said. "*We* were brought up by the principle"—he said it in English: "right or wrong, my country." I was impressed by his response; I could not answer him and thought about it for a long
time, feeling, however, that there was something wrong with
this. Many years later I read Chesterton with delight: "My
country right or wrong is like saying, 'My mother, drunk or
sober.'" Still Chesterton's profound aphorism related to an England, stiff and swollen with pride, in the aftermath of the
mafficking and the jingoism of the Boer War. We in Hungary,
another generation later, were stiff and swollen not with pride
and possessions but with hunger and hatred, including self-
hatred. I was struggling against the Communist subjugation of
my country; yet, if someone had offered me American or Swiss
or Portuguese citizenship, I would have accepted it in an instant. "Right or wrong," I thought, "*my* country?" From this
time on not much remains to be said: Year Zero was about to
run out and I was about to run away from my country.

Fleeing to the West. For a while it seemed that Hungary,
even though remaining under the Soviet thumb, would not become entirely Communized or Sovietized. Most people thought
that the Communists were not popular enough to rule by them-

selves; consequently the country might continue to be governed
by the coalition of the so-called democratic parties of which the
Communists were members. I thought that, too; only I had come
to the conclusion, early during Year Zero, that labels and names
mattered little. What mattered was the possession of power,
something which will *always* attract a sufficient number of people for its disposal. Within every one of the officially non-Communist parties and associations there were men and women who
were willing to go along with the Russians and with the Communists; they had some of the key positions; eventually they
would be the local representatives of power; and this was what
counted in the end. I also came to the conclusion, later in the
year, that the British and the Americans would do little or nothing for Hungary; the Americans might do something, but at a
time when it would be too late. I thought that not only the
Communists but the Russians were less sure of their power than
it seemed; but I also knew that the Americans were not really
aware of this—in a subdued way they may have respected the
power of the Russians almost as much as the Russians respected,
and feared, both American power and American prestige. In
early October there occurred a significant event. In the city elections of Budapest the Communists lost. They had made the
Socialists run on a joint ticket with them: even so, the majority
of the people of this industrial city, including the majority of the
working class, voted for the Small Holders' Party, an originally
rural party and now the relatively most conservative one of the
coalition. I was a member of this party, with its ungainly name,
in the electoral success of which now the majority of hopes resided. One month after the Budapest election the national elec-

tions were to be held. The Russians now moved. Their commanding general called for a confidential meeting of the parties, including some of the leading Small Holders, telling them that there ought to be but one ticket in the election, that of a Democrat Front. The seats in the forthcoming parliament would then be distributed according to a prearranged schedule between the parties—I think that the Small Holders were offered 47 percent of the seats. It was a sort of Russian ultimatum, to be decided immediately.

I was told about it by a family friend, Paul de Auer, a leading member of the Small Holders. A few of us had gathered in his apartment. We speculated that the Russians might be stalled at their game *if* the Americans were informed about this as promptly as possible, and if this clumsy Russian intervention were publicly revealed by the American press and radio. I volunteered to go straight to the Americans. My mission consisted of two parts: to tell the Americans what was up, and to try to ascertain whether they would accordingly and quickly protest against this Soviet interference in Hungarian politics. It was late afternoon; I bounded across the city in the rain; I found no one at the American Legation but I caught Admiral Dietrich in the military mission building as he was about to leave. I was very excited; it took me some time to convince him that speed was of the utmost importance. I did not know whether I had succeeded in both of my tasks; I informed the Americans but could not elicit any commitment from them. I now decided to lie. I rushed back to Uncle Paul's apartment. He had already gone to the headquarters of the party, where the matter was under discussion. I had great difficulty in pushing my way through the various anterooms of the old County Casino, which served as the present headquarters of the Small Holders' Party. Finally Paul emerged, slightly irritated at my insistence. I breathlessly told him that I had talked to the top Americans, adding that I had reason to believe the Americans would intervene. I did this because I thought this piece of news might be decisive in tilting the decision in the party conclave in favor of the resisters and against the compromisers; I think that I did it, too, because it may have made me look more important and influential than I actually was.

It was a cold night; I lingered in the cavernous foyer of the building until, around eleven, the news came from upstairs: the Small Holders' Party had chosen to decline the Russian suggestion; they refused to take part in the election on a joint ticket with the Democratic Front including the Communists. For months, indeed years afterward I prided myself on my role that day, in having influenced, if only in the short run, the fate of Hungary, of Europe, perhaps of the world. Many years later I found out that the Americans had already learned about the Russian intervention independently of me; also that Paul had chosen not to announce my news at the party conclave, for a variety of reasons—*surtout pas trop de zèle*. The election took place on 4 November. I voted, for the first time in my life, and for the last time in Hungary. The Communists got 17 percent of the vote, the Small Holders nearly 60. I felt not much of a sense of triumph, rather the contrary: the composition of the new government reflected not so much the people's choice as the supreme reality, which was that Hungary belonged to the Russians. The key positions in the new government were allotted either to men whom the Russians wanted, or to others whom the Russians would tolerate, at least for the time being, no matter to which party they might officially belong.

I convinced myself that the jig was up; or, rather, that it was not coming down, not at all. The year was drawing to its end; the atmosphere was chilly; I enveloped myself in a cocoon of self-indulgent gloom. My mother was not well. We had little money and little food. My personal life was unattractive, in more ways than one. On the day before Christmas I sat with my mother in darkness at noon in our erstwhile dining room, with the electricity hardly flickering, with everything around us, including my mother's beauty, in ruins. The radio hissed and babbled while we were eating our soup. There was a program about what was going on citywide on this day. In a downtown square the staff of the American military mission had put up a Christmas tree. The voice that came on the radio was that of Margit Schlachta, the head of a Catholic religious order, who was famous for her untiring, and sometimes heroic, efforts during previous years in helping the victims of Nazis. She made a brief statement thanking the Americans for their gifts and then she suddenly said: "A little boy had come up to me just now. He asked me: 'Sister, what kind of soldiers are these?' My answer was: 'These are soldiers whom you don't have to fear.'" My mother burst into tears; so did I, I am ashamed to say.

I wasn't ashamed of it then. I was full of illusions about America, about the West. "The West": this term that the Germans, calculatedly and rather shamelessly, used in their propaganda toward the end of the war, began to have a meaning for us only now, during Year Zero, when we lay under the big greasy thumb of the Orient Bear. (No one in Hungary ever thought that we belonged to "Eastern Europe" before.) I knew how backward and unattractive the Communists and their Russian masters were, ridden with corruption and with their own sense of inferiority. I had not the slightest doubt that Americans were better, stronger, richer, more dynamic, and infinitely more attractive. One day the Russians would retreat and the Americans would advance. But it would take a long time, perhaps decades. The Sovietization of Hungary was, for the time being, irreversible. I was right, for all that, but not entirely for the right reasons. This kind of pessimism was, at least in part, a rationalization. I was convincing myself that things were turning not to the better but to the worse: that I had no future in this Hungary, that next year my university studies would be over, that because of my merits the Americans would grant me a preferential visa, that sooner or later the Communist political police would reach out for me, in sum, that my situation in Hungary was becoming dangerous, that it was intolerable. In December 1945 some of this was still exaggerated. How much of my decision to skip was spurred by a sense of adventure, by a desire to escape these gloomy surroundings, perhaps even including the sad presence of my mother, I cannot tell. All immigrants lie, also to themselves.‡ I was a political refugee par excellence: yet I know now what I refused to know then: that, in escaping to America, my motives as well as my purposes were more mixed than I chose to think then, and for a long time thereafter. I was

‡ This is one of the reasons for the difficulty of truthful literature about them, about which I wrote above, p. 287.

desperate and impetuous, pessimistic and impatient at the same time. As I have said, "intolerable" is simply what one doesn't want to tolerate.

Many years later, in the memoirs of a Hungarian political figure who, like many others, took the route of exile two or three years after me, I read a passage I have since thought about often. He related his conversation with a friend, a political colleague from the Small Holders' Party, with whom they had struggled against the Germans and their many followers but a few years before. Only now this man decided to go along with the Russians: he was a leader among the accommodationists, not the resisters. His friend reminded him that they had been sitting in the same restaurant only three or four years before, talking about the politicians who had thrown in their lot with the Germans, and who would be soon gone with the wind, destroyed, or, at best, scattered in disgrace, which was indeed what happened. Wasn't he doing the same thing now: choosing the side of disgrace and of certain defeat? No, the other man said: the comparison was incomplete. Then the Germans were bound to be defeated in one or two years at the most. Now the Russians would stay for a long time. True, the Americans had begun to oppose them (this was in 1947) but the Americans had no staying power. Ten or twenty years would pass, and the Americans would give up this kind of struggle. They were an immature people; and they were going to have enough troubles of their own.

That, too, was a rationalization, I thought when I first read this, and I still think so: this man was trying to convince himself that, after all he had been living through, it was better for him to stay in Hungary and earn some kind of living under the Sovietish regime than to go abroad and be an exile in a foreign country. He, too, had just enough courage to be a coward. But of course he was not entirely wrong.

He was wrong in one sense, however, as indeed I was, coming from a different direction, and for different reasons. When I returned to Hungary on a visit in 1972, more than a quarter of a century after my escape, I found that the Americanization of my native country was nearly complete. The largest building along the once destroyed Danube riverfront was an Intercontinental Hotel, a concrete pile looking like a large American airport building, furnished and inhabited by the clientele of the latter. A Hilton Hotel was being erected; it would soon dominate the skyline of Buda. Hungary had become a democratized, industrialized and bureaucratized society, with hordes of young people wearing American blue jeans. The principal interest of the majority was cars. The only handwriting on a wall that I remember was not a political, or even an obscene, scrawl: it was the name of a world-famous American rock group, I forget which. The red, white, and blue pennant of Pepsi-Cola flew in many places, from sailboats on lakes to the doorways of restaurants.** I saw

---

** A small memory survives. Toward the end of 1945 a few taxis appeared in Budapest again. Their license plates were imitations of those of Russian vehicles, yet their doors were marked by a strip of black-and-white checkers. This was how American taxis were marked, I had seen them in American movies. So I wondered why. I was told later that this, too, followed the Russian pattern, since taxis in Moscow were checkered accordingly. Many years later I learned that a promoter from New York had started taxi service in the Soviet capital in the 1920's. Like Pepsi, the checkered taxi had thus come from New York to Budapest, via Moscow.

large family parties ordering Pepsi after the main course in restaurants, with pride and panache, as if it were champagne. During twelve days in Hungary I saw less than a handful of Russians, while the city was full of Germans and Americans. In the better hotels and restaurants Russians were virtually nonexistent: if they ventured to trudge in, wearing dusty sandals and soiled open shirts, they were relegated to tables in the back, near the kitchen or the lavatory. More important was my realization that thirty years of Russian rule had left the culture and the civilization of my native country largely untouched. Russian fashions were nonexistent, Russian customs ignored, Russian art, Russian writing, both new and old, unpopular and left unread; after thirty years not more than a handful of Russian words had been adopted or transformed into Magyar, whereas the everyday language teemed with new words that had come from the proletarian, the city argot, the gypsy, the American, or the computer-English languages. Of course this was but one side of the coin. The other side was the sovereign reality: the Russians were still the masters of the Hungarian state. The government would do nothing against their consent; and not a single critical suggestion about them would be uttered in public or in print. Here, too, I thought, not much has really changed since Year Zero. The strange coexistence—or, rather, codominion—of America and Russia ruled the world, including Hungary. The levels of their influences may have changed but the proportions remained largely the same. Had Hungary ended up on the western side of the iron curtain, she would have been spared much terror, brutality, and suffering; yet, so far as her social transformation went, the end result may not have been terribly different. But that, too, is another story.

My story, that of Year Zero recalled, ends with a moral and with a failure. What I learned during that year was something I had found to be true well before Zero, under different circumstances, when the Germans had been dominant, and something that I was to find again and again later, under even more different circumstances, in the United States. It was stated by Karl Stern in his spiritual autobiography, *The Pillar of Fire,* as he spoke about life under the Nazis in the thirties; but the very same thing was true under the Soviets in the forties. "In the 1930's," he wrote, "it first dawned on me that the Great Dividing Line in Europe, in fact in the entire world, is not the line between Right and Left. All of us who grew up in the intellectual atmosphere of the twenties were sincerely convinced that people who were politically to the Left of the middle acted under a moral incentive. Indeed, as I have said, in most radicals there had been during the early post-war period, underneath it all, a love of justice and a compassion for the multitude. Conversely, it was held that people were conservative out of material motives for conservation, no matter how much some of them were able to deceive themselves. In this respect the Nazi years taught us a lesson. It happened not infrequently that you met a friend whom you had known for years as a 'staunch liberal,' and he turned out to be eager for any compromise to save his skin. On the other hand, we saw people whom we had disclaimed as 'reactionaries' go to concentration camps and to the gallows. In the beginning it seemed confusing. But gradually the issue became clearer and it was obvious that the only thing that counts in this world is the strength of moral convictions."

How true this was, and how it corresponds with what I had seen! Only I wanted to have my cake and eat it, too. At the end of Year Zero my decision was made. I would get out, preferably to America. (The rest is autobiography; it does not belong here; in any event it would carry this odd account beyond Year Zero.) Next July I fled from Hungary. Fifteen years later (and fifteen years before this is being written), I reminisced about those days, in a private letter. I was about to be smuggled across the Austrian frontier, with American help. At noon on the day I was to flee I went to say goodbye to my grandparents. "So you are going, after all?" my grandmother said. There was something infinitely sad about these words. "*Hát mégis elmész?*"

Once more, that afternoon, something gripped my heart. At Györ I left a bus and took a dirty, broken-down train for the frontier town where I was to meet the man who would take me across next morning. Passing through abandoned fields, torn-up sidings, ruined stations, that train wheezed painfully forward during the hot, yellow dusk of a Hungarian evening in July. I saw a signalman in his pathetic, torn uniform of the Hungarian State Railways, with a thin and hungry face, stand in front of his signal house and give the customary salute with his signal flag to that rattling wreck of a train. At that moment I had an almost irresistible impulse to turn around, to cut my escape short: I knew it was my duty to return to my now almost manless family; the voice and shape of my grandmother swam before me in a small rising pool of tears; I felt not nostalgia and not homesickness but the deep impulse of a very human and solemn responsibility—surely to them, perhaps to my country, perhaps even to myself. As I just wrote, however, the compulsion was almost irresistible; and, no matter how true and deep its source, the small pool of my tears was shallow. Even now I sometimes think that to follow that impulse may have been the right thing to do. But I don't have enough of that stuff of self-sacrifice that I otherwise so much admire.

NOTES

Chapter II

1. John Lukacs, *The Last European War: September 1939/December 1941* (New York, 1976), pp. 158 et seq.
2. P. E. Schramm, *Hitler: The Man and the Military Leader* (Chicago, 1971), Appendix II, p. 204.
3. *Das Reich,* 23 February 1945.
4. *The Testament of Adolf Hitler: The Hitler-Bormann Documents, February–April 1945* (London, 1959), 2 April 1945.
5. Ibid.
6. Ibid., 26 February 1945.
7. Ibid., 14 February 1945.
8. Ibid., 15 February 1945.
9. Ibid., 26 February 1945.
10. Ibid., 2 April 1945.
11. Ibid.
12. Ibid., 4 February.
13. Ibid., 2 April.
14. Ibid., 13 February 1945.
15. Ibid.

Chapter III

1. H. Nicolson, *Diaries and Letters* (London, 1967), Vol. II, p. 453.

Chapter IV

1. *Actes et documents du Saint-Siège relatifs à la Seconde Guerre Mondiale* (Vatican City, 1974), Vol. V, p. 193.

Chapter V

1. M. Djilas, *Conversations with Stalin* (New York, 1962), p. 82.
2. Ibid., p. 14.

Chapter VI

1. Charles L. Mee, Jr., *Meeting at Potsdam* (New York, 1975), p. 9.
2. Winston S. Churchill, *The Second World War.* Vol. VI: *Triumph and Tragedy* (Boston, 1953), p. 480.
3. Ibid., pp. 456–57.
4. W. Averell Harriman and Elie Abel, *Special Envoy to Churchill and Stalin, 1941–1946* (New York, 1975), p. 502.

5. *Foreign Relations of the United States, 1945: Diplomatic Papers,* Vol. V, p. 253; also cited in Lisle A. Rose, *Dubious Victory: The United States and the End of World War II* (Kent, Ohio, 1973), p. 102.

6. *Correspondence Between the Chairman of the Council of Ministers of the USSR and the Presidents of the USA and the Prime Ministers of Great Britain During the Great Patriotic War of 1941–1945* (Moscow, 1957), pp. 219–20.

7. Cited by Rose, *Dubious Victory,* p. 277.

8. Truman, *Memoirs,* Vol. I, p. 426.

9. George F. Kennan, *Memoirs 1925–1950* (Boston, 1967), p. 300.

10. Churchill, *Triumph and Tragedy,* p. 455.

11. Edgar Snow, *Journey to the Beginning* (London, 1959), p. 357; cited by Vojtech Mastny, "The Cassandra in the Foreign Commissariat: Maxim Litvinov and the Cold War," *Foreign Affairs,* January 1976, p. 373.

12. Vladimir Petrov, *A Study in Diplomacy: The Story of Arthur Bliss Lane* (Chicago, 1971), p. 248.

13. *Foreign Relations of the United States, 1945: Conference of Berlin,* Vol. I, p. 257.

14. Petrov, *A Study in Diplomacy,* p. 235.

15. Harriman and Abel, *Special Envoy,* pp. 510–11.

16. Petrov, *A Study in Diplomacy,* p. 235.

17. Kennan, *Memoirs,* pp. 294–95.

Chapter VII

1. Julian Marías, *Generations: A Historical Method* (University, Ala., 1972), pp. 7–8.

2. From an article in the Autumn 1945 *American Scholar* by James Bryan, managing editor of *New York Medicine* and executive secretary of the Medical Society of the County of New York.

3. *The New Yorker,* 24 April 1945.

4. *American Scholar,* Summer 1945.

5. *The New Yorker,* 5 January 1946.

6. *Commonweal,* 12 January 1945.

Chapter VIII

1. Tony Sharp, *The Wartime Alliance and the Zonal Division of Germany* (Oxford, 1975), p. 30.

INDEX

Acheson, Dean, 135, 162 ff.
Adamic, Louis, 194 n.
Albania, 124
Allen, Frederick Lewis, 188
Alsace-Lorraine, 122
American Scholar, The, 182, 189, 190 n., 196 n.
Anders, General Wladyslaw, 65 n.
Ardennes offensive (1944), 16, 19
Atlantic Monthly, 178 ff., 187 ff., 196, 207 ff.
Augsburg, Treaty of (1555), 229-30
Austria, 58, 67, 120, 154, 222 ff.

Barmine, Alexandre, 185
Barzun, Jacques, 191
Basso, Hamilton, 199
Belgium, 16, 143
Berle, A. A., 163 n.
Bernanos, Georges, 211, 239, 244
Bevan, Aneurin, 75
Biddle, Francis, 161
Bilbo, Theodore, 205-6
Bismarck, Otto von, 109, 115, 121, 225, 240
Bock, General Fedor von, 18
Bohr, Niels, 103 n.
Borgese, G. A., 195 n.
Bormann, Martin, 31 ff.
Bowra, Maurice, 191
Braun, Eva, 45

Brooke, General Alan, 79 n.
Brown, Tillie, 135
Bruenn, Dr. C., 84
Bryan, William Jennings, 87
Bulgaria, 90, 112, 153
Burckhardt, Carl J., 26 n.
Bush, Vannevar, 150 n., 207
Byrnes, James F., 130, 134-5, 141, 148, 166 ff., 195 n.

Cadogan, Sir A., 76 n., 78 n.
Cameron, Meribeth, 182
Carr, E. H., 251-2
Catholic Universe Bulletin (Cleveland), 209 n.
Chamberlain, John, 185, 195 n.
Chamberlain, Neville, 64
Chesterton, G. K., 76
Chiang Kai-Shek, 110, 236
China, 124, 146 ff., 182 ff., 236 ff.
Christowe, Stoyan, 194 n.
Churchill, Lady Randolph, 69
Churchill, Winston Spencer, 4, 12, 23, 43, 45, 49 ff., 81 ff., 100 ff., 109, 113, 119, 138 ff., 143 ff., 152, 157-8, 179 ff., 199, 213 ff.
Ciechanowski, Jan, 156 n., 201 n.
Clemenceau, Georges, 12
Close, Upton, 203-4
Cohen, Benjamin, V., 91
Columbia Broadcasting System, 184

Columbia Teachers College, 173 n.
Commonweal, The, 173 n., 205 n.,
   208–9
Communism, 13–4, 26 ff., 33,
   62 ff., 88, 96, 100, 109 ff.,
   117 ff., 128 ff., 137 ff., 154 ff.,
   160 ff., 176 ff., 189–90, 200 ff.,
   236 ff., 253 ff., 260 ff.
Conant, James, 150 n., 190, 196
Coolidge, Calvin, 87
Cugat, Xavier, 12
Currie, Lauchlin, 99, 162
Curzon Line, 56 n.
Czechoslovakia, 153, 167

Daniels, Jonathan, 99
Darrow, Clarence, 87
Darwin, Charles, 241
Das Reich, 26 n.
Davies, Joseph, 144, 164
De Gaulle, Charles, 10, 60, 89 n.,
   92 n., 115, 128, 155 n., 228,
   237 n.
Denmark, 61
Descartes, René, 251
Disney, Walt, 27 n.
Displaced persons, 11
Djilas, Milovan, 114, 117
Djugashvili, Svetlana, 116
Djugashvili, Vasili, 114
Djugashvili, Yakov, 114
Dmitri, Ivan, 197
Doctorow, E. L., 189 n.
Doenitz, Admiral Karl, 30
Dolivet, Louis, 194 n.
Douglas, William O., 134
Dulles, Allen, 23
Dulles, John Foster, 63, 86, 104,
   139 n., 164, 217

Durbrow, Elbridge, 156 n., 162
Dutourd, Jean, 267

Eden, Anthony, 55, 59 n., 71 n.,
   90, 230
Edward VII, 49, 71
Einstein, Albert, 191, 199
Eisenhower, Dwight, 61 n., 63 ff.,
   138 ff., 141, 158 n., 217, 223,
   232–3
Elizabeth I, 115, 230
Esquire, 281
Ethridge, Mark, 130

Farley, James, 94
Fascism, 13, 28–9, 93, 96
Fielding, Temple, 185 n.
Finland, 120
Fishbein, Morris, 200
Fisher, John, 185
Foot, Michael, 75
Ford, Gerald, 158
Forrestal, James, 143
Fortune, 182
France, 6, 8, 10, 47, 50, 57, 152,
   204
Franco, Francisco, 30, 37
Frankfurter, Felix, 99, 162
Franklin, Benjamin, 94
Franz, Josef I, 49 n.
Frederick the Great, 17
Freud, Sigmund, 241

Gallup poll, 22, 174
Genêt (Janet Flanner), 205
Genoud, François, 32
Georgia (USSR), 131–2
Germany, 3 ff., 15 ff., 111 ff.,
   145 ff., 167 ff., 195 ff., 216 ff.
Gladstone, William Ewart, 94

Goebbels, Josef, 19, 26 ff., 36, 164, 233

Goldwyn, Samuel, 174 n.

Göring, Hermann, 16, 19, 24

Grafton, Samuel, 186

Great Britain, 16 ff., 49 ff., 217 ff.

Greece, 51, 59–60, 73 n., 90, 143, 179

Hague, Frank, 94

Halifax, Lord, 223 n.

Hamsun, Knut, 46

Hanfstaengl, Ernst, 50

Hannegan, Robert, 134, 136

Hansen, Alvin, 197 n.

Harper's, 178, 181, 185

Harriman, Averell, 123 n., 130, 140, 143, 148, 151, 165

Harvard University, 178 ff., 189 ff.

Hauser, Heinrich, 195 n.

Hemingway, Ernest, 240

Hibbs, Ben, 203

Himmler, Heinrich, 23, 24, 27–8, 119, 129 n., 218

Hiroshima, 147–8, 150, 210

Hiss, Alger, 159–60, 199

Hitler, Adolf, 5, 12 ff., 49–50, 52, 62, 67, 74, 76, 82 n., 93, 97, 109 ff., 115, 127–8, 136, 147, 152, 176, 262–3

Hoffman, Paul G., 197

Holmes, Oliver Wendell, 85

Hoover, Herbert, 86, 97, 107, 203

Hopkins, Harry, 99, 140–1, 150 n., 162, 167

Hughes, Charles Evans, 86

Hull, Cordell, 163 n.

Hungary, 5, 57 ff., 66 n., 119, 125, 129 n., 167, 251 ff.

Hurley, Patrick, 146

Hutchins, Robert, 213

Ivan the Terrible, 94, 145, 230

Izvestia, 178

James, Henry, 193

Japan, 9, 111 ff., 122 ff., 133 ff., 145 ff., 233 ff.

Jeffers, Robinson, 244–5

Jefferson, Thomas, 94, 221

Jews, 11, 23–4, 38 ff., 106, 123, 127–8, 263–4

Jodl, Field-Marshal Alfred, 18, 20

Johnson, Lyndon B., 105

Johnson, Samuel, 70

Kaliningrad-Königsberg, 126, 154, 224 n.

"Kapos," 29

Kempis, Thomas à, 272

Kennan, George F., 91, 150, 166 n., 169

Kennedy, John F., 105, 158 n.

Khrushchev, Nikita, 131

King, Admiral William, 146

Kinsey, Dr. Alfred, 242 n.

Korea, 127, 217

La Guardia, Fiorello, 105

Lampman, Ben Hur, 198 n.

Lane, Arthur Bliss, 162 ff.

Lattimore, Owen, 179 ff., 186

Lauterbach, Richard, 184

Lawrence, T. E., 68

League of Nations, 87, 89

Leahy, Admiral William, 141–2

Lenin, Nikolai, 12, 13, 46, 55, 111 ff., 127, 216

Leslie, Kenneth, 204 n.

Lessner, Erwin, 194–5

Lewis, Fulton, Jr., 203–4
Lewis, Sinclair, 191
Ley, Robert, 29 n.
Life, magazine, 184, 197–8
Lilienthal, David, 181
Lincoln, Abraham, 41, 97, 240
Lippincott (Publishers), 183 n.
Litvinov, Maxim, 156
Lloyd George, David, 12
Lombardo, Guy, 6, 12
Louis XIV, 81, 115
Luce, Henry, 198
Luhan, Mabel Dodge, 193 n.
Luther, Martin, 229 n.

MacArthur, General Douglas, 135, 141, 235
McCarthy, Joseph R., 104, 206 n.
McCloy, John, 149 n.
McIntire, Admiral Ross, 83
MacLeish, Archibald, 162
Mailer, Norman, 242 n.
Mann, Thomas, 199
Mao Tse-tung, 46, 120, 124 n., 236
Marías, Julían, 171
Marshall, General George C., 135, 142
Marshall Plan, 155, 167
Marx, Karl, 21, 111, 127, 227, 241
Mary I (Mary Tudor), 230
Masur, N., 23
Matthiessen, F. O., 193
Mili, Gjon, 197
Model, Field-Marshal Fritz, 25
Molotov, Vyacheslav, 59 n., 123, 129, 135, 141 ff., 151, 166, 187–8

Montgomery, Field-Marshal Bernard, 61 n.
Morgenthau, Hans, 195 n.
Morgenthau, Henry, 161
Moscow Conference (1944), 58 ff., 90
Munich Conference (1938), 68
Murrow, Edward R., 206 n.
Mussolini, Benito, 6, 19, 40 n., 82 n., 93, 109, 113, 216

Nabokov, Vladimir, 198, 201 n.
Nagasaki, 148
Napoleon I, 33, 45, 47, 81, 220
Napoleon III, 240
Nation, The, 28, 189, 193
National Socialism, 31 ff., 46 ff., 136 ff., 227
NATO, 167
New Republic, 189
New Statesman, 28
New Yorker, The, 74 n., 168, 178, 185 ff., 199, 205 n., 212–3
New York *Herald Tribune,* 208
New York *Post,* 186
New York *Times,* 99, 189 n.
Nicolson, Harold, 52
Nixon, Richard M., 86, 156, 232, 236

Oder-Neisse Line, 154 n., 224 ff.
Ortega y Gasset, José, 77

Pan American Airways, 198
Panter-Downes, Mollie, 74
Partisan Review, 193
Pascal, Blaise, 135, 207
Patton, General George, 27 n., 140 n.

Pauker, Ana, 125
Paulding, C. G., 204–5
Péguy, Charles, 186
Pepper, George Wharton, 172
Perón, Juan Domingo, 227 n.
Pétain, Marshal Henri Philippe, 30
Phelps, Maggie, 135
Pius XII, 94, 96, 173 n.
Poland, 4, 38, 56, 65, 95 n., 101–2, 142 ff., 152–3, 162 ff., 179
Politics, 186 n., 209 n.
Poor, Henry Varnum, 181
Potsdam Conference (1945), 9, 65–6, 119, 142, 145, 224 ff.
Pravda, 178
Primo de Rivera, José Antonio, 37 n.
Protestant, The, 204 n.
Public opinion (American), 173 ff.
Pynchon, Thomas, 25

Quebec Conference (1944), 83

Rajchman, Ludwig, 161 ff.
Rákosi, Mátyás, 125
Renner, Karl, 120
Reves, Emery, 194 n.
Ribbentrop, Joachim, 19, 24
Robeson, Paul, 189
Rockwell, Norman, 11–2
Rommel, Field-Marshal Erwin, 19
Roosevelt, Mrs. Eleanor, 87, 97 ff., 122 ff., 129 ff., 133 ff., 141 ff., 185, 194, 199, 213 ff.
Roosevelt, Elliott, 83
Roosevelt, Franklin D., 4, 6, 13, 23, 39 ff., 51, 68, 72, 81 n., 82 ff., 109, 202 ff.

Roosevelt, Theodore, 86
Roper, Elmo, 174
Rosenberg, Alfred, 29 n., 43, 64
Rosenbergs (Julius and Ethel), 180 n.
Rosenman, Samuel, 99, 141, 145, 162
Rostow, Eugene V., 185 n.
Rumania, 60 n., 90, 119, 129, 153
Russia. *See* Union of Soviet Socialist Republics (U.S.S.R.)

Saki, 68
Sandburg, Carl, 191
San Francisco Conference (1945), 141 ff.
Santayana, George, 194 n., 200–1
Saturday Review of Literature, 99, 183
Schellenberg, Walter, 29
Schlesinger, Arthur, Jr., 194, 207
Seversky, Alexander de, 209 n.
Shaffer, Blanche Weber, 183 n.
Shakespeare, William, 115
Shapley, Harlow, 190, 301
Shaw, George Bernard, 191, 199
Sherwood, Robert, 99
Sikorski, General Wladyslaw, 56 n.
Simonov, Konstantin, 194
Simpson, General C. A., 139
Sinclair, Upton, 199
Skinner, B. F., 242 n.
Snow, Edgar, 156
Snow, Mrs. Edgar (Nym Wales), 182 n.
Solzhenitsyn, Alexander, 132, 243–4
Spain, 37
Speer, Albert, 17, 21, 24

Stalin, Joseph, 4, 9, 12–3, 38, 39, 43, 46, 51, 55, 58 ff. 81 ff., 109 ff., 136 ff., 142 ff., 166, 213 ff.
Stettinius, Edward, 141, 165, 188–9
Stimson, Henry L., 135, 141, 143, 148, 152
Strong, Anna Louise, 179, 183 n.
Swing, Raymond Gram, 181, 186 n.
Switzerland, 23
Szilárd, Leó, 195–6

Taft, Robert, 100, 104, 137, 164, 203
Tardini, Monsignor Domenico, 96
Teheran Conference (1943), 92, 221
Thompson, Dorothy, 194–5
Time magazine, 97, 184, 198, 205 n.
Tito, 119, 124 n., 185 n.
Tocqueville, Alexis de, 133, 176, 242
Torgau meeting (1945), 7
Trans World Airlines, 198
Trevor-Roper, Hugh, 32 n.
Trieste crisis (1945), 119 ff.
Trotsky, Leon, 67 n., 110
Truman, Harry S, 12, 66 n., 78, 103 ff., 121 ff., 132 ff., 195
"Truman Doctrine," 167, 213 ff.
Tucker, Sophie, 200

Ukraine, 126
Union of Soviet Socialist Republics (U.S.S.R.), 4 ff., 15 ff., 53 ff., 109 ff., 122 ff., 174 ff.

United Nations, 7, 71, 87, 89, 122, 187 ff., 212, 233 ff., 241 ff.

Vandenberg, Arthur, 97
Victoria, Queen, 49, 71, 240
Vietnam, 105
Vonnegut, Kurt, 25
Vyshinsky, Andrei, 123, 181 n.

Wallace, Henry, 134, 161, 198
Wallenberg, Raoul, 129 n.
Waln, Nora, 196
Walpole, Horace, 214
Warsaw Rising (1944), 101
Waugh, Evelyn, 200
Weeks, Edward, 200
Weil, Simone, 81
Wellington, Arthur Wellesley, Duke of, 232
Wells, H. G., 199
Westphalia, Congress of (1646–48), 229
White, E. B., 187–8, 199
White, Harry Dexter, 161
White, William S., 184
William II of Germany, 228, 234
Williams, Michael, 208
Wilson, Edmund, 160 n., 185
Wilson, Gill Robb, 208–9
Wilson, Woodrow, 12, 83, 85 ff., 94, 106, 218 n., 232

Yalta Conference (1945), 4, 65, 73 n., 92 ff., 97, 101, 118, 141 ff., 168, 186 ff., 231 ff.
Yugoslavia, 57, 60, 119 ff., 124

Zhukov, Marshal Georgi, 118, 140

T